Notes on
mathematics for children

Notes on
mathematics for children

by members of the
Association of Teachers of Mathematics

CAMBRIDGE UNIVERSITY PRESS
Cambridge
London · New York · Melbourne

Published by the Syndics of the Cambridge University Press
The Pitt Building, Trumpington Street, Cambridge CB2 1RP
Bentley House, 200 Euston Road, London NW1 2DB
32 East 57th Street, New York, NY 10022, USA
296 Beaconsfield Parade, Middle Park, Melbourne 3206, Australia

First published 1977

Typeset in Malta by Interprint (Malta) Ltd.
Printed in Great Britain at the
University Press, Cambridge

Library of Congress Cataloguing in Publication Data
Association of Teachers of Mathematics.
Notes on mathematics for children.
Bibliography: p.
Includes index.
1. Mathematics – Study and teaching (Elementary)
I. Title.
QA 135.5.A827 1976   372.7'3'044   76-14026
ISBN 0 521 20970 6 hard covers
ISBN 0 521 29015 5 paperback

Contents

7

Prefatory note

The following members of the Association of Teachers of Mathematics shared in writing the book:

A. W. Bell   (Mrs) R. M. Fyfe
A. J. Bishop   A. J. McIntosh
P. S. Boorman   S. A. Morley
(Miss) B. I. Briggs   J. W. Oliver
W. M. Brookes   (Mrs) A. I. G. Renton
(Miss) B. Carter   L. F. Rogers
J. Dichmont   P. Vallom
       D. H. Wheeler (executive editor)

Introduction

Mathematics is a notable human achievement. The men, known and unknown, who made it have contributed to our world some of the most penetrating and subtle awarenesses that the human mind has reached, awarenesses that have incontrovertibly established their significance and their usefulness for a wide range of human endeavours. A world with men but without mathematics is unthinkable. Mathematics is an inheritance belonging by right to everyone who chances to be born into our civilisation.

The vision of such a birthright, claimable by anyone, may sometimes seem an extravagant picture when looked at from inside a primary classroom, where some children apparently find great difficulty in taking even the first few steps along the path to mathematics. But we believe it is right and reasonable to be optimistic about the possibility of putting everyone's mathematical inheritance within reach. There is first of all the fact that mathematics has marked our culture and that some of its byproducts are embedded in the fabric. No one can grow up without encountering numerals – the primary raw material of so much mathematics – without learning how to count, without performing some simple measurements, playing some simple mathematical games, handling coinage, telling the time, reading some double-entry tables and some graphs, noticing the presence of some simple geometrical shapes. These items are an inescapable part of the environment, like the spoken language, and children will learn something of them without the assistance of schools. Whatever teachers do or do not do, children will meet some mathematical tools and have opportunities to use them.

The second reason for optimism, and much the more significant, lies in the learners themselves, the children. When it is acknowledged that all children, save only a few with gross somatic defects, can learn to speak their native language and can master a range of physical and social skills, and when a second and a third look have been taken in order to appreciate the complexity of the challenges they successfully surmount in their early years, it is easy to see that there is no *a priori* reason why they should not be able to learn some significant mathematics and every reason why they should. Being born a human being is, in principle, enough to guarantee an entry into mathematics because it confers all the powers that are required to make a good start. Mathematics begins with bodily actions, perceptions and speech – is, indeed, implicitly present in these somatic activities although not in itself the object of the learner's attention. It cannot be an accident that an analysis of the structure of everyday speech is forced to use words such as class, intersection and inclusion of classes, relation, substitution, transformation, etc., which belong to the specialist vocabulary of mathematics. If they are the right words to describe what the grammarian finds, they must be the right words to describe the awarenesses which have to be achieved by a learner in becoming an autonomous speaker of his adopted language.

The powers of children include the power to mathematise. Children are acutely aware of the kinds of relationships that are called mathematical; their minds spontaneously anticipate the activities that mathematicians have chosen to cultivate and structure. It is no surprise to children that what has been done can often be undone, that what has been combined can often be decomposed; that the eye can find patterns and that the mind's eye can generate them; that an exemplar can stand for a class and that words and signs represent classes; that properties can be singled out for attention and others ignored; that objects and images can be transformed without losing their identities. These awarenesses not only produce mathematics – indeed, they are employed in almost all human activities – but they are the fundamental awarenesses that led to the mathematics we know. Since children can, in the terms of this description, function as mathematicians it should be possible for them to enter into their inheritance in the narrower sense of learning the mathematics that our society judges important and that its schools are asked to teach.

Such a view of children's capacities brings genuine optimism because it says that there is good reason to believe that teaching mathematics to everyone is possible and not impossible. It does not imply that teachers are redundant, or that teaching mathematics is a trivial activity, but it does put in question the traditional picture of what a teacher must do. The classroom folklore suggests that children come to school with virtually no mathematical experience and with blank mathematical minds; that it is the teacher's job to force impressions on their minds by providing them with mathematical experience, by showing them how to express the experience in regular mathematical form, and by demonstrating some necessary mathematical skills; and that the children must hold these impressions in their minds by continuing to rehearse them until they stick. This model is sufficiently plausible, because it is constructed of part-truths rather than downright lies, to have dominated the practice of mathematics teaching in the majority of classrooms until now. Yet the orientation of the model is at right angles to the proper direction if children actually come to school with the impressions of a wealth of mathematical experience and with mental powers which are algebraic by nature. The traditional model can only make a teacher into an opponent of natural learning rather than an ally and gratuitously increase the obstacles that the children who want to learn must overcome.

Wanting to be an ally of children's learning is not enough, and finding how to be an ally is not always easy, as we show in the last section of this book. A teacher who would be, as it were, a midwife needs to know exactly what to do to help; an arsenal of techniques and sound judgment about which to use are of more value to children than any amount of goodwill. We believe that a proper degree of professionalism involves paying much more attention to how children learn, how their minds work, so that teaching can accommodate to the facts of learning. But we notice that not all those who can agree with what we have just said seem to mean what we mean.

We have no patience with the kind of teaching that judges itself to be satisfactory if the learner can show that he has learned exactly what he was taught. Admittedly this is successful teaching when the learners are dogs or dolphins, but it does not seem to us to be good enough for children. The significant characteristic of human learning, the quality that distinguishes it from the learning of all other organisms, is that it is at the disposal of the learner: he owns it and can use it in ways that he chooses. Because the human learner powers his learning with energy assembled by his affectivity and directed by his will, he knows that he is the one who decides how much of himself to give, when to stop giving it, and what to do with what he has learned. He knows that he must recognise the imperatives in each learning situation and voluntarily submit to the demands of each of the tasks that he wants to master until it is sufficiently in his grasp for him to relax his obedience. Each new item of learning is incorporated into himself and he can integrate it with related learning already in his possession to increase its potential usefulness and give it longer life. Human learning always goes beyond what it was given because of the personal contribution of the learner.

In the sense of the last paragraph, all human learning is 'individualised' and can only be the responsibility of the learner himself. There are genuine questions that the teacher must face about how to act so that the placing and acceptance of this responsibility are not fudged, but there are no easy answers to be found by merely reorganising the classroom, installing packages of materials, and allowing each child to work at his own pace. If the new situation can only function by reverting to the principle that children have to learn exactly what they are given to learn, then it has nominally individualised teaching by dehumanising learning and everyone is back where they were before.

We would prefer to conceive, even if we cannot yet achieve, an education in mathematics which is consonant with all the facts of human consciousness and the aspirations of a human education. The idea of transformation, to which we give considerable prominence in this book, is an example which may bring some threads together. We find that transformation is a natural capacity of the human mind and that children much younger than those in primary classrooms are already masters of its use. Speech depends on transformation since it changes itself to match changes in what is being experienced, and changes again when the frame of reference shifts from one speaker to another. Visual perception depends on transformation since the variety of retinal images derived from any object seen at different angles at different times have to be linked in the mind if recognition is to take place. Imagination is a personal world in which transformation rules unchallenged. But we also know that 'transformation' is a word adopted by mathematicians to refer to certain actions, such as the permutation of a set of objects or the translation of all the points of a plane. The clue sets us looking for other, more elementary, examples and we see that counting is a transformation, and that computation is a set of transformations. A bridge therefore exists between what we know children can do and some of the mathematics we would like them to learn. The idea of transformation becomes a tool that a teacher can use, a tool that does not dehumanise learning because it corresponds to one aspect of the voluntary activities of the mind.

Transformation can act as a tool because it encapsulates an awareness, a precise awareness that permits a teacher to seek and find definite and detailed ways of being on the side of the students as they learn, and that also makes clear to the students that they own a personal resource which will bring learning nearer if they choose to use it. But transformation is also a tool in a less metaphorical sense. As we show in this book the awareness of transformation becomes a technique for dynamically exploring the articulation of mathematical situations so that the learner becomes familiar with the interconnections and how the movements of his mind define the structure.

Perhaps we should point out here that although our emphasis on transformation may make it look as if it can be applied everywhere in the learning of mathematics, we do not want to leave readers with the impression that it is a multi-purpose tool capable of teaching anything. Complex learning jobs require a variety of tools, most of which have not yet been invented. We talk about one that we know and that has proved useful. There is no implication that it is the only one or the only kind. A box of rods is a tool; a geoboard is a tool. But these are very well known even if not very well used, and it seemed to us better to show how an observation of a characteristic of children's learning can be associated with some properties of mathematics and then fashioned into a powerful and precise tool for bringing children and mathematics together. This process seems to us to serve as a paradigm for the invention of tools to aid the teaching of mathematics.

In our earlier book [1] we tried to show how it is possible for teachers to enlarge the mathematical space in which their students can be encouraged to move. We gave little attention to the conventional number work that has always held a prominent position in the early years of schooling. This time we have given much more attention to this area of elementary mathematics, not because we have retreated from our earlier position, but because we did not want to write the same book again and because we wanted to back up our assertions that the subject of numbers, and operations with numbers, is as suitable a medium for mathematical dialogues between students and teacher as any other.

Until a few years ago the teaching of mathematics in the early years in school was exclusively concerned with numbers, number operations and numerical computations. The shift that has taken place reflects a realisation that number work is not the only kind of mathematics that is accessible to children, but it also represents a desire to eliminate the routine learning and drill that had become too closely identified with the teaching of elementary arithmetic. At the same time the work of some psychologists and epistemologists has contributed to a belief that the foundations of the number concept in children are vastly more complex than teachers had always supposed. A considerable confusion about the 'what', 'when' and 'how much' of number work in the early years at school has resulted, currently exacerbated by a vigorous backlash from those ignorant of, or unsympathetic to, the causes of the confusion.

We believe it is possible to rehabilitate the teaching of elementary arithmetic and rescue it from its present uncertainties without putting any clocks back. Moreover we think that there are good mathematical and pedagogical reasons for including more, not less, arithmetic in schools. For example:

Numbers have not been dislodged from their primary place in mathematics.

They are the most concrete of mathematical entities, readily accessible to beginners.

The association between number and quantity exemplifies, from the simplest to the most complex cases, the binding of pure ideas and tangible objects in the peculiar intimacy characteristic of mathematical thinking.

The sequence of numbers allows us to approach the infinite.

Computation is quite the most dramatic application of the economy of operation of the human intellect – so little effort applied to so little knowledge produces so much.

The family of numbers is workmanlike, orderly and reliable, and yet the members are infinitely various in their endowments and most are totally unknown.

Numbers play a significant role in magic and ritual, fairy tales and fantasy.

There is nothing drab or routine here, unless the way that arithmetic is taught systematically extracts all its potential excitement. Unfortunately, it seems as if school arithmetic is not only dogged by a regrettable past but somewhat hamstrung at present by the well-meaning interference of psychologists and mathematicians too.

It seems obvious that the teaching of mathematics should draw upon the insights of mathematicians into the nature of mathematics since they are the people who know it best, and it is a valid criticism of the development of the teaching of elementary mathematics that it has not generally tapped this source of assistance, and of professional mathematicians that they have not generally shown a very positive interest in how their subject is taught in the early stages. The story of the development of the teaching of elementary mathematics during this century shows it subjected to a variety of social forces and swayed by a variety of changing social attitudes, but all the time having to grapple with the growing pains associated with establishing a system of mass education and the concomitant blurring of distinctions between the training of a semi-skilled labour force and the education of a professional elite. Forced by this evolutionary movement to face very difficult questions about the contribution mathematics can make in this new situation, teachers could have been helped to get some perspective on their problems by mathematicians who, in the same period, were turning more and more to considerations of the nature and foundation of their own activity and its relation to the phenomena of the physical world and of mental processes. As it happened, however, neither group was sufficiently aware of the implications of what it was doing, let alone aware of the preoccupations of the other, for more than a small handful of people to see the mutual advantages of an exchange of information. When some sort of effective liaison eventually emerged it turned out to have unfortunate consequences, as the last few years have shown.

As we said in the introduction to our earlier book, we welcome the impact of modern mathematics on teaching because it points to important characteristics of the nature and role of the subject that passed unnoticed in traditional classrooms. Yet when we look at the tangible outcomes of the recent modern mathematics reforms, particularly in North America and some European countries where the intervention of professional mathematicians is more evident than in Great Britain, we see that most of the message was misunderstood by those who brought it and garbled by those who had to implement it. Some of the mathematicians were more concerned with the preparation of future professionals than with the general education of children, most of whom would never become makers or users of mathematics. Even those who glimpsed the illumination that modern mathematics could bring to teachers and to students did not, by and large, know enough about the classroom situation or about the way that mathematics is acquired to be able to show how their intentions could be realised. The recommendation, for example, that the elementary teaching of numbers should be based on the explicit teaching of sets now seems a monumental folly. It was proposed because mathematicians knew that the theory of sets had not only added a powerful weapon to their armoury but had succeeded in illuminating and strengthening the foundations of their subject. For them, indeed, it seemed important that all the familiar properties of numbers, gradually made explicit over some thousands of years of history, could be shown to derive from a handful of more primitive notions and that mathematics could be reorganised into a hierarchy of increasingly complex abstract structures. But instead of having the wisdom to ask themselves what, precisely, might be the implications, if any, for pedagogy, they went right ahead and inferred that if the classroom followed the lead given by mathematics the advantages would be comparable. It is a matter for regret that in several countries, our own not altogether excepted, this example of non-rigorous thinking won a temporary victory.

We would not bother to mention these things here, most of them now being common knowledge, if they did not raise a question that was often in our minds when we met to discuss and to write the material in this book. It can be formulated in a variety of ways: How can mathematics teaching protect itself from reckless innovation and yet not stagnate? Where are the criteria that will sort the wheat from the chaff, the worthwhile reforms from the non-starters? Does a discussion of the teaching of mathematics always have to be a battle of opinions? Can anything be *known* about mathematics teaching?

To the last form of the question we give a hesitant affirmative, conscious of a multitude of qualifications with which we must hedge it, yet sure, from our own experience, that we do find we know more when we have studied a problem in the right way, freeing ourselves from as many of our preconceptions as we notice and focussing on an aspect of the problem that looks as if it might be soluble. Although what we discover we have come to know often seems very little, a long way from accumulating into 'a body of knowledge' about teaching, nevertheless we are sure of its quality when we put it alongside many of the statements that pass for knowledge in the educational world. We recognise when an observation or an idea rings true and we can go on from there. There is nothing special to us in this and we know that any teacher or anyone close to children who is interested in mathematics could experience it too.

Everyone knows that mathematics teaching exists, but opinions are divided on the existence of mathematics education. By the latter we mean the disciplined study of the practical and theoretical aspects of the teaching of mathematics, a study with its own intrinsic character, ready like any other serious study of common phenomena to go public – that is, freely to open its values, rules of evidence, know-hows and knowledge to inspection, criticism and experimental validation. To become accountable, in other words. It seems to us that this present time does display some signs that mathematics education is beginning to find itself, that a few people here and there have noticed that an advance in knowledge requires sharply different questions to be posed and new styles of investigation to be evolved.

In our more optimistic moments we fancy we see a parallel with the time when chemistry was struggling to emerge from the stranglehold of alchemy. The image at least indicates the degree of difference that we are looking for.

However, there is no point in trying to prove an existence theorem. No one doubts the existence of a bird in the hand and when a sufficient number of people have given themselves to acting on their belief that the disciplined study of mathematics education is a possibility and that it can in principle produce significant statements which can be shown to be true or false, and when there is a growing public that has learned to discriminate between truths and folklore, mathematics education will have become, and will be seen to have become, a field of study with an honourable future.

In the meantime we offer this book to those who are not looking to be told what to think but who value the stimulus to their own thinking of encountering the thoughts of others. If it turns out that some readers find in some of our words a sign that thinking about the teaching of mathematics in a certain way yields results, not opinions, we will have been given the best of possible rewards.

1

Language and Experience

When I talk with someone I rely on the other person sharing the context in which I am talking. Were this not so then every conversation would be a long drawn out affair where every word was defined and accepted before it was used. It would be impossible in the sense that common sharing of experience and activity is the precursor to a constructed spoken language. When I cannot rely on the other person sharing the context there is as much a problem of finding an appropriate context to share as finding appropriate words. One could say that the latter is impossible without first establishing the context in some way.

Most of the time this situation doesn't arise as context and words go together without too much ambiguity.

As this is written, a soccer match is to be shown on television. People have talked about the match in the last few days and casually one has become aware that from their conversation it was not clear whether they were going to see the match or going to see the match on television. When people of either intent use only the words 'Are you going to see the match?' there is little to tell one whether they are going to travel to the football ground or sit in their room with the television set. The reader can react to this by saying that normally people would indicate in some way what they intend. And he might follow it by suggesting some alternative phrases that would normally be used. For instance, people going to the match would say just that and not use 'see' or 'watch'. But this attempt to distinguish is an irrelevant intellectual exercise as soon as one has experienced an actual happening. A happening where there is sufficient ambiguity to make one uncertain. 'Did you see Arsenal (or whatever the team was called) on Saturday?' has for me a very definite flavour of actually being there, whereas it could perfectly well refer to television, and not even to the live programme. And then you have the feeling sometimes that two people arguing about what they saw couldn't have been at the same match.

But what is a soccer match? The ground is clear of players, there is a period when they are watched by thousands and then the ground is clear again. During the play there is incessant movement and because most people who read this have had some experience of soccer matches I can leave it at that.

How do you watch a match? Do you follow the ball? The referee? A player? The spectators? What governs your watching? Do you watch one thing? Do you exclaim or describe or move with your own body? Do you talk to others as you watch? Do you move about a great deal or a little? The question could go on because the event is a complex, changing experience. A goal is scored. Was it a good goal? A fluke? An advantage taken of a scramble? What team do you support when you answer these questions? The game begins and ends as games do; time out, cutting into our experiencing a definite swathe of changing forms and diverse emotions. It is easy to refer to an event such as a game of soccer because in recall it can be isolated, identified by its formal beginning and its formal end. We know the emotions of expectancy and anti-climax that can pre-- cede and follow an event so clearly marked out for us. We can talk as a consequence of the experience and attempt to live in a new way (re-live?) excitement that we recall. Perhaps recalling is easier to know as a dream rather than by an at- tempt to use words which limit and eventually exasperate. Whatever we do, the game seems to have an entity, sometimes separate, sometimes merging with other experiencing.

The experiencing we can talk easily about has a characteristic of 'entity' or 'wholeness' which is summed up in a descriptive noun. But such easy talk about 'the match' does not express the range of emotions experienced by those involved. Nouns used like this to express our awareness of events invite us to consider how the event is marked off from the rest of our awareness. Think of such things: a meal, a journey, a rest, a concert. Notice the difference from: eating, travel- ling, resting, listening, which are words expressing the actual experiencing.

An experiencing always has two possibilities of expression: the one which separates it, which identifies a beginning and end; and the other which says something of what is felt during its happening.

Sometimes the language of expression confuses these two and when we wish to be more abstract it is even more difficult to reconcile the two pos- sibilities. Consider 'a sum':

$$63 + 28.$$
Answer?

Now consider the experience of doing the sum. The object called sum starts with seeing $63 + 28$ and finishes with 91, but the experience of doing it is not easily expressed.

There is something about the ease of description which stops us thinking about the consequent change in ourselves during such an event. It may even reduce the possibility of change so that we fall into a set of habits. Habits are ritualised actions triggered off by certain needs but which then follow a pattern which is so repetitive that nothing happens to disturb the train of events that have been triggered off. Not all action is thus. There are actions which we take which involve some kind of triggering that invokes known skills and yet which still may imply a conscious awareness of the possibility of change. This very act of writing, for example. I have a facility in the skill of moving the pen across the paper and yet as I do this I am continually being faced with decisions and conflicts in what I actually allow to flow as a consequence of the skill.

Some may argue that it would be intolerable if we were all encouraged to be maximally aware of the possibilities all the time. They would argue that habits and the ability to repeat in the way I have described are a protection against the wildness that could take over if the protection were not possible. This may be so, but my feeling is that too often the encouragement to accept these notions of regularity, habit, conformity, discipline, is not offset by adequate acceptance of wildness, of imaginative leaps, of freeing oneself in order to think. In asking for a balance this too often means encouraging people to stand at the fulcrum, at the point of balance where little or nothing happens. Balance can also be achieved by wildness offset by extreme discipline. The inadequacy of our language inhibits us from realising that these can co-exist. 'I am surprised that such an imaginative person is capable of so systematic a piece of work.' In mathematical activity we hold our cards too close, fearful that people will charge off in too many directions, uncertain what will happen if they do. The mathematical information available to a teacher allows him to develop that kind of control which tends to become inhibiting. It is one which sees mathematics as a set of methods, of symbols to learn, of procedures to master, of problems to solve, of statements to make, conclusions to draw and applications to discuss.

Examples of this are not easy to give without being invidious, but phrases like 'the four rules', 'formulæ for area and volume', 'solving simple equations', 'percentages', 'formulæ for a circle', have about them a circumscribed air. They imply that the set forms through which these can be recognised are the important goals to be reached at all costs. And this restrictive thinking is not confined to traditional subject matter. 'Number patterns', 'sets', 'symmetry', 'pictorial representation', can have exactly the same narrow outcome. It is largely because they are seen as objects, as events to effect a definite end rather than as particularly useful activities identified from amongst all the other possible activities with numbers, shapes, space and relations.

That these are valid descriptions of possible activities is not in question; that they are adequate to say what the vigour of mathematics consists in certainly is. To discover connections, to alter the conditions, to ask 'What if . . . ?', to perceive in a different way, to doubt someone else's certainty, to struggle with someone else's understanding or non-understanding, to see the consequences of someone else's different perception of what you have seen.

These are the other things, and immediately the differences can be seen. The first group closes and the second group opens. Both are useless on their own. It is no good having flights of fancy if, having a purpose, there are no skills for expressing the flights in some form or forms which may be effective in bringing about some change that you wish to see.

Mathematical activity has always been a responding, vigorous, iconoclastic affair as well as a precise, careful, structure-building process. Unfortunately, unless you are acquainted with people involved in the former, the only things that are offered are expressions from the latter: formalised instructions, textbooks of theorems, treatises on topics. All of these are manifestations of the latter care, but all depended in the first place on imaginative leaps and jagged intellectual and physical struggles.

How can we have an environment where both these experiences are clearly available to children growing?

One of the first things that we need is confidence to recognise that we can go in all kinds of directions without necessarily having all the facility to be careful and precise. On the other hand the imagination needed to climb mountains or go surfing would be useless without care in developing appropriate skills. But real and valuable skills cannot be developed in a vacuum.

One of the ways in which we can develop confidence in mathematics is to know that it is to do with *change*. Every piece of mathematics has some characteristic of change. Let us look more closely at what can be achieved by thinking about the mathematics we know in terms of changing or transforming.

Examples of Change

In arithmetic we change numbers into other numbers by carrying out operations. Starting with one number, for instance, we can finish with another and these will be different depending on what we do to the first.

Given 4 as a start:

$$4 \quad \rightarrow \quad 20 \quad \text{after multiplying by 5,}$$
$$\rightarrow \quad 16 \quad \text{after squaring,}$$
$$\rightarrow \quad 7 \quad \text{after adding 3,}$$

or if we use a combination of operations,

$$4 \quad \rightarrow \quad 20 \quad \text{after adding 6 and multiplying by 2,}$$
$$\rightarrow \quad 14 \quad \text{after multiplying by 2 and adding 6,}$$
$$\rightarrow \quad 20 \quad \text{after squaring and adding 4.}$$

On the other hand, one may have a number in mind which is to be the finish, and the problem is to find the necessary starting number using a given operation.

Given 24 as the finish:

24 ← 3 if multiplying by 8 is used,

24 ← 5 if multiplying by 4 and adding 4 is used,

24 ← 22 if halving, followed by subtracting 3 and followed by multiplying by 3.

Or one may have the starting and finishing numbers and decide on different operations which will fit. Given 28 as the finish and 7 as the start:

7 → 28 multiply by 4,
add 21,
subtract 3 and multiply by 7,
subtract 2, multiply by 5 and add 3.

Note that although some knowledge is required of simple operations (four rules?), these are not needed at a very high level of sophistication in order to explore the possibilities hinted at in the above examples. *The reader is invited to investigate similar examples for himself.*

Sometimes when considering space it is convenient to change to numbers in order to organise more clearly the relations we wish to consider. The game of battleships makes use of a co-ordinate system to identify precise position: a submarine instead of being two squares becomes D1, D2.

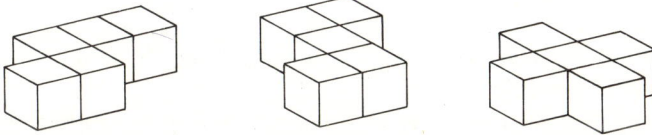

Fig. 1.1

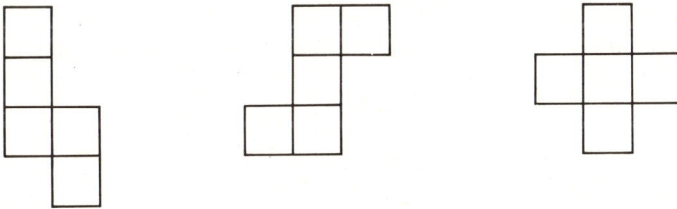

Fig. 1.2

We use pictures to change from a concrete situation to one which we can control when we have particular relations in mind. The picture will not be the *same* as the original and will lose some of its properties, but in the change we would try to ensure that what we were wanting to think about was still there. Fitting five cubes together on a flat surface could be seen as in Fig. 1.2

if we were concerned with the variety of patterns, but would not be helpful if we were concerned with, say, the number of outside faces.

This is not unconnected with an architect's problem of drawing plans on paper (two dimensions) for a house (three dimensions). This also implies the builder's problem of converting the two-dimensional plans into a three-dimensional house with his materials.

We struggle to simplify our imagery with symbols. x as an 'unknown number' has left many people irritated and bewildered besides allowing others the freedom to use it efficiently to deal with problems. There is a vast difference in emphasis between a decision to symbolise as an aid in helping to contain a problem and work with it, where the problem itself helps to carry the meaning of the symbolisation, and a decision to give children practice in 'the use of symbols' away from any meaningful context. It is another example of the difference between a real experiencing of mathematical activity on the one hand and the narrowness of a set form which can be labelled on the other. More care is needed at the point when the struggle to deal with a problem leads to a decision to symbolise.

If someone thinks of a number and is then asked to operate on it, as in the example above, he can give us the finishing number and we can set about trying to find the number he started with. After being asked to multiply his number by 2, add 5 and divide by 3 he tells us that he has arrived at 9. What do you think he started with?

Knowing that there was a number there in the first place we can set about returning to it from 9. Multiply by 3, subtract 5 and divide by 2. Where did this sequence come from?

This kind of work has led to a way of introducing people to simple symbolisation of numbers. Yet it would be a mistake to presume that it was simply a method of sweetening the x pill. A more sophisticated problem develops with the use of the sign x which cannot arise in the 'think of a number' situation.

The example given could be symbolised in a conventional way,

$$\frac{2x + 5}{3} = 9,$$

leading possibly to

$$2x + 5 = 27, \quad (A)$$
$$2x \quad\;\; = 22,$$
$$x \quad\quad\; = 11. \quad (B)$$

This symbolism is itself a mathematical situation so that we can ask: 'With a starting point which is a thing like (A) how can we arrive at a thing like (B)?' So we can set about writing down

$$3x + 7 = 28, \quad \text{(i)}$$
$$4x - 3 = 9, \quad \text{(ii)}$$
$$2x + 9 = 3, \quad \text{(iii)}$$
$$5x + 2 = 13. \quad \text{(iv)}$$

(i) and (ii) fit the possibility of working on the 'think of a number' principle, presuming that it is a whole number which is in mind. (iii) and (iv) do not, but that would not stop them being written down in the pattern

$$\square x \pm \triangle = \bigcirc,$$

where numbers can be arbitrarily chosen to take the place of $\square$, $\triangle$ and $\bigcirc$. The question could then be: 'Is there a number which can replace x and make the equality true?' The answers would depend on one's skill in sorting out the properties of each potential equality, and what kind of number one is allowing – whole number, negative number, rational number.

Originally $2x + 5 = 27$ described the build up of a 'think of a number' game ($x \times 2 + 5 = 27$ is closer to what actually happened) and we were able to use the written form to '*hold*' the problem for us so that we could work on it. (Of course the memory doesn't require the conventional written form. Something like

$$\times\ 2$$
$$+\ 5$$
$$27$$

would do equally well as long as it was meaningful to the writer.) It is so easy to be deceived into thinking that we have found an honest way of including the accepted writings into our work! We changed or *transformed* the situation into a written form because it served our purpose better. But as we have seen, the symbolism itself can then become a starting point for further mathematical activity. In this case, we decided to keep a certain pattern, viz. $\square x \pm \triangle = \bigcirc$, but change the numbers arbitrarily and examine the consequences of this decision.

This indicates how the symbol system can subtly change what was originally a fairly simple problem.

We change situations into others which we think we can handle. The rule for dividing fractions is an example. Having learnt how to multiply, it is a reasonable procedure to change division into multiplication by an appropriate transformation. It is not reasonable to introduce this as a completely blinding bit of magic.

There are other ways of converting division of fractions into a known operation, for example,

$$\tfrac{3}{4} \div \tfrac{2}{5} \quad \text{to} \quad \tfrac{15}{20} \div \tfrac{8}{20} \quad \text{to} \quad 15 \div 8.$$

This sequence involves the recognition (*a*) that fractions can be changed into *equivalent* fractions by taking equal multiples of their numerators and denominators, and (*b*) that in dividing two fractions with equal denominators, the denominators can be dropped.

As we look into many of the characteristics of arithmetic and ask about how changes take place, it should be possible to see more clearly the reasons for many rules which appear as if by magic.

The act of classification is another kind of change, especially when one can take the same set of things and classify them in different ways. Try classifying the set of shapes in Fig. 1.3. Give the question to other people

Fig. 1.3

and compare results. Is there a right way? Are some decisions better than others? Were there any surprises in the choices other people made? What kinds of decisions were made in order to carry out the classification? Let us look at some of the interpretations we might give to

'2 and 3 makes 5'.

It seems obvious. What makes it obvious? 2 and 3 can make 6 if we take the product; or 1, or $\frac{2}{3}$, or 8 if we raise 2 to the power 3, or 9 if we raise 3 to the power 2.

The obviousness rests in what we assume we are meant to do with the 2 and 3. This depends on the usage of 'makes'. But 'makes' is a powerful word to use in such a limited way and when we can feel the large variety of things that we can make with 2 and 3 we begin to see that what '2 and 3 make' depends on what we are thinking of doing with them.

Once we know this we can really go on inventing rules. All we need is a pair of numbers and a rule. The result may be a single number, another pair of numbers or it may be that for a given rule we would have to invent an answer.

A pair of numbers with no particular consequence in mind is often written (2, 3).

Look at the consequences as rules are invented:

2, 3)	'product'	→ 6
2, 3)	'difference'	→ 1
2, 3)	'first is the units figure, second is the tens figure in a numeral'	→32
2, 3)	'raise the first to the power of the second'	→ 2^3 →8
2, 3)	'add the sum to the product'	→11
2, 3)	'take 1 from the product of one more than the first with one more than the second'	→11
2, 3)	'double the second less the first'	→ 4

There is no need to produce only one number:

2, 3)	'square the first, square the second'	→ (4, 9)
2, 3)	'form a pair by adding the first and second and then forming the product'	→ (5, 6)

Some of these are familiar, others not; some of the ones that are not are not familiar because they have just been invented. To what purpose? Because it is possible.

A Heap of Stones

Separate them into two heaps, three heaps, twenty heaps. Put some of the heaps together. Sort out the stones into size, into colour, into shape, into feel.

Put the stones together. Choose one: now choose another and another and another.

The patterns form and dissolve. Some stay longer than others.

He wants some of the bigger stones. Sort out some of the bigger stones.

Is this big enough? Take away the collection of big stones. Shovel the others into a bucket. How many buckets? Shall I fill the bucket or will it be too heavy to carry? Fill it as full as you think you can carry.

All the stones have been cleared away.

Getting Right Answers

'8 multiplied by 3 is 24' carries with it meanings that are unexpressed. Meanings which, for those who know, convey a conviction that the statement is correct. We are so used to accepting these meanings that we feel cheated if someone says 'But 8 multiplied by 3 could be 4', as if some trick had been played. And it is so; a trick has been played. By deliberately using the same

sounds '8 multiplied by 3' one can righteously feel that whatever validit
is given to 'could be 4', it is somehow less correct that the statement w
actually know to be correct. Yet we can use the symbol 8 and the symbol
and put them into a sufficiently strong situation which makes 4 inevitable
Thus, in Fig. 1.4, if we start from zero we can count on 8 three times an

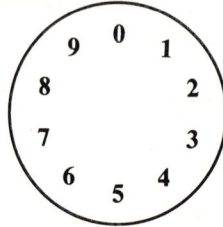

Fig. 1.4

arrive at 4. There is nothing strange about this – it could be a dial on a
gas-meter. But now you may want to use a different way of reporting the
fact. Suppose I ask you what happens if 8 is replaced by 7 and three by
six? In this new situation I see the answer as 2. What way would you
choose to let someone else know that, when working in this way, 7 and 6
give 2?

We have become used to knowing correct answers because particular
procedures are associated with particular words. These associations are
often very tightly made so that a child of eleven may well not know the
answer to 8 multiplied by 5 but know straight away what 8 times 5 gives
Most of us have been taught mathematics in such a way that these associations have formed strong organising forms which it is difficult for us to break
We can subtract

547
189

———

and we each will have a procedure that makes another set of digits appear
in the bottom line. It is surprising how many personal procedures there are
and yet we shall all respond to the same instruction: 'Subtract 189 from
547.' Though, as with 'times' and 'multiply', some of us will be even happier
to be asked to 'take 189 from 547'. Each one of us can explore his own ways
of tackling procedures and can with care identify the ease (or not) with which
they are carried out with particular associations of words or other actions.
Look at this:

$$547 - 189 = 1 + 10 + 347 = 358.$$

Not many will have seen subtraction written down like this and it could well be difficult to convince someone that it is a method which is easy to grasp. When I first saw it written down it was some time before I detected that it was a statement that could be a written form of how I often do subtractions of that kind in my head. There had never been any need for me to attempt to express in writing or in symbols this method of transforming the pair of numbers to be subtracted into the answer. It was something I just did.

But having seen it written symbolically in this way, there is something about the written form which draws my attention to the generality of the procedures. As long as I went on doing it in my head when I needed to, my attention was taken up with the subtraction I was doing at the moment and not with any generalisable pattern. What happened inside me was not exactly as written.

Given that subtraction I think I would have said

189 : 11
11 and 47 is 58
and there are 5-less-2 hundreds
358.

This does not destroy for me the other ways of subtracting that I know. Rather it expands for me the range of choice I have for subtracting. I do not want to ask questions like 'What is the best method?' without counter-demanding 'For what purpose?'

The particular incident that led to this way of subtracting awkward numbers was a consequence of a teacher working with children who found symbols difficult. She had found, ironically enough, that this method was closer to what they could actually do in their heads.

I once asked a general teacher, having to take mathematics with a class of not very clever twelve-year-olds, and being troubled by subtraction, to do such a sum in her head. The method she reported was precisely this one. When I expressed interest she apologised, saying that she learned it from working in a market when she was young.

This raises an important point concerned with the degree of closeness between a calculation carried out mentally and the written symbolic representation of that calculation. In the previous example I recognised that the written form was an adequate description of the way in which I do subtractions in my head.

Look at the following addition:

$$3\tfrac{3}{4} + 2\tfrac{1}{3} = 5\frac{9 + 4}{12}$$
$$= \tfrac{13}{12}$$
$$= 1\tfrac{1}{12}$$
$$= 6\tfrac{1}{12}.$$

We have all seen this kind of writing. At one level we may worry at the misuse of the equality sign but at another, recognise that what is written to the right of the equality signs resembles quite closely what we do in our heads. Having added the 3 and 2 together what do we do? Drop the 5 from our thoughts and give attention to $\frac{3}{4} + \frac{1}{3}$. Only at the end do we bring back the 5 and combine it with the $1\frac{1}{12}$. This written form is a half-way house. It disobeys some of the rules under which the symbols are used so that it is not acceptable in the written space. It also contains extra bits which are irrelevant in the mental space and so there is a distortion there too. The mental space in which we operate allows us to scatter bits of the question and part of the solution to the winds provided that we gather them up again at the end. A very controlled calculation done in one's head can appear chaotic when transformed on to paper. Take Margaret's example. She is $6\frac{1}{2}$. What is written is as near as possible what she said.

> How many 3s in 200?
> 100 and 100
> 90 so 30
> 30 and 3 and 1
> 33 and 1
> 66 and 2
> so 66 3s and 2 left over.

Recording is sometimes a handicap or sometimes a help to the recorder. It is a handicap if he has to fit his thinking into a form which feels alien and constricting. It can be a help if the written page acts as a memory for him.

Take $3684 - 426$. I personally find it difficult to hold each partial complement in my head:

$$4 \quad 54 \quad 200 \quad 3000$$
$$3258$$

I don't of course need the ' + ' signs or an ' = ' sign as an aid to memory. I carry the 'add' in my head. I only write down what I know I need to write down. So it is not for me that the form

$$3684 - 426 = 4 + 54 + 200 + 3000$$
$$= 3258$$

is required. That is for communication with another who may not be carrying ' +, = ' in his head.

There is another point. So far we have put emphasis first on the mental act of calculating and secondly on a corresponding written form. But suppose we put the emphasis first on the written form. Let's take

$$\begin{array}{r} 234 \\ +169 \\ \underline{37} \\ 440 \end{array}$$

where we first add the units, then the tens and lastly the hundreds. It is possible to be so trapped by a particular written form that we are unable to break away and look for ways of expressing an addition which is done differently. This particular method in which numbers are 'carried' and in which the answer appears immediately requires that we start at the right-hand side with the units. But as we know, there is nothing obligatory about starting there and as long as we feel free to change the written form we can accommodate a start from anywhere: left, right or indeed middle.

$$\begin{array}{r} 234 \\ +169 \\ \underline{37} \\ 300 \\ 20 \\ \underline{120} \\ 440 \end{array}$$

Running through all the examples discussed we can see transformations of one kind or another. Change is at the heart of doing mathematics. We can substitute numbers for other numbers, change numbers into others, change the shape or position of an object, change our point of view with respect to it, change the form of a problem so that we can now solve it, change to solving another problem which we see in some way to be related to the first, change the representation of an idea using objects, speech, written words, symbols, diagrams.

Some of these changes may be given more formal labels; many could be called transformations with various adjectives being used to classify them. But within this category are many which are already familiar in the mathematics taught to younger children. In some of the following chapters we shall develop this particular viewpoint with both familiar and unfamiliar topics in mathematics. We hope to see how transformations help us to move between topics and how they help to explain changes and arguments within topics.

Algorithms

The study of mathematics from the point of view of transformation is important because it can widen the range of actions that the teacher can take in responding to children learning and making their own mathematics. For many people the procedures of arithmetic are considered to be basic and our examples so far have drawn on several. In our view, awareness of transformation offers the best opportunity for any one of us to take maximum responsibility for our own learning. In particular it becomes clearer now to see the role of algorithms or routine procedures in a very positive and fruitful setting. They can appear as a sequence of transformations chosen frequently by one person, and, over a period of time, by several people. Eventually they become well-known paths. Usually the word algorithm refers to a commonly used *written* procedure which carries the maximum conciseness concomitant with carrying out the computation and which can be universally adopted for that particular computation, irrespective of the numbers involved. Often it is so brief that someone looking at it for the first time may have to struggle hard to see what is happening.

For instance, this may well be what is seen as a multiplication algorithm.

$$\begin{array}{r} 23 \\ \times\ 14 \\ \hline 92 \\ 230 \\ \hline 322 \end{array}$$

It is concise. The following are examples of other possibilities. Compare them for clarity.

$$
\begin{array}{ll}
\text{(i)} & \begin{array}{r} 23 \\ \times\ 14 \\ \hline 12 \\ 80 \\ 30 \\ 200 \\ \hline 322 \end{array}
\qquad
\text{(ii)} & \begin{array}{r} 20 + 3 \\ \times\ 10 + 4 \\ \hline 12 \\ 80 \\ 30 \\ 200 \\ \hline 322 \end{array}
\end{array}
$$

(iii) $(10 + 4) \times (20 + 3) = (10 \times 20) + (10 \times 3)$
$$+\ (4 \times 20) + (4 \times 3)$$
$$=\ 200 + 30 + 80 + 12$$
$$=\ 322$$

(iv) $14 \times 23 = 2 \times (7 \times 20 + 7 \times 3)$
$$=\ 2 \times (140 + 21)$$
$$=\ 2 \times 161$$
$$=\ 322$$

$$
\text{(v)} \quad
\begin{array}{r} 23 \\ 14 \\ \hline 161 \\ \text{double } 322 \end{array}
$$

Once more we shall find ourselves choosing, as a consequence of our experience, what we feel to be the best. It is hoped that we also recognise that for different purposes and for different people the 'best' will be different.

Looking again at our original 'subtraction' example we can see two things. First, that we need to know how to subtract and second, that there are many ways in which such a transformation can be carried out. An over-concern in the past for rapidity has led many teachers to believe that if children did not learn quickly they must therefore be less able – 'slowness equals dimness'. This is dangerous because it does not allow the individual response to such situations time to accommodate; especially when the response does not resonate with the teacher's offering. It means that judgments as to what is 'best' will often be distorted.

Looking at subtraction symbolically we have two numbers a, b and an answer to find: c. We know how to confirm the answer c because if we add c to b we should get a. This means that the first transformation $(a, b) \rightarrow c$ is confirmed by an earlier transformation of a different kind $(b, c) \rightarrow a$. But how do we carry out the first transformation?

There are clearly many ways. Which do we choose? The criteria for choice now depend on who is to do it, what aids are available, whether the purpose limits the choice. Must it be done as quickly as possible, accepting the high risk of error, or can it be done slowly, so decreasing the probability of error? Many people have been made fearful of arithmetic by being forced to use what, to them, is a blindly incomprehensible juggling of symbols associated with 'carry one, 'borrow one', 'pay it back' . . . This has often led to people being characterised as without number ability simply because the self-same methods have been acceptable to a sufficiently large number of others.

Looking at these activities in terms of the possible transformations should give us more confidence to create conditions for more people to feel confident in dealing with mathematics.

Transformations and Equivalence

Once the seed of the idea of transformations has taken root we see that all our thoughts and actions involve them in some way. Such great generality might make the observation of little importance – rather as if transforming were on a par with breathing: something that had to be done to allow anything else to take place. But the essence of the idea is that by talking about transformations we make explicit the links that we can find between different perceptions; the power of it is that it educates perception.

Suppose we consider two simple arithmetical statements:

$$5 = 2 + 3, \qquad \tfrac{1}{2} \times 10 = \sqrt{4} + 2^2 - 1.$$

All readers of these statements will immediately recognise the first statement and accept it. The second is not so familiar, although it involves familiar ingredients, and may prompt the reader to check its truth. (If any of the signs are not, in fact, familiar – that is, recognisable and associated with meaning – the reader cannot know whether the second statement is true. He may *assume* that it is true and then deduce the meaning of an unfamiliar sign, in which case the statement will act as a definition of meaning for him.) What is involved in checking the truth of the second statement? Since as it stands it is not recognisably true, the only procedure is to reduce it in some way to a statement which is recognisably true or false. The reduction is a transformation of the whole by transformation of its parts. So, for instance, we look at $\frac{1}{2} \times 10$ and know that we can change it into 5. Then we look at $\sqrt{4}$, change it to 2, look at 2^2 and change it to 4, and then assemble the parts into $2 + 4 - 1$ which we can transform by 'adding and subtracting' into 5. Since $5 = 5$ is recognisably true we now know that the original statement was true.

It is clear that throughout this activity our perceptions of the signs on the paper are triggering associations with particular transformations that we have built up. Taking the same example again, perhaps struck by the fact that 5 appeared after reduction, we may now see that if our perception had been sufficiently awake to a direct comparison of the two statements it could have instructed us at once that they were merely different ways of saying the same thing.

The second statement was in fact produced by direct transformations of the parts of the first. The links are indeed two-way.

None of us could link any of our perceptions together if we did not have at our disposal the transformations which allow us to bridge the gaps. Transformations are the binding agents which enable us to say, for instance, that we 'recognise' or 'remember' certain situations, that this perception is the 'same as' or 'similar to' that. Since we are able to do this from birth, we must have an inherent capacity to perform transformations on our perceptions. So we put a strong emphasis on transformations in this book, not because we believe that children have to be taught to use transformations, but because we believe that we can serve them by bringing into awareness those transformations which will offer them opportunities to develop their abilities to become mathematicians if that is what they find they want to be.

Transformations bring perceptions into relationship – they say, essentially, that one perception is related to another because it can be transformed into it according to whatever transformational rules are used at the time.

We can notice the distinctive quality of this formulation of what has long been recognised as central to mathematical activity – the perception of relationships. It stresses two things. First, that it is perceptions that are brought into relationship, not objects or situations independent of a perceiver and, second, that there is an inherent dynamism in the process because it rests on an awareness that perceptions can be changed. Both aspects help to make it clear that all this activity is taking place exclusively in active, personal, idiosyncratic minds.

If the human mind is always and all the time 'into' the business of making transformations, it would seem common sense for teachers to be aware of this universal power and harness it if they can. At the very least, awareness of transformation makes us look at mathematical relationships in new lights.

Consider any pair of numbers which sum to 10, say (6, 4). The transformation which *subtracts from one number of the pair while it adds the same amount to the other* generates a class of pairs, each summing to 10. Omitting negative numbers (although they can be included without invalidating the argument) this transformation generates the class:

(0, 10), (1, 9), (2, 8), (3, 7), (4, 6), (5, 5), (6, 4), (7, 3), (8, 2), (9, 1), (10, 0).

With this transformation it is possible to get from any one pair to any other in one step.

We can say we have an *equivalence class* of pairs, because all the pairs are equivalent *with respect to their sum*, and that the transformation that generated the whole class is an *equivalence transformation*. An equivalence transformation preserves some property which we judge to be significant, in some connection, for some purpose, and which is taken as the basis of the equivalence.

If we work with sets of pairs of whole numbers we can have, as we shall see in later chapters, equivalence transformations that preserve the difference, or the product, or the ratio, or less obvious properties of the pairs they are applied to. In the field of plane geometrical shapes, reflection and rotation are equivalence transformations that preserve shape and size but not position; shears preserve area but not shape; projections onto another plane preserve certain parallels and intersections but not lengths and angles, and so on.

But not all transformations are equivalence transformations. Many, perhaps most, chemical and biological transformations can hardly be regarded as equivalence transformations – since they are generally not reversible, for one thing. The geological forms of carbon are not obviously equivalent, even if they may all be seen as transformations of the same original organic matter.

It seems as if we must have some conditions other than the simple preservation of some particular property before we can agree to the presence of an equivalence transformation. The clue provided by our number-pair example is that the transformation generates the complete set of pairs *in the sense that* it links any two pairs of the set in either direction.

Symbolically, for example,

$$(1, 9) \xrightarrow{\ T\ } (7, 3) \quad and \quad (7, 3) \xrightarrow{\ T\ } (1, 9).$$

Furthermore the repeated application of the transformation can generate the complete set whichever pair is chosen as a start, and there are no inconsistencies between alternative generations.

For example,

$$(1, 9) \xrightarrow{\ T\ } (7, 3) \xrightarrow{\ T\ } (3, 7) \xrightarrow{\ T\ } (0, 10) \xrightarrow{\ T\ } (5, 5) \xrightarrow{\ T\ } (9, 1)$$
$$\xrightarrow{\ T\ } (10,0) \xrightarrow{\ T\ } (2, 8) \xrightarrow{\ T\ } (4, 6) \xrightarrow{\ T\ } (6, 4) \xrightarrow{\ T\ } (8, 2).$$

We can notice in passing how the commutativity of certain pairs of pairs is automatically taken care of by this transformation. Commutativity can itself be regarded as a transformation. Is it an equivalence transformation?

We can conveniently summarise the above by saying that an equivalence transformation must be *reversible* and *transitive*.

If we apply the transformation *add a number to, or subtract a number from, one member in a pair* to an element in our set of pairs, it will take us out of the equivalence class generated by the first transformation. But if we apply this new transformation (*T′*) in this way, it will give us a new pair which can become the nucleus of another equivalence class generated by *T*.

For example,

$$(1, 9) \xrightarrow{\ T'\ } (1, 5);$$

$$(1, 5) \xrightarrow{\ T\ } (2, 4) \xrightarrow{\ T\ } (3, 3) \xrightarrow{\ T\ } (4, 2) \xrightarrow{\ T\ } (5, 1) \xrightarrow{\ T\ } (6, 0)$$
$$\xrightarrow{\ T\ } (0, 6).$$

The following array shows some of the pairs that can be generated by the

(0, 11) (1, 10) (2, 9) (3, 8) (4, 7) (5, 6) (6, 5) (7, 4) (8, 3) (9, 2) (10, 1) (11, 0)
(0, 10) (1, 9) (2, 8) (3, 7) (4, 6) (5, 5) (6, 4) (7, 3) (8, 2) (9, 1) (10, 0)
(0, 9) (1, 8) (2, 7) (3, 6) (4, 5) (5, 4) (6, 3) (7, 2) (8, 1) (9, 0)
(0, 8) (1, 7) (2, 6) (3, 5) (4, 4) (5, 3) (6, 2) (7, 1) (8, 0)
(0, 7) (1, 6) (2, 5) (3, 4) (4, 3) (5, 2) (6, 1) (7, 0)
(0, 6) (1, 5) (2, 4) (3, 3) (4, 2) (5, 1) (6, 0)
(0, 5) (1, 4) (2, 3) (3, 2) (4, 1) (5, 0)
(0, 4) (1, 3) (2, 2) (3, 1) (4, 0)
(0, 3) (1, 2) (2, 1) (3, 0)
(0, 2) (1, 1) (2, 0)
(0, 1) (1, 0)
(0, 0)

Fig. 1.5

combined use of T and T'. In fact, the whole pattern can be generated from any one pair appearing in it. *Where are the equivalence classes? Can the array be extended?*

Although the most powerful transformations are those which generate equivalence classes, their scope is still wider if they are combined with the other kind as the example above shows. Equivalence transformations enable one to travel round an equivalence class, but non-equivalence transformations enable one to leap into another. If we can have at our disposal sufficient examples of both kinds of transformation we can span enormous regions of elementary arithmetic and geometry, bringing together vast quantities of relationships that are customarily treated atomistically.

Because mathematical transformations are essentially generative devices, they are an important tool for the production of clusters of mathematical relationships, as in Fig. 1.5. They enable us to get a great deal at relatively little cost.

The metaphor of cost and economy in relation to learning is worth pursuing.* There is no doubt that learning anything exacts a price, if only in terms of the investment one must make of one's attention, one's energy and one's time. But who could want the cost to be more than it need be?

In the field of learning mathematics, awareness of transformations is an efficient source of low-cost energy.

There is no need to over-sell the case. Transformations cannot do everything, even in mathematics, In particular, they cannot deal with the acquisition of all those arbitrary and conventional items that are part of the current language of mathematics and that have to be 'paid for' if the learner is to be able to function in this field. Neither do they eliminate the need for the learner to practise skills in order to achieve a functional degree of fluency. But these admissions do not give all the ground away. Within every part of mathematics, awareness of transformations brings personal power and control – to an extent that anyone who has not experienced for himself this awareness will find utterly astonishing.

The whole-hearted enlisting of the aid of awareness of transformations can do more to humanise the teaching and learning of mathematics than any other single act.

* See the article 'A Prelude to a Science of Education' by C. Gattegno in *Mathematics Teaching* No 59, 1972.

Miss Mountain's Arithmetic

Miss Mountain was born in April 1865 and on 1 April 1876 she was doing Compound Division on the first page of her new exercise book:

Rule: Divide the first denomination on the left hand and if any remain, multiply them by as many as the next less as make one of that, which add to the next, and divide as before.

Proof. By Multiplication.

Lest you should think all her calculations were 'abstract', we hasten to say that she solved problems of gentlemen distributing 6£ . . 6s . . 8d. among the poor, buying 'frails' of raisins, a hogshead of sugar, 2 fine laced lippets and 6 sets of knots;

she calculated: In 27 yards how many nails? *thus*

$$
\begin{array}{r}
\text{yards} \\
27 \\
4 \\
\hline
108 \\
4 \\
\hline
432
\end{array}
$$

and to How many barleycorns will reach round the world which is 360 degrees each degree $69\frac{1}{2}$ miles? *she found the answer* 4755801600.

Next time you have trouble with 'mixed numbers' try this method:

To reduce a mixed fraction to a single one.

Rule. When the numerator is the integral part, multiply it by the denominator of the fractional part, adding in the numerator of the fractional part for a new numerator; then multiply the denominator of the fraction by the denominator of the fractional part for a new denominator.

Reduce $36\frac{2}{3}/48$ to a simple fraction.

$$
\frac{36 \times 3 + 2 + }{48 \times 3} = \frac{110}{= 144} = \frac{55}{72} \text{ Ansr.}
$$

When the denominator is the integral part, multiply it by the denominator of the fractional part, adding in the numerator of the fractional part for a new denominator, then multiply the numerator of the fraction by the denominator of the fractional part for a numerator

This should be easy after the previous rule. Miss Mountain only needed to work one example, apparently. If it isn't quite clear try the rule on this:

Reduce $47/65\frac{4}{5}$ to a single fraction.

Perhaps you've seen answers more like this one:

Reduce $\frac{3}{5}$ of a month to its proper time.

$$
\frac{3}{5} \times \frac{4}{1} = \frac{12}{5} =
\begin{array}{ccc}
\text{Wks} & \text{dys} & \text{hours} \\
2 & 2 & 19\frac{1}{5} \text{ Ansr.}
\end{array}
$$

We also have *Miss Mountain learning* Rule for multiplying Duodecimally *and by example we find that* Multiply 8 ft. 5 in. by 4 ft. 7 in. *yields as* Ansr. 38 − 6 − 11. (*Can the 6 be 'finches'?*)

Let us pass over the prices of wainscotting, the debts of the merchant at Amsterdam who would pay another in London £642 in Spanish guilders, and the butcher who sent his man with £216 to a fair to buy cattle: oxen at £11, cows at 40s, colts at £1. 5s and hogs at £1. 15s a piece and of each a like number, *and leave with you two of the young lady's final problems:*

A person said he had 20 children, and that it happened there was a year and a half between each of their ages: his eldest son was born when he was 24 years old, and the age of his youngest was 21. What was the father's age?

Bought a cask of wine for £62. 8s. How many gallons were in the cask, when a gallon was 5s. 4d?

And what will the present-day Miss Mountain's exercise book look like a hundred years from now?

The currency is, of course, the £ s d currency, used in Britain until 1971, with the pound (£) made up of twenty shillings (s) each of twelve pence (d).

2

Transforming in Order to Count

Questions of the 'how many' variety give us a chance to catch ourselves at work in a situation where counting is required. In simple counting questions, it may escape our notice that our procedure for counting is determined by the way in which we look at the situation. We only need to ask others to say *how* they arrived at their answer to know that an element of personal choice is involved.

Let's look at some examples.

'Find the area of a rectangle 6 cm by 5 cm.'

What meanings are carried by these words?

Someone's reaction will be 30 sq cm fairly quickly. The product of 6 and 5 being 30 is implicit in the belief that there are 30 centimetre squares. This is easy, compared with the attempt to find the area of Fig. 2.1, where each of the squares is a centimetre square.

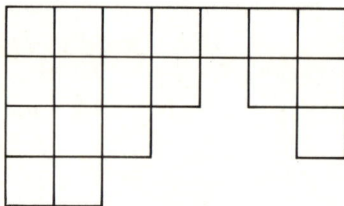

Fig. 2.1

We organise the squares for counting in the simplest way for us. One reader does it one way; another will do it another. Counting requires that a sequence be put on the separate squares so that the person counting can assure himself that he has counted each square once, but not more than once. That this is in effect a transformation of the perception can be appreciated by becoming aware that it is equivalent to the action of arranging the squares in a straight line, or touching each square and moving it aside as it is counted, or some other intervention by the one who is counting.

Each part of Fig. 2.2 is a personal transformation of the shape into a countable object. The agreement at the end that there are nineteen squares

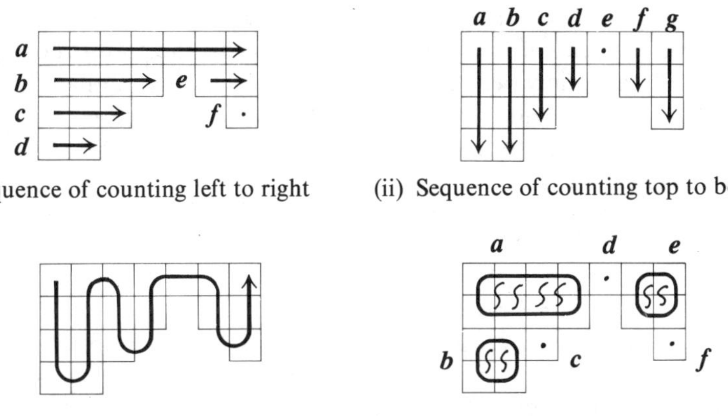

(i) Sequence of counting left to right

(ii) Sequence of counting top to bottom

(iii) Following through

(iv) Blocks and bits

Fig. 2.2

often hides the different transformations that have been in action in order to arrive at the same endpoint. Compare with the 'sum' $63 + 28 = 91$ mentioned earlier (p. 2) where we can think mainly of getting the right answer or we can focus attention on the variety of actions, each of which produces 91.

Now, how many squares are there in Fig. 2.3? The act of counting demands that there be a physical eye movement from object to object or from

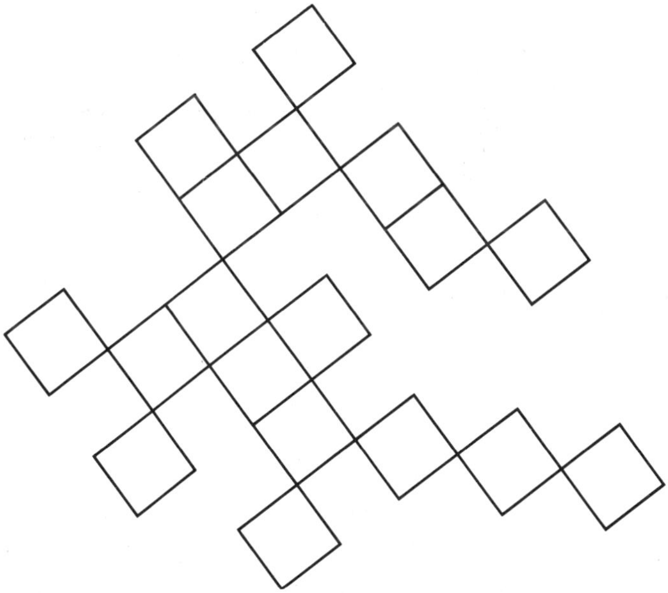

Fig. 2.3

readily recognised group (say a pair) to readily recognised group (say another pair) when counting in twos. Objects, like the patterns of squares looked at already, may be seen to be arranged in easily assimilated patterns so that counting is simple. The last example may have required a little more care to ensure that no squares were missed. Now try the following.

Ask a group of people to close their eyes. Mark on a board some nineteen or twenty dots scattered all over the board. Ask them to open their eyes and count the dots.

The task is completed when all agree to the number.

Then ask how each arrived at this number.

Consider the implications of the answers given – press people who merely say 'the same as him' to consider whether it was exactly *the same.*

Are some actions better than others?

When?

Consider what criteria you have in mind when you use the word 'better'. Better for whom?

And was it necessary for anyone to keep a careful track on what had been counted, perhaps by putting rings round certain groupings or crossing out the dots to indicate that they had been counted? The randomness of the dots compared with the more orderly pattern of squares requires the person counting to impose some order onto the chaos. Otherwise he may remain with the dizzy feeling of confusion that results from the necessarily random eye movements needed in the attempt to count. But to know the confusion is an essential part of the experiencing, for through it can come the awareness that one can control the situation, instead of letting the situation take control. Thus counting is possible.

What we have discussed about the examples so far can be summarised in the following way:

Task	Actions	Conclusion
(a) Find a measure of the area in square centimetres	Choice	A number
(b) Count the number of dots	Choice	A number
(c) 63 + 28	Choice	A number

Find the area of each of the triangles (i)–(vii) in squares of the lattice in Fig. 2.4. The second line of the figure shows attempts to build up the areas in whole squares and obvious bits of squares. The third tries alternative approaches.

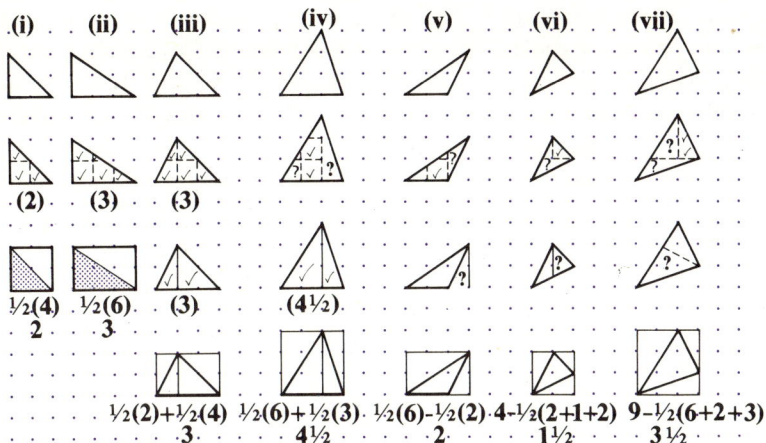

Fig. 2.4

The fourth becomes indirect in that each triangle is seen as part of a sur-rounding rectangle. (This happened to triangles (i) and (ii) in the third line.) The diagram offers just a small number of the possible journeys that can be made.

It is vital not to scorn the variety of possibilities in the choice of journey by the simple conclusion that all valid alternatives finish with the same answer.

For instance, the method shown in the last line of Fig. 2.4 is one which will cope with the area of *any* simple closed straight-line shape drawn on the vertices of a square grid. The method is shown with two more complicated looking shapes in Fig. 2.5.

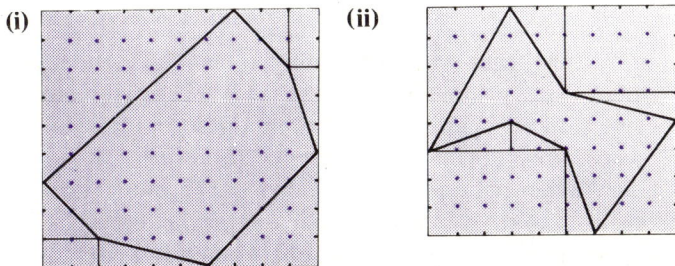

Fig. 2.5

Did the original demand to find the area of triangles in terms of squares arouse any feeling of conflict? For indeed it is not possible to make any of the triangles out of a whole number of whole squares. Perhaps the use of the word 'area' already carried with it the possibility of 'cutting up' whole squares. But without some awareness that the question requires the actual or virtual transformation of shapes, it would not have made sense – or not the sense that we have made of it.

The second line in Fig. 2.4 shows attempts to transform the triangles by cutting them into smaller pieces. Some are recognised as easy parts of squares to identify. This action involves a second transformation of a different kind (Fig. 2.6).

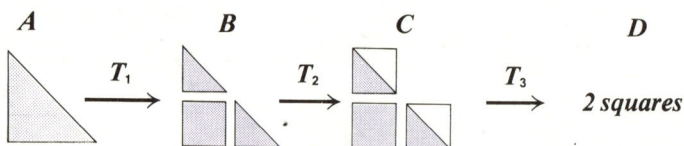

Fig. 2.6

T_1 is the transformation which results in the triangle being in bits.
T_2 is the transformation by which one recognises the bits of triangles as bits of squares.

The film Dance squared* *uses this notion in the animation sequences where triangles, squares and rectangles come in and out of different combinations; Fig. 2.7 is an example.*

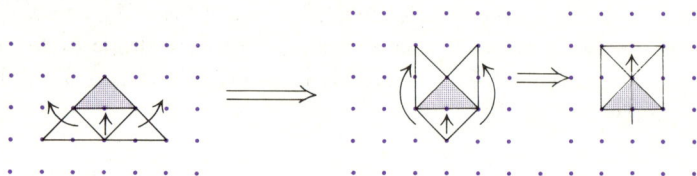

Fig. 2.7

T_3 will be a third transformation leading to the total number of squares, that is, T_3 produces the number 2 from 1, $\frac{1}{2}$ and $\frac{1}{2}$. The first method fails for the more awkward triangles. Looking along the second row in Fig. 2.4 we find parts whose areas are largely a matter of guesswork. ('It looks as if it is about $\frac{1}{4}$ . . .') We can see from this sequence of figures that, for example, a triangle like Fig. 2.4 (ii) can be built up in this way in terms of squares and bits of squares, but we may become uncertain about (iv) or (v) and look for

---

* National Film Board of Canada. Also see *Notes on mathematics in primary schools*, p. 243.

another method. In these examples we can connect the areas with the rectangles which contain the triangular parts.

Figure 2.8 shows both methods: the building up in squares and bits of squares, and the area of the triangle as half the area of a rectangle. The co-existence of these two methods will possibly help to establish an understanding. More formally, it can be seen as the establishing of an equivalence between the number arrived at: 3 (the number of squares from the dissection) and $\frac{1}{2}$ of (2×3) ($\frac{1}{2}$ the number of squares in the rectangle). The equivalence may be guessed and then confirmed by working on other triangles.

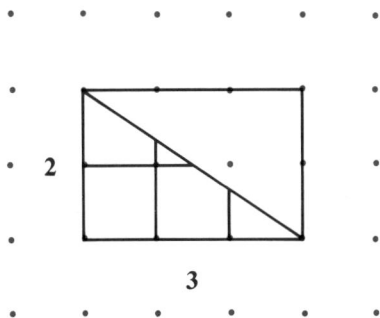

Fig. 2.8

Throughout this example one may discern a pattern: starting, doing something, finishing: $A \xrightarrow{\ T\ } B$. *If we can be clear about where we start (A), conscious of how we proceed (T) and intrigued by where we finish (B), then we have a powerful mechanism.*

It can become the basis of other attempts to deal with the more awkward triangles. We have used T_1, T_2, and T_3 for the transformational steps before, now we shall alter them slightly.

Start again. T_{1a} becomes: split the triangle into convenient right-angled triangles, not merely 'bits'.

T_{2a} becomes: relate the right-angled triangles to parts of squares or blocks of squares.

T_{3a} is the same as T_3, that is, count and arrive at a number. But we still do not solve the problem easily for triangles (v), (vi), (vii). Triangle (v) looks more tractable than (vi) or (vii) and this can lead to another connection being made.

T_3 so far has been accomplished by adding numbers together. In the case of the sequence

$$A \xrightarrow{\ T_1\ } B \xrightarrow{\ T_2\ } C \xrightarrow{\ T_3\ } D,$$

T_3 was accomplished by adding one square at a time as the various bits were recognised.

In the case of the sequence

$$A \xrightarrow{T_{1a}} B \xrightarrow{T_{2a}} C \xrightarrow{T_3} D,$$

T_3 involved adding the number of squares in the two blocks.

The new connection for (vi) or (vii) is that T_3 could be accomplished by subtracting numbers of squares. T_3 as originally defined can be dealt with in this way as it invites one to use any necessary knowledge of calculations to find the total number of squares.

So now,

T_{1b} is: form the rectangle whose edges contain all the vertices of the triangle. This is not to split the triangle up but to so transform the space that the triangle itself is seen as one of the bits of a rectangle. And moreover so that the remaining bits are all right-angled triangles.

T_{2b} involves recognising all the bits, except the original triangle, as parts of blocks of squares.

T_3 now sometimes involves a subtraction as well as additions, and certainly does in the case of (v), (vi), (vii).

So now we have a sequence.

$$A \xrightarrow{T_{1b}} B \xrightarrow{T_{2b}} C \xrightarrow{T_3} D$$

which effectively deals with the last of the triangles and is a description of the general method suggested for the shapes in Fig. 2.5.

All this is one way of describing what is wrapped up in some of the possible consequences of the demand to: 'Find the area in squares of the triangles'. We do not need to use this transformation language unless we want to be clearer about what is involved. The fact that there can be a number of paths starting from the statement of the problem to the arrival at an answer needs a language both to help one to distinguish between the paths and, in the case of the teacher, to be able to clarify the ways in which others attempt to solve the problem.

The reader is invited to construct a number of polygonal shapes on a geoboard and consider the transformations that will yield their areas.

Often the possession of knowledge of a 'formula' leads to 'no problem'.

How Many?

Counting problems give us a chance to observe how we look at situations and work on them so that in the end we can say, 'There are so many'.

And then?

If a number of people are working on a problem, several different answers may be given. Some may be changed when a check is made, but others persist. This leads us to look more closely at the methods used, and the problem

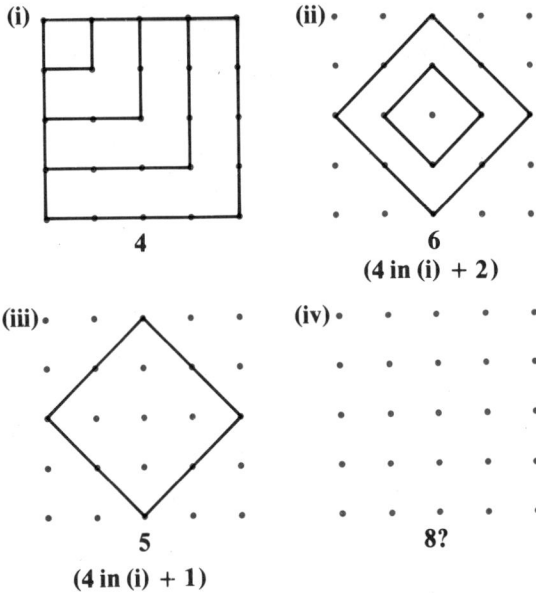

Fig. 2.9

now lies in whether we can justify that a pattern of counting has in fact done the job. Have we missed some out? Counted some twice? We can be very confident of a procedure – but how often we are fooled. And even if everyone in the group agrees, how certain are we?

A group of teachers was finding out how many different-sized squares there were on a 5 × 5 pin geoboard (Fig. 2.9). Somebody said 'Four', somebody else 'Six', another 'Eight', another 'Five'.

Eventually, everyone agreed there were eight.

'But why are we so sure that we have them all'?

Is it sufficient proof if no one in the group can find a ninth? For some, yes; for others . . . ? There were times as they worked, when an answer like 'Four' was given very confidently by somebody. Only when he heard 'Six'! did he look again – either at his own board or at the board of the teacher who had said 'Six'.

One teacher suggested that a more sure way would be to count the number of different-lengthed segments on which squares could be built. But how do we know when we have solved that problem? Is it more convincing than concentrating on the squares? Another teacher tackled the situation as follows:

(i) With a 2 × 2 board there is one square (Fig. 2.10).

Fig. 2.10

(ii) With a 3 × 3.

1, 2, or 3 pins can be used for the side of a square (Fig. 2.11). There are three possibilities, one of which we already have.

(iii) With a 4 × 4, four possibilities; only the last is new (Fig. 2.12).

(iv) With a 5 × 5 board, ... Wait a minute. One has been missed out on the 4 × 4 board (Fig. 2.13).

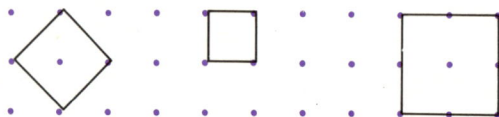

Fig. 2.11

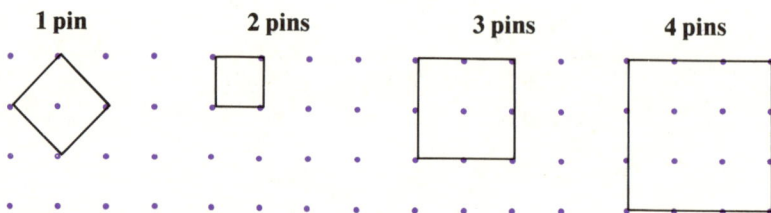

Fig. 2.12

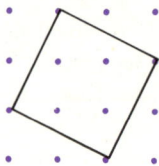

Fig. 2.13

If we proceed step by step, increasing the size of the board in this way, we still have to watch that squares don't escape us. How about this? If we use up two or more pins along the edge of the board, the squares must have their sides parallel to the edges of the board, and for a 5 × 5 pin board, there are certainly only four of them – those using 2, 3, 4 or 5 pins. So all we have to watch are the successive situations when one pin only is used along the edges (Fig. 2.14). At this point, someone suggested rotating the band around the point, attaching it to each nail in turn and checking for a square or not (Fig. 2.15). By symmetry we shall have repeats if we turn about R. And for a 5 × 5 pin board (Fig. 2.16) – no more from Q – the same for S, by symmetry. And R will give a further square (Fig. 2.17).

3 × 3

1

4 × 4

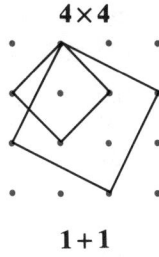

1 + 1

Fig. 2.14

P   Q   R   S

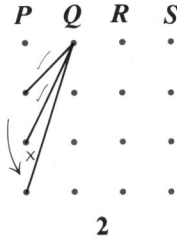

2

Fig. 2.15

P   Q   R   S   T

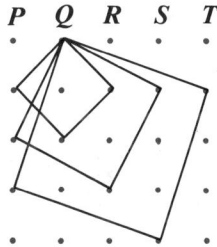

Fig. 2.16

P   Q   R   S   T

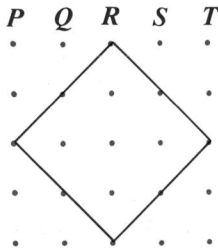

Fig. 2.17

Counting the new ones at each stage, we have

$$1\,[3 \times 3] + 1\,[4 \times 4] + (1 + 1)\,[5 \times 5]$$

which, with the original four parallel to the edges, gives eight. And at the end one teacher said, 'We needn't have built up from a 2 × 2 to a 5 × 5 board. All we needed to do was to study the single pins in turn along the edge of the 5 × 5 board and symmetry required that we only looked at P, Q, R' (Fig. 2.18).

Counting in one sense is easy – 1, 2, 3, 4, 5, ... The problem lies in the patterns we superimpose on the situation in order to count.

(For further discussion of this point see *Notes on mathematics in primary schools* pp. 181–6 and 289–94.)

And how about counting goldfish in a fish tank?

Here are some 'How many'? questions. Work on some of them with a group of children and notice the various actions taken. Try some on your own and if possible compare your results with someone else.

1. How many different paths can be drawn which start and finish at S and pass through all the other four points once only (Fig. 2.19)? Try for other numbers of points.

P   Q   R

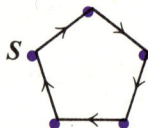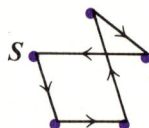

Fig. 2.18   Fig. 2.19

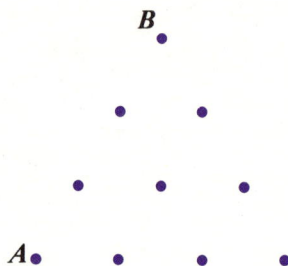

Fig. 2.20

2. How many three-digit even numbers are there using any of the digits 1, 2, 3, 4, 5 without repetitions?

3. By putting rods end-to-end, make rows equal in length to the yellow rod. How many different rows can be made? (Assume that order matters, that is, red followed by green is different from green followed by red.)

4. Taking the distance between any two neighbouring points in Fig. 2.20 to be 1 unit, how many paths are there from A to B of length 4 units? Of length 5 units?

5. There are 12 counters, 3 of them red and the remainder yellow. In how many distinct ways can they be arranged in a circle?

6. What is the total number of squares that can be made on a 6 × 6 pin geoboard?

The chief problems with the solution to a 'how many'? question are:

(i) how do you know when you have finished (exhausted all possibilities)?
(ii) how do you know that there are no repetitions?

In the end someone might not be satisfied that he has the answer until he has in some way shown that these two problems have been resolved.

Equivalence Transformations

We shall now look at a few examples involving number in which the transformations used preserve a particular equivalence. Earlier (p. 17), we examined number pairs and the transformation: *subtract from one number in the pair what is added to the other* – and saw that the sum of the two numbers was unaffected by the change. The relation 'has the same sum as' held. If we apply the same transformation to a number pair and observe the effect on the product we see that the change in the number pair does effect a change in the product. Starting with (12,9) and adding and subtracting 2, for example, we have:

$$\text{product } 108$$
$$\downarrow$$
$$\ldots \leftarrow (16, 5) \leftarrow (14, 7) \leftarrow (12, 9) \rightarrow (10, 11) \rightarrow (8, 13) \rightarrow \ldots$$

The relation 'has the same product as' is not induced by the transformation.

But the transformation: *multiply one number of the pair and divide the other by the same number* would not affect the product and it can be called an equivalence transformation, provided it is the product which is being kept in mind. Starting with (16, 9), we have:

$$(16, 9) \rightarrow (8, 18) \rightarrow (4, 36) \rightarrow (2, 72) \rightarrow (1, 144)$$

if we restrict our choice to whole numbers, but if we include fractions, an infinite set of pairs is potentially available to us.

$$\ldots \leftarrow (64, 2\tfrac{1}{4}) \leftarrow (32, 4\tfrac{1}{2}) \leftarrow (16, 9) \rightarrow (8, 18) \rightarrow (4, 36) \rightarrow (2, 72)$$
$$\rightarrow (1, 144) \rightarrow (\tfrac{1}{2}, 288) \rightarrow (\tfrac{1}{4}, 576) \rightarrow \ldots$$

Once we recognise that such a transformation allows us to travel around an equivalence class of pairs, then, given any product, or in the earlier example, any sum, we can choose either to work on it to get the answer, or to select, through transformation, an equivalent product which, for one reason or another, we prefer the look of – we may find one for which we know the answer immediately. (*Note* that within the equivalence class, the 'answer' can be 'seen' in at least one of the number pairs: in the case of a product, one number in the pair will be 1, and for the sum, one of the numbers will be 0.) But how we choose to make a change and what we prefer is a very personal matter, depending upon what each of us knows, and a positive reason for working with transformations is that it allows so much individual choice, at the same time providing a firm basis on which to build.

Of course, we are only able to move around an equivalence class in this way if we have some facility to carry out the appropriate transformation – to double and halve, for example, in the case of products, to add and subtract in the case of the sum, and so we need to provide children with experiences which help them to do this.

Partitions

One possibility is the study of the partitions of a given number, sometimes introduced as 'the story of . . .'. Not infrequently this is limited just to *pairs* of numbers adding up to the given number. Yet given the condition that the partitions must sum to the fixed total, and if we know one such partition, we can generate *all* the others by substitutions which have as their basis what, in hindsight, we can call the *commutative and associative properties of addition*. But how can these properties emerge as significant ideas in the thought of young children? We think that the replacement of lengths by other equivalent lengths using Cuisenaire rods is ideal material for this purpose, since the changes are physically enacted in a way which captures closely the way in which the mind carries out substitutions.

Using Cuisenaire Rods

For any length we can build up a pattern or a set of partitions using the rods. There are decisions to be made about the number of rods in each line (two only, or any number perhaps) and whether we shall take order into account or not. At a certain stage it may largely be trial and error which enables us to add more rows to the pattern; a scanning procedure may be used to see if a new line has already been included or not. It is possible, too, that we may use equivalences already available to us in order to move from one line to another: for example, we see a light green rod in a line and knowing that it is equivalent to red end-to-end with white we can make another line using that equivalence. By a substitution we have transformed one line into another. By observing such a pattern and by being conscious of our ability to go on making new lines, we can simply see *that there are many equivalent lengths.* Although it is necessary to know that there are many, it is not enough. In addition, we need to look for ways in which we can generate many from one so that we are in a stronger position to use what we know, *however little that may be*, to generate what, until that time, we did not know. ('Know' in the sense of being able to recall.) This places emphasis not on the memory, but on the control which each person can have on the situation through his ability to transform it in ways appropriate to the problem in hand. The control is uniquely his because it is his perception of the situation which triggers his selection of a suitable transformation from those available to him. For this to happen, it must be worked for, and we need to provide activities for children which focus attention on transformations, so that it becomes conscious and deliberate.

Taking the first letter of the colour of each rod as the symbol for the rod we can write for the colours white, red, light green, pink, yellow, dark green, black, brown (tan), blue, orange, the letters w, r, g, p, y, d, b, t, B, o, respectively.

Consider $\qquad\qquad\qquad y + p.$

In what ways can we pay attention to it in order to perceive other equivalent expressions through transformations of it and through transformations of transformations of it? The question is a personal one to each reader simply because of the different perceptions it will propose to each one.

My attention is drawn to the pink rod and I know that it is equivalent to $r + r$ *or* $2r$. *I also know that* $y = p + w$ *and so I can write*

$$y + p \rightarrow y + r + r \rightarrow y + 2r$$
$$\rightarrow p + w + 2r$$
$$\rightarrow r + r + w + 2r$$
$$\rightarrow w + 4r$$

if I know that I can change the order without affecting the sum. A variety of games can be played with children in order to make them more sensitive to the multiplicity of possibilities. A challenging game to play when they already have experience in making partitions is to choose a line of rods like $y + p$ and ask them to name other lines equivalent in length, one of the rules being that no one is allowed to touch the rods. This gives a chance for them to recognise that they can transform in their minds and so produce many equivalent expressions, most of which they don't carry around in their memory – nor have they need to if they can generate them at will. I found, when working with children of 5 – 7 years that *they could between them build up large networks of expressions through games like this and they enjoyed the challenge of not being able to touch the rods. I noticed too, that unless I produced games with rules which deliberately forced attention to be given to virtual actions – transformations from one perception to another in the mind independent of any corresponding physical action – many children remained unaware, as far as I could see, of the power they had and could develop. Few discovered it for themselves: most required attention to be drawn to it and then they could, if they chose, work on it (Fig. 2.21).*

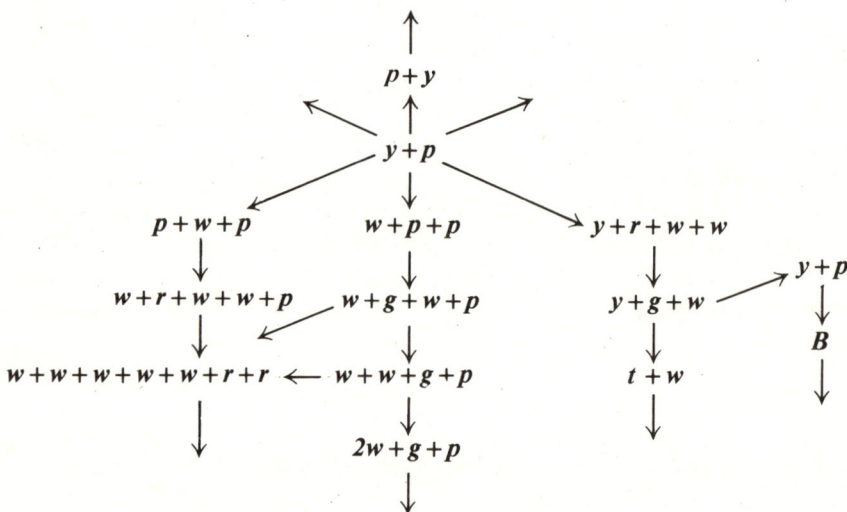

Fig. 2.21

So far we have been concerned with changes which keep length constant. We started by physically making a pattern of rods, line by line, and went on to the mental generation of a number of partitions from any given line. We suggest that the source of confidence and power in the situation comes from a child knowing how to get from one partition to another. This is the key to the degree of freedom we have within the restrictions we have imposed. These are, that we are partitioning one particular length and that we use only the addition operation.

Although rods have been used here to convey the action of generating a set of partitions through transformations, it is of course not essential to use rods in order to do the job. If other materials such as Unifix cubes, pebbles, or even written numerals are available, then it is necessary, as with the rods, to see what is required so that the material models as closely as possible the actions which the mind makes when it shifts its viewpoint and transforms the situation.

If we assign a unit of measure to the rods, we can carry out the transformations as before and use numerals to record them.

1. *Choose any partition for a number and see if it is possible to generate all the others from it (taking order into account) using only the associativity of addition and not commutativity.*

2. *Is it possible to find* all *the products of a given number, taking a* × *b to be different from b* × *a, using only the associativity of multiplication?*

The last question is briefly taken up on p. 51.

It is worth mentioning in passing that, with any apparatus, there are actions which are simple to carry out and which produce a desired result at the physical level with the manipulation of the apparatus, but which do not prompt efficient mental operations when the apparatus is no longer there.

For example, suppose a child meets such questions as $13 + 15 =$ for the first time and uses rods to find the answer.

10	3	10	5

The train, $10 + 3 + 10 + 5$ is made and it is measured by making another train $10 + 10 + 8$ (say) at the side of it. A number is associated with the second train – that is, 28 – and he can write $13 + 15 = 28$. A simple physical action. 28 is arrived at by naming the second train and not by a direct transformation of the first. If the rods are no longer available and he proceeds to operate mentally as he did with his hands previously, then the procedure is quite a difficult one. In other words, the physical operations with the rods and the mental operations going hand-in-hand with them are of different complexities. If, on the other hand, he knows that he can change the order of the rods in the first train to say, $13 + 15 = 10 + 3 + 10 + 5 = 10 + 10 + 3 + 5$, then he is in a position to read off 28 (measurement of $3 + 5$ may be needed). Children sometimes say at this stage, 'I don't need to move the rods. I can do it with my eyes', or something similar. The physical and mental operations are now much closer.

Another example concerns a 'take away': $17 - 8 =$. A child has a pile of 17 pebbles and he takes away 8. He then counts those left and finds 9. Hence $17 - 8 = 9$. If he now works on similar questions mentally without the pebbles, what is the complexity in the handling of the mental operations corresponding to the physical actions, compared with the complexity of the physical actions alone?

Complementary Pairs

If, out of the set of partitions for a number, we consider the subset which contains pairs of numbers only, we can develop a vast amount of computational know-how based on equivalence transformations on the pairs. (Reference is also made to this on p. 17). This work has been developed in considerable detail by Gattegno (particularly in *The common sense of teaching mathematics*). We give an outline of his work here because we feel it to be fundamental to our consideration of computation, based on transformation and equivalence, but refer readers to his book for a detailed development.

The complementary pairs for 9 are:

$$9 \to (1, 8), (2, 7), (3, 6), (4, 5), (5, 4), (6, 3), (7, 2), (8, 1),$$

and we can move within the equivalence class by adding 1 to one member of the pair and subtracting 1 from the other. If we know about the transformation – that is, if we can bring it to mind in order to use it – then any one of the pairs together with the transformation will generate all the others.

$$[(a, b), T] \to \text{set of complements.}$$

If we also have the commutative transformation available to us, then only half the pairs need to be found using the first transformation. As we saw earlier, if we have the transformation *add to one member of the pair what is subtracted from the other*, then we can move directly to pairs more than one step away from the given pair; and so with the set of complementary pairs for any number.

Let's now look at the special cases of complementary pairs for 10, 100, 1000, that is, for powers of 10. This approach is based upon the idea that the transformation and conventions used in writing the number pairs that add up to 10 can be re-used in a simple way in more complicated computations involving the other powers of 10.

(*a*) The fundamental complementary pairs are:

$$
\begin{array}{lll}
10 \to 1 + 9 & \left[\begin{array}{l}\text{by the commutative} \\ \text{property of addition} \\ \text{these are the same as:}\end{array}\right. & \left.\begin{array}{l}9 + 1 \\ 8 + 2 \\ 7 + 3 \\ 6 + 4\end{array}\right] \\
\quad\; 2 + 8 & & \\
\quad\; 3 + 7 & & \\
\quad\; 4 + 6 & & \\
\quad\; 5 + 5 & &
\end{array}
$$

(*b*) Given one pair, we can generate the others by transferring a unit from one number to the other.

Suppose we start with $6 + 4$:

$$9 + 1 \leftarrow 8 + 2 \leftarrow 7 + 3 \leftarrow \boxed{6 + 4}$$
(right to left transfer)

$$\boxed{6 + 4} \to 5 + 5 \to 4 + 6 \to 3 + 7 \to 2 + 8 \to 1 + 9$$
(left to right transfer)

Here are two of many models we can use to show these number pairs:

(i) If I hold up ten fingers and bend down four, I have a model of (6, 4) and I can generate all the other pairs by bending or unbending fingers.

(ii) If we make a stair of Cuisenaire rods, the rods which make each step the same length as the orange rod are their complements with respect to the orange rod.

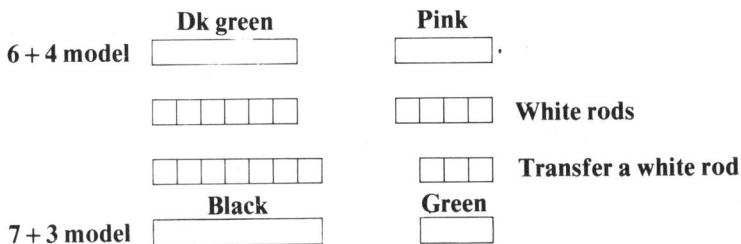

Fig. 2.22

We can generate other pairs from any starting point (Fig. 2.22).

(c) The relationships

$$10 \rightarrow 6 + 4 \rightarrow 5 + 5 \rightarrow 4 + 6 \rightarrow \text{etc.}$$

lead to

$$100 \rightarrow 60 + 40 \rightarrow 50 + 50 \rightarrow 40 + 60 \rightarrow \text{etc.}$$

and

$$1000 \rightarrow 600 + 400 \rightarrow 500 + 500 \rightarrow 400 + 600 \rightarrow \text{etc.}$$

So we can generate complementary tens with respect to 100, and complementary hundreds with respect to 1000, just by writing zeros on the right of the original numerals.

(d) We can transfer units in two-digit numerals:

$$62 + 38 \leftarrow 61 + 39 \leftarrow \boxed{60 + 40} \rightarrow 59 + 41 \rightarrow 58 + 42 \rightarrow 57 + 43 \rightarrow$$

and tens:

$$\leftarrow 71 + 29 \qquad 49 + 51 \rightarrow$$

and tens and units:

$$39 + 61 \rightarrow 38 + 62 \rightarrow 37 + 63 \rightarrow$$

$$29 + 71 \rightarrow 28 + 72 \rightarrow 27 + 73 \rightarrow$$

And all these number pairs are complements with respect to 100.

(*e*) We can transfer 'tens' in three-digit numerals:

$$620 + 380 \leftarrow 610 + 390 \leftarrow \boxed{600 + 400} \rightarrow 590 + 410 \rightarrow 580 + 420$$

and units:

$$602 + 398 \leftarrow 601 + 399 \leftarrow \boxed{600 + 400} \rightarrow 599 + 401 \rightarrow 598 + 402$$

Suppose now we start with one number in a pair

$$4 + ? = 10, \quad 40 + ? = 100,$$
$$400 + ? = 1000, \quad 4000 + ? = 10\,000.$$

With experience of the pairs it is also possible to find the missing one.
Try the following examples, the aim being to get the answer mentally as quickly as possible.
Find complements to 100 *of the following:*
40, 70, 20, 63, 28, 71, 19, 44, 53, 59

Find complements to 1000 *of:*
399, 200, 600, 325, 714, 463, 827, 481, 264, 48, 103

Find complements to 10 000 *of:*
5000, 4000, 4327, 2498, 5871, 7233, 1927, 9782, 184, 378

Describe what is required in order to give the complements quickly.
Let's look at one or two of these to see what happens:

complement of 63 to 100 → 37
complement of 548 to 1000 → 452
complement of 7273 to 10 000 → 2727

We only require the complements to 9 and to 10.
For the units digit the complement to 10 is needed, and for all the other digits, the complement to 9 (if we don't absorb the place value into our thinking then the requirement is complements to 90, 900, 9000 etc.).
So for the complement to 100 000 of 67 346 we have: 67 346
32 654
↑↑ ↑↑↑
99 9910

All the complementary pairs for addition can be rewritten in terms of subtractions. For example,

$$543 + 457 = 1000 \rightarrow 1000 - 457 = 543 \text{ and } 1000 - 543 = 457,$$

or
$$\begin{array}{ccc} 543 & 1000 & 1000 \\ + \ 457 & - \ 457 & - \ 543 \\ \hline 1000 & 543 & 457 \end{array}$$

$$543 + 457 \rightarrow 1000 - 457 \text{ and } 1000 - 543$$

This provides an example of how a whole area of number experience can be developed from a very small number of facts required to be committed to memory. Going back to the beginning of this section, we began simply with a number pair and a transformation. Once the complements to 9 and 10 are available for use, all the rest follows.

Finding All the Partitions of a Number

Earlier in the book, in connection with 'How many?' questions, we discussed the problem of the adequacy of procedures for ensuring that all cases had been included and that none had been counted more than once. In this chapter we have seen how it is possible to start with any line of rods and generate *some* other partitions. The emphasis was placed on an ability to produce *some* from a given *one*, depending upon what the mind was able to read into the line of rods. (See equivalence diagram on p. 36).

To complete this section we shall look at some possible procedures for arriving at the *total* number, while stressing that in computation the ability to transform from a given expression to another appropriate one is what really matters. To find them all is a special kind of exercise. In *Notes on mathematics in primary schools*, p. 292, examples were given showing ways in which two children had tackled the question. We give them again here.

JOHN

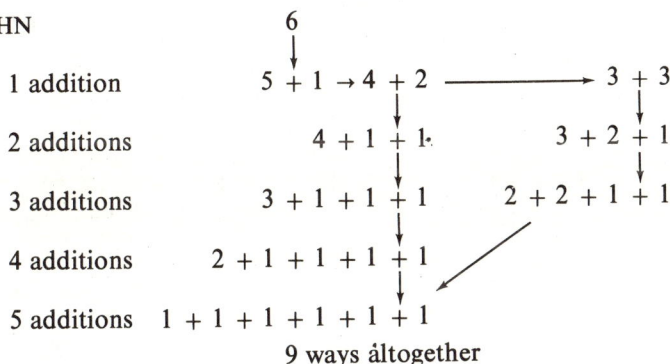

9 ways altogether

ROBERT

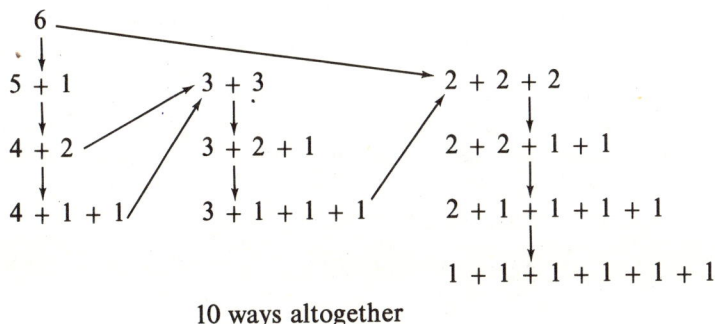

10 ways altogether

Notice that order has not been taken into account and the starting number 6 has not been counted, since the pattern was drawn up in terms of additions. No repetitions in either list. 2 + 2 + 2 is missing from John's. Did John's routine not allow for 2 + 2 + 2? Can it be inserted without upsetting the pattern?

Roderick (11 years) worked in the following way. The order in each pattern is his.

5

$1 + 1 + 1 + 1 + 1$
$1 + 1 + 1 + 2$
$1 + 1 + 3$
$1 + 4$
$2 + 3$

6

$1 + 1 + 1 + 1 + 1 + 1$
$1 + 1 + 1 + 1 + 2$
$1 + 1 + 1 + 3$
$1 + 1 + 2 + 2$
$3 + 3$
$3 + 2 + 1$
$4 + 2$
$4 + 2 + 1$
$5 + 1$
$2 + 2 + 2$ (This was produced after scanning the lines already found.)

7

$1 + 1 + 1 + 1 + 1 + 1 + 1$
$1 + 1 + 1 + 1 + 1 + 2$
$1 + 1 + 1 + 1 + 3$
$1 + 1 + 1 + 4$
$1 + 1 + 5$
$1 + 6$
$2 + 5$
$2 + 2 + 2 + 1$
$2 + 2 + 1 + 1 + 1$ $\qquad$ $2 + 2 + 3$
$2 + 1 + 1 + 3$ $\qquad$ $2 + 4 + 1$
$\qquad$ $3 + 3 + 1$
$\qquad$ $3 + 2 + 2$
$\qquad$ $4 + 3$

'How did you work out the lines for 7?'
  'I did the ones beginning with "ones" and another number first.' Then I started by finding all the combinations containing "twos", not repeating the already discovered ones, and finally the three and fours.'
(*This repeat was not noticed, however.*)
  'I have some more. Can you find any missing ones?'
  After some thought he inserted 2 + 1 + 1 + 3 and 2 + 2 + 1 + 1 + 1 as shown.

Find all the partitions of 7 and 8 (ignoring order) and examine the procedures you have used. Were you confident at the end that you had included them all? Do you think that your routine would be satisfactory for finding the partitions of a bigger number, say 10?
Can you avoid writing them all out?

Here are some possible ways of tackling the problem.

1. This routine has an order in it which corresponds to the ordering of words in a dictionary.

Begin with the partitions of 6

$$6 = 5 + 1$$
$$= 4 + 2$$
$$= 4 + 1 + 1$$
$$= 3 + 3$$
$$= 3 + 2 + 1$$
$$= 3 + 1 + 1 + 1$$
$$= 2 + 2 + 2$$
$$= 2 + 2 + 1 + 1$$
$$= 2 + 1 + 1 + 1 + 1$$
$$= 1 + 1 + 1 + 1 + 1 + 1$$

Does it ensure that none is omitted?

Try the same method for some other numbers.

Here, we started with a number and broke it down into its set of partitions.

The next method begins with the partitions of any number and from it, builds up the partitions of the number above it.

2. Can we obtain the partitions of 7 from the partitions of 6?

Yes, by adding a 1 to each partition of 6.

In how many ways can the 1 be added?

It can be added to each summand (name given to any number in a partition, for example, in 2 + 3 + 1, 2, 3 and 1 are summands) in turn or written as an extra summand, and these are the only possibilities. For example, beginning with 2 + 3 + 1, the possibilities are:

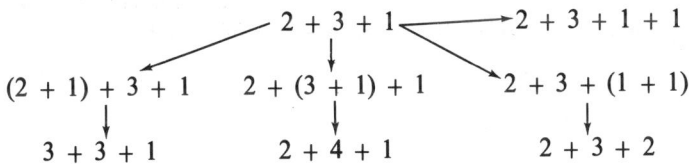

$$2 + 3 + 1 \qquad 2 + 3 + 1 + 1$$
$$(2 + 1) + 3 + 1 \qquad 2 + (3 + 1) + 1 \qquad 2 + 3 + (1 + 1)$$
$$3 + 3 + 1 \qquad 2 + 4 + 1 \qquad 2 + 3 + 2$$

When this is done to each of the partitions of 6 we shall have *all* the partitions of 7. However, we shall have repeats since this method does not in itself take care of repeats and these will have to be eliminated.

Try this method to obtain the partitions of another number from the one preceding it.

3. Another routine, which again includes repeats, illustrated by finding the partitions of 5.

For this we need the partitions of the previous numbers 2, 3, 4.

$$2 = 1 + 1,$$
$$3 = 2 + 1 = 1 + 1 + 1,$$
$$4 = 3 + 1 = 2 + 1 + 1 = 1 + 1 + 1 + 1 = 2 + 2.$$

Add 1 to the partitions of 4:

$$4 + 1, \quad 3 + 1 + 1, \quad 2 + 1 + 1 + 1, \quad 1 + 1 + 1 + 1 + 1, \quad 2 + 2 + 1$$

Then add 2 to the partitions of 3:

$$3 + 2, \quad 2 + 1 + 2, \quad 1 + 1 + 1 + 2$$

and 3 to the partitions of 2:

$$2 + 3, \quad 1 + 1 + 3$$

This gives all of them but, again, with some repeats.

Postscript on Complete Partitions

There are many ways of looking at partitions. In the end the properties of number with which we are all familiar can be traced back to partitions of numbers. When partitions are investigated using pegs in pegboard, or simply dots in rows and columns, the graphs that result show up some interesting properties.

We can write a positive integer as the sum of other positive integers in various ways.

$$5 = 4 + 1 = 3 + 1 + 1 = 2 + 1 + 1 + 1$$
$$= 3 + 2 = 2 + 2 + 1 = 1 + 1 + 1 + 1 + 1.$$

These are the seven *partitions* of 5 if we don't take order into account and we can write this: $P(5) = 7$.

In a partition like $4 + 1$ above, the numbers 4 and 1 are called *summands* and order is ignored so that $1 + 4$ is the same partition as $4 + 1$. One way of classifying the partitions is by the number of summands they have:

5 has
1 partition into 5 summands	$1 + 1 + 1 + 1 + 1$
1 partition into 4 summands	$2 + 1 + 1 + 1$
2 partitions into 3 summands	$3 + 1 + 1, 2 + 2 + 1$
2 partitions into 2 summands	$4 + 1, 3 + 2$
1 partition into 1 summand	5

Another way of classifying them is by the size of the summands in them:

5 has
1 partition with 5 as the largest summand	5
1 partition with 4 as the largest summand	$4 + 1$
2 partitions with 3 as the largest summand	$3 + 1 + 1, 3 + 2$
2 partitions with 2 as the largest summand	$2 + 2 + 1,$
	$2 + 1 + 1 + 1$
1 partition with 1 as the largest summand	$1 + 1 + 1 + 1 + 1$

It looks as if the number of partitions with a given number of summands is equal to the number of partitions with that number as the largest summand. *Try it for the partitions of* 6

Taking these partitions of 5 in turn, we can represent them by 'graphs' in which each summand is represented by the appropriate number of dots in the rows (Fig. 2.23).

A Reading by rows		*B* Reading by columns
$1 + 1 + 1 + 1 + 1$	⋮	5
$2 + 1 + 1 + 1$	⁞	$4 + 1$
$3 + 1 + 1$		$3 + 1 + 1$
$2 + 2 + 1$		$3 + 2$
$4 + 1$		$2 + 1 + 1 + 1$
$3 + 2$		$2 + 2 + 1$
5	•••••	$1 + 1 + 1 + 1 + 1$

Fig. 2.23

However, each of these dot 'graphs' can also be added in columns to give the readings shown in column *B*. These also give partitions of 5 since we are merely counting the total number of dots in a different way. Moreover, the 'graphs' can be paired so that each member of any pair is a reflection of the other in the line in Fig. 2.24.

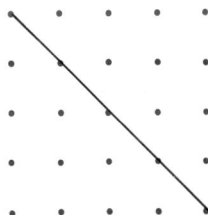

Fig. 2.24

The pattern ⦂ being symmetrical about the diagonal line is not paired off.

1. *Find the set of partitions for P*(2), *P*(3), *P*(4), *P*(7), *P*(8) *and analyse them in a similar way. Can you pick out,* before *drawing the graphs, which, if any, of*

the partitions will give a graph which is symmetrical about the line shown in Fig. 2.24? Check.

2. Conjecture the properties required of a partition so that it has a symmetrical graph. For example, is it necessary for the number of summands in the partition to be equal to the largest summand in the partition? Is this sufficient? How many symmetrical graphs has P(8)?

3. Can you find a way of working out values for P(1), P(2), P(3), . . . , P(n)? These and more ideas are developed in I. Niven, *Mathematics of choice.*

Products Associated with Partitions

We have looked at partitions in general with no restrictions on the numbers used. We also considered the subset in which pairs of numbers only were allowed, giving us a chance to work on complementary pairs.

The following sequence describes the use of rods where work with another subset of partitions is employed: that in which rods of the same colour only are permitted. This of course corresponds to repeated addition of the same number. For example,

$$3 + 3 + 3, \qquad 7 + 7, \text{ out of which products can emerge.}$$

Knowledge assumed:
numerals, written and spoken

1 2 3 4 5 6 7 8 9		units
11 12 13 14 15 16 17 18 19		teens
10 20 30 40 50 60 70 80 90		tens and 100
meanings: for example, $4 + 10 = 10 + 4$		*defines* 14
5 tens or $10 + 10 + 10 + 10 + 10$		*defines* 50

transformations of the kind:
$$7 + 8 = (7 - 2) + (8 + 2) = 5 + 10 = 15$$
(with the object of 'making tens')

Stage I

Factors are defined with rods, and a writing suggested in which $\times$ represents the meaning of 'of the'. For example (Fig. 2.25).

Factors of 10

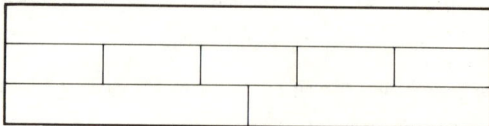

Fig. 2.25

$$1 \text{ orange} = 5 \text{ 'of the' red,}$$
$$10 \quad = 5 \times 2,$$
$$1 \text{ orange} = 2 \text{ 'of the' yellow,}$$
$$10 \quad = 2 \times 5.$$

Awareness of reversibility as such is not certain, as long as only trains of rods are used. Only when a rectangle, say of four yellow rods ($4y$), is seen together with the corresponding one, a rectangle of five pink rods ($5p$), is there a chance to direct the children's attention to reversibility. One can 'see' a rectangle $7g$ when confronted with a rectangle $3b$, but not with three black rods in a line. The side-by-side comparison of these sets of rods arranged in rectangles and squares brings comments and further awarenesses. Such numbers as 4, 6, 8, 9, 10, can now be called *product numbers.*

Stage II

If we have plenty of orange rods but only one each of d, b, t, B, can we find other product numbers?

Suggestions are invited for pairs that will lead to a product number. Opportunity is given for the children to express any results that they already know; the teacher can 'go with' the class and find out which are the easy ones for them. Examples they may give are:

1. Even numbers   12, 14, 16, 18, 20, . . . as doubles of
                     6, 7, 8, 9, 10, . . .

2. Counting in fives   5, 10, 15, 20, 25, . . . yielding
                   . . . , $3 \times 5, 4 \times 5, 5 \times 5, \ldots$

3. Tens, implicit in the definitions of the numerals

$$2 \times 10, 3 \times 10, 4 \times 10, 5 \times 10, 6 \times 10, 7 \times 10, 8 \times 10, 9 \times 10$$
$$20 \qquad 30 \qquad 40 \qquad 50 \qquad 60 \qquad 70 \qquad 80 \qquad 90$$

4. Factor patterns of rods can give other pairs for 12, 16, 18 or we can use associativity as follows:

$$12 = 2 \times 6 = 2 \times (2 \times 3) = (2 \times 2) \times 3 = 4 \times 3 = 3 \times 4$$
$$16 = 2 \times 8 = 2 \times (2 \times 4) = (2 \times 2) \times 4 = 4 \times 4$$
$$18 = 2 \times 9 = 2 \times (3 \times 3) = (2 \times 3) \times 3 = 6 \times 3 = 3 \times 6$$

Stage III

WHAT ELSE?

There may or may not be a store of suggestions from stage II. The chart may have fewer entries than are shown in Fig. 2.26. It is probable that the unfilled boxes in this chart will now prove stimulating.

	2	3	4	5	6	7	8	9	10	
10										100
9										90
8						•	•			80
7							•			70
6					•	•	•			60
5				25	30		40			50
4			16	20	•	•	•	•		40
3		**9**	12	15		•				30
2	**4**	**6**	**8**	**10**	12	14	16	18	20	20

Key: heavy figures — numbers found at stage I
other figures — numbers found at stage II
dots — numbers found at stage III *A* and *B*

Fig. 2.26

The teacher may have to create an atmosphere of restraint at this point. It is all too easy for children to become identified in a feverish activity to fill the empty boxes as fast as possible, with little regard for the rightness of the entry, and no storing in their minds of the results, or even of the methods used to find the answers.

What we now attempt is to help the children to discover for themselves, and each other, methods by which they can find other results, not by counting on their fingers, but by several routes which lead to identical answers. Some examples follow:

A. It is required to find 4 × 7, which also gives 7 × 4.
   (i) Using associativity 2 × 7 = 14   (already found)
      4 × 7 = (2 × 2) × 7   (since 4 = 2 × 2)

$$= 2 \times (2 \times 7) = 2 \times 14 = 14 + 14$$
$$= 10 + 4 + 10 + 4$$
$$= 10 + 10 + 4 + 4$$
$$= 20 + 8$$
$$= 28.$$

(ii) Partitions of 7

$$7 = (6,1) = (5,2) = (5,1,1) = (4,3) = (4,2,1) = (4,1,1,1)$$
$$= (3,3,1) = (3,2,1,1) = \ldots$$

which shall we use?

(a) $7 = 5 + 2$: $4 \times 7 = (4 \times 5) + (4 \times 2) = 20 + 8 = 28.$
(b) $7 = 4 + 3$: $4 \times 7 = (4 \times 4) + (4 \times 3) = 16 + 12 = 10 + 6 + 10 + 2$
$$= 10 + 10 + 6 + 2 = 20 + 8.$$

B. Associativity with a further doubling.

(i) $2 \times 2 = 4$
$4 \times 4 = (2 \times 2) \times 4 = 2 \times (2 \times 4) = 2 \times 8 = 8 + 8 = (8 + 2) + 6$
$$= 16.$$
$4 \times 6 = (2 \times 2) \times 6 = 2 \times (2 \times 6) = 2 \times 12 = 12 + 12 =$
$$= 10 + 2 + 10 + 2$$
$$= 20 + 4 = 24.$$
$4 \times 8 = 4 \times (4 \times 2) = (4 \times 4) \times 2 = 16 \times 2 = 2 \times 16 = \ldots = 32.$
$4 \times 9 = 2 \times 18 = 18 + 18 = 20 + 16 = 36.$

(ii) $2 \times 4 = 8.$
$8 \times 8 = 2 \times 4 \times 8 = 2 \times 32 = 60 + 4 = 64.$
$8 \times 9 = 2 \times 4 \times 9 = 2 \times 36 = 60 + 12 = 72.$

(iii) $2 \times 3 = 6 = 3 \times 2.$
$6 \times 6 = (3 \times 2) \times 6 = 3 \times (2 \times 6) = 3 \times 12 = 30 + 6 = 36$
or $6 \times 6 = 2 \times 3 \times 6 = 2 \times 18 = 20 + 16 = 36.$

By this method we can also work out results for $3 \times 8, 6 \times 8, 7 \times 8, 6 \times 7$.

The strings of notation in the above examples may appear to be more than most children can manage. This may be because they are seen out of context, divorced from the intensive discussions that give rise to them, and from the initiatives of the children who propose the steps themselves. Nevertheless, if the above activities remain at the level of games with notation, they cannot serve their purpose. Most of the children will be able to see that all of the apparent complexities in the writing are only what they can do in their heads, with ease, provided they are in control of what their minds are doing.

As results are found they can be used, which means that the number of steps in the working gets fewer. However, at a few points above, the rule known as *distributivity* has slipped in, as it is almost indispensable for finding products. More important, it underlies place value – the scheme by which numbers are recorded.

For example, to say that $2 \times 18 = 20 + 16$ implies that, knowing

$$18 = 10 + 8, \text{ then } 2 \times 18 = 2 \times (10 + 8) = 2 \times 10 + 2 \times 8.$$

Algebraically, the rule is expressed as $a(b + c) = ab + ac$, the reverse of which we call 'factorising' viz. $ab + ac = a(b + c)$.

Work can be done, in both directions and using small numbers, to establish this rule, so that by the time we need it for 'tens and units' it has become an interesting game. Rods can be used (Fig. 2.27).

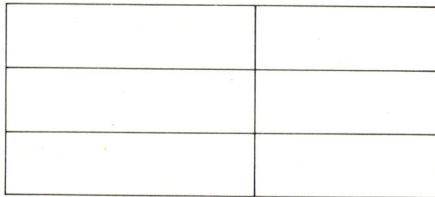

3×4	+	3×3	=	3×7
12	+	9	=	21

Fig. 2.27

C. The spaces in the chart (Fig. 2.26) not yet filled are the odd-number products:

$3 \times 7, 3 \times 9, 5 \times 7, 5 \times 9, 7 \times 7, 7 \times 9, 9 \times 9$ together with 6×9.

(i) 3×7 might be determined as in Fig. 2.27, by partitioning 7 as $3 + 4$, but any other partition of 7 would do:

$$3 \times (6 + 1) = 18 + 3 = 21,$$
$$3 \times (5 + 2) = 15 + 6 = 21,$$

or we could partition 3 as $(2 + 1)$ to find $14 + 7 = 21$. It could also be found as $\frac{1}{2}$ of $42 = (\frac{1}{2} \times 6) \times 7 = 3 \times 7$; but do the children already know that $\frac{1}{2}$ of 42 is 21?

(ii) It is tempting, and perhaps desirable, to think of $\times 9$ as an exploration of adding 10 and subtracting 1. Diagrams can be made of the satisfying pattern of the results (Fig. 2.28).

1	2	3	4	5
09	18	27	36	45
90	81	72	63	54
10	9	8	7	6

Fig. 2.28

(iii) There remain only 5×7 (which is half of 70) and 7×7.
If this situation arises, the whole of a lesson might be devoted to finding 7×7 by as many different ways as possible.
One of these could well be $7 \times 7 = 7 \times (10 - 3) = 70 - 21 = 70 - 20 - 1 = 50 - 1 = 49$.

Some checks may help to confirm results. By looking at a completed chart we can colour in odd numbers, and then bring to awareness that odd $\times$ odd = odd, whilst all others are even.

The diagonal numbers are the squares. From the product of two numbers with a given (even number) sum, the square is always the largest. For example, for $a + b = 16$, $ab = ?$

$$a = b = 8, ab = 64; \quad a = 7, b = 9, ab = 63.$$

This can be explored in detail. If $a + b = 10$, all the products $a \times b$ can be listed:

$1 + 9 = 10$	$1 \times 9 = 9$	$2 + 8 = 10$	$2 \times 8 = 16$
$3 + 7 = 10$	$3 \times 7 = 21$	$4 + 4 = 10$	$4 \times 6 = 24$
$5 + 5 = 10$	$5 \times 5 = 25$		

The Associative and Commutative Properties of Multiplication

In contrast to partitions where the associativity of addition is sufficient to generate all the other partitions from a given starting one, to find *all* the products of a given number we require both the associative and commutative transformations of multiplication, assuming that in both cases we are taking order into account, that is, $a + b$ and $b + a$, $a \times b$ and $b \times a$ are to be counted as different. For example:

(i) $8 = 5 + 3 = (3 + 2) + 3 = 3 + (2 + 3) = 3 + 5$
and similarly for other partitions.

(ii) $24 = 3 \times 8 = 3 \times (4 \times 2) = (3 \times 4) \times 2 = 12 \times 2 = (6 \times 2) \times 2$
$$= 6 \times (2 \times 2) = 6 \times 4$$

using only associativity.

But to get 4×6 from the same starting point, we must use commutativity,
$3 \times 8 = 3 \times (4 \times 2) = (3 \times 4) \times 2 = (4 \times 3) \times 2 = 4 \times (3 \times 2) = 4 \times 6$.

commutativity

Notice that underlying these changes is another kind of transformational rule which we can call a symmetrical substitution rule. *When we know a particular 'addition fact' such as* $3 + 2 = 5$, *we may use it to make the substitution 5 whenever we see* $3 + 2$, *or, equally important, make the substitution* $3 + 2$ *whenever we see 5. The same is true for 'multiplication facts'. Knowing that* $4 \times 7 = 28$, *we can substitute* 4×7 *for 28 and vice versa. Concentration on 'finding the answer' to an addition or multiplication places emphasis in the direction* $a + b \rightarrow c$ *and* $a \times b \rightarrow c$, *whereas concern for ways of transforming numbers or expressions in order finally to reach a single number as answer, emphasises* $c \rightarrow a + b$ *and* $c \rightarrow a \times b$. *This second direction opens up many possibilities from which a choice can be made, while the first closes by only having one end point (Fig. 2.29).*

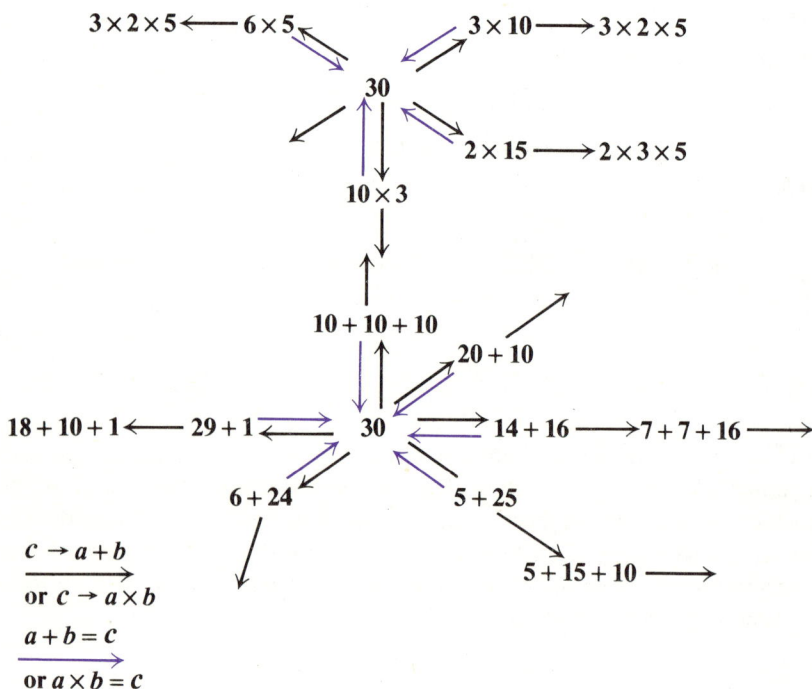

Fig. 2.29

But how do associativity and commutativity of multiplication emerge for children? With rods we can ask children to make trains using only rods of the same colour in a given train, and this will give us all the factors. But it does not encourage the activity of creating from one set of factors all the others, except where 'halving and doubling' is possible (see Fig. 2.30). In a sense it gives us commutativity, since, for example, four light-green rods give the same length as three pink rods, but the role of the different operators is so strongly emphasised in this arrangement that commutativity does not necessarily present itself to the awareness.

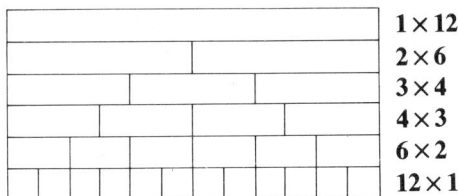

	1×12
	2×6
	3×4
	4×3
	6×2
	12×1

Fig. 2.30

With trains of rods, for example, $p + p + p$ and $g + g + g + g$, we can see that the lengths are the same so that we can say $p + p + p = g + g + g + g$, or $3p = 4g$ which, if the white rod is 1 unit, becomes 3 *four-unit lengths* = 4 *three-unit lengths*. But given one of the trains, say $p + p + p$, it is not obvious by looking at it, that it will be equivalent to $g + g + g + g$. It is true that someone may know that

$$p = g + w,$$
$$p + p + p = (g + w) + (g + w) + (g + w)$$
$$= 3g + 3w$$
$$= 3g + g$$
$$= 4g.$$

But in terms of immediate recognition it is not obvious, and if we take something harder like seven blue rods, it is not possible to superimpose an image of nine black rods on it as a result of one transformation. A series of transformations is required, for example,

$$B + B + B + B + B + B + B = (b + r) + (b + r) + \ldots$$
$$= 7b + 7r$$
$$= 7b + (3r + w) + (3r + w)$$
$$= 9b,$$

whereas we are looking for a single transformation which we can label *the commutative rule for multiplication*. This important-sounding name can interfere with the clarity which we ought to bring to this aspect of number work. In *Notes on mathematics in primary schools* (pp. 320–6) there is some discussion of these matters.

No matter what materials one uses, the response to five threes, 5 threes, 5 of the threes, 5×3, is to have to construct the answer directly by building up five threes. Other actions imply other transformations. To decide that one can *also* find five threes by building up three fives is a necessary insight before the descriptive commutative rule for multiplication can be understood. Many believe that it is actually this particular insight which is the commutative property of numbers. This is largely because we fail to distinguish between number symbols used to represent active operations and symbols used to describe relations. After experiences of the kind hinted at, and which we discuss in terms of rods, it may be fruitful to think of pairs of numbers and products so that we can associate, for instance, 30 with (5, 6): 24 with (8, 3), (2, 12), (4, 6), (3, 8) amongst others. The commutative rule for multiplication is defined on these pairs so that we always discover in every set of pairs corresponding to a number, not only (*a*, *b*) but (*b*, *a*).

When we talk of children 'knowing their tables' the practical virtue is in knowing those products which can generate further exploration of numbers. Even when we know the commutative property we will tend to choose one form or the other when we actually have to *find* a product. Thus 29 × 432 is unlikely to be calculated as

$$
\begin{array}{r}
29 \\
\times \\
432 \\
\hline
58 \\
87 \\
116 \\
\hline
12528
\end{array}
\qquad \text{but probably} \qquad
\begin{array}{r}
432 \\
\times \\
29 \\
\hline
3888 \\
864 \\
\hline
12528
\end{array}
$$

(This is also a nice example of lack of flexibility.

Why not

$$
\begin{array}{r}
432 \\
\times \\
29 \\
\hline
12960 \\
432 \\
\hline
12528 \ ? \ )
\end{array}
$$

Let us make a distinction between the two numerals when we look further at some rectangles of rods.

Look at the pairs of congruent rectangles in Fig. 2.31.

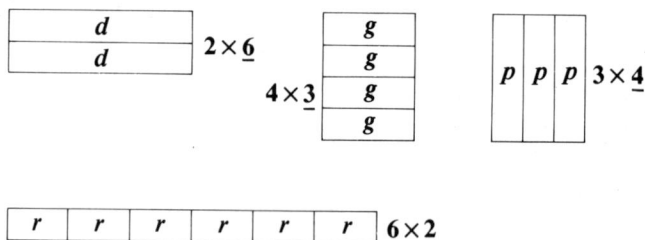

Fig. 2.31

Would you be reluctant to write 3 × 4?
Which form appears more realistic, 6 × 2 or 2 × 6?

It seems reasonable to put

$$2 \times \underline{6} = 6 \times \underline{2} \text{ and } 4 \times \underline{3} = 3 \times \underline{4},$$

or, if you prefer it $\underline{6} \times 2 = \underline{2} \times 6$ and $\underline{3} \times 4 = \underline{4} \times 3$.

Now, given any one rectangle, say the one consisting of 2 dark green rods $(2 \times \underline{6})$ it is possible to evoke the image of the other (6 red rods $(6 \times \underline{2})$). How?

Fig. 2.32 shows another example. The 3 indicates which rods we need

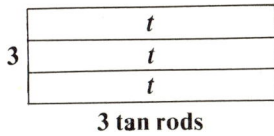

3 tan rods

Fig. 2.32

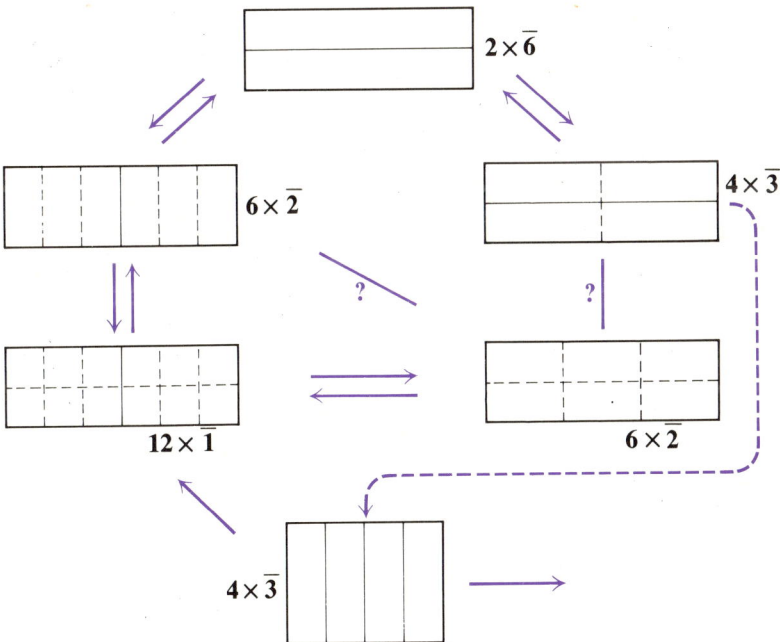

Fig. 2.33

for the second rectangle – green, and the tan rod indicates the number of greens needed – 8.

Hence $3 \times \underline{8} = 8 \times \underline{3}$

or $\underline{8} \times 3 = \underline{3} \times 8.$

A further transformation of our awareness is required for us to agree to ignore the differences between these two sets of numbers and to stress their similarities and so consider the set of pairs of natural numbers with the operation of multiplication and the transformational rule of commutativity.

But discussions and explorations with children are never as clear cut as this. The rectangles of rods and our ability to transform them into new arrangements still in rectangular form offer a variety of experiences (Fig. 2.33). There is a great variety of transformational paths to follow governed by the conserved material form (Fig. 2.34). Can you see

$$2 \times \underline{12},$$
$$3 \times \underline{8}?$$

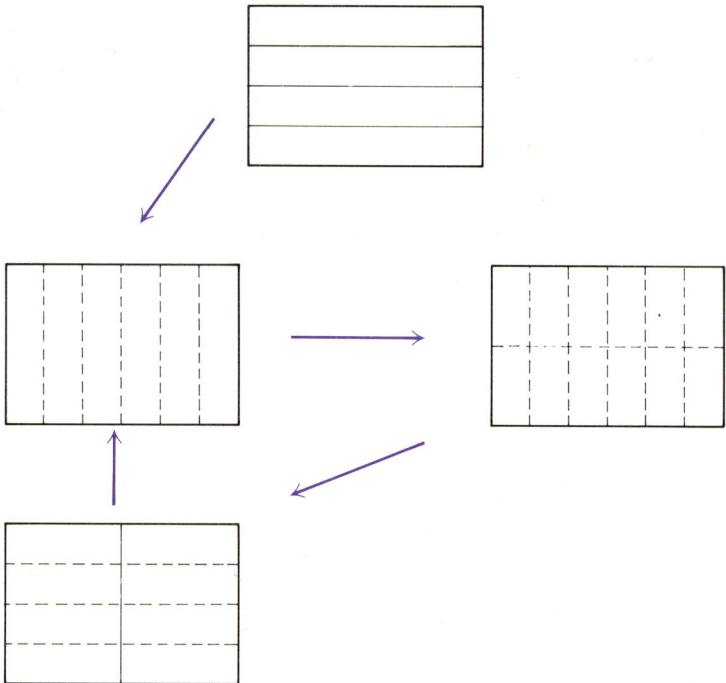

Fig. 2.34

The use of two rods crossing to symbolise multiplication implies that we are ready to work with the set of pairs of natural numbers and multiplication. A replacement activity of the kind used in partitions is now possible involving extending the cross to towers of crossed rods and transformations with such towers. The transformations will be those of substitution, commutativity and associativity, and so there will be generated all the products equivalent to a given product. This three-dimensional model enables us to be as free in our movement around the equivalence class of products as we were with the equivalence class of additions (partitions). As with addition, some products need to be known by us to provide a set of starting points, but once again, provided we have these few transformations available, the number of products required to be known can be minimal.

Commutativity

Commutativity, limited to special cases, 'came' to Yvonne aged six through 'doing the same' in Unifix cubes as she'd just done with Colour Factor — the tug on my sleeve showing that she just *had* to tell someone that, '4 threes are the same as 3 fours!' 'So they are! Does it work for anything else?' 'I don't know', she said, with interest and purpose clearly discernible in her voice, 'I'll find out.'

She then made 6 twos and 2 sixes in both materials, with satisfaction, and said 'It works for 2 sixes and 6 twos.' 'Anything else?' 'I don't know', she replied with finality. Enough is enough!

For Keith, however — a little older — it was 'multiplication' on a pegboard that brought the insight. He had made 5 rows of 3 and said so. 'No', said Vaughan, sitting at the next side of the table. 'It's 3 rows of 5.' 'You're not looking at it right' said Keith, turning the board round for Vaughan to see it properly. 'Oh! Now I've got 3 fives. Of course, it's the same — bound to be.'

Matching, say, Colour Factor products like $3(y + p) = 3g$ with 3 rows of pegs in two colours on the pegboard also seems helpful to realising the characteristic property of distributivity, too, especially when compared with Mummy giving 3 children their pocket-money in two similar coins each.

Once these transformations have become reversibly familiar they do indeed give power and economy in a whole variety of situations.

Equivalent Differences

Whereas the number of partitions or products of a given number is finite, as long as we work only with natural numbers, the set of number pairs with a given difference is infinite. Take 3:

$$3 = (5, 2) = (10, 7) = (8, 5) = (21, 18) = (621, 618) = \ldots$$

It is worthwhile to gather a long list of such differences so that children gain some sense of the enormous choice of pairs open to them which satisfy the requirement of 'same difference'. A strip of length 3 units moved either way along a number line gives an easy visual method for producing pairs (Fig. 2.35). Alternatively, using rods, and, for example, the light green to

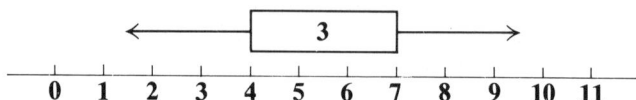

Fig. 2.35

represent the difference, pairs of rods can be found each showing a difference in length equivalent to the light-green rod.

In this way, we can build up classes of number pairs, equivalent from the point of view of difference.

In the methods mentioned for finding number pairs we have not at all been concerned with order – which number came first. If the number strip has its ends on 8 and 11, then we are indifferent to which number we read off first. There is a difference of 3 between them. Similarly with the rods. When we find the pairs of rods, we focus attention on the 'gap' and can say 'the difference between the orange and the black is the green' *or* equally well 'the difference between the black and orange is the green'.

Contrast this with the equating of difference with *subtraction*, where order is now taken into account. $2 - 5$ is not equal to $5 - 2$. Too often, we insist that children use the written form of subtraction when the first interpretation of difference is more appropriate.

Jane has 8 sweets; John has 15. How many more has John than Jane? All we need to do is to bridge the gap between 15 and 8. Subtraction as such is irrelevant. We could use $\sim$ to indicate an indifference to order, that is, we need both numbers – that's all.

$$8 \sim 15 = 7,$$
$$15 \sim 8 = 7.$$

This recognition of indifference to order is simpler because it is closer to what happens when faced with questions of this kind.

Indeed subtraction is really only associated with 'take away' in an elementary and introductory sense. If the context always indicated (a) the value of the difference and (b) the sense of its use (John has more than Jane as against Jane has less than John) then there would be no need to develop the abstract ordered system we know as subtraction.

Thinking now of the implication of possible order in a difference and the development of subtraction, we shall write $a - b$ as the number pair (a, b); (b, a) will indicate $b - a$.

Is it possible to find a transformation which allows us to travel around a class of equivalent differences just as we can within the classes of number pairs having the same sum or the same product? What kind of transformation will change the number pair without at the same time changing the difference?

Add or subtract the same number to/from each number in the pair will do this. Starting with the pair (7, 4) we can generate the following:

$$\ldots \leftarrow (3, 0) \leftarrow (4, 1) \leftarrow (5, 2) \leftarrow (6, 3) \leftarrow (7, 4) \rightarrow (8, 5) \rightarrow (9, 6)$$
$$\rightarrow (10, 7) \rightarrow (11, 8) \rightarrow \ldots$$

The transformation add or subtract 1 *from each number in the pair* gives the pairs step-by-step from (7, 4) but, of course, we are free to add or subtract any number.

$$(7, 4) \xrightarrow{\text{Add 5}} (12, 9) \xrightarrow{\text{Add 3}} (15, 12) \xrightarrow{\text{Subtract 10}} (5, 2) \xrightarrow{\text{Subtract 2}} (3, 0) \ldots$$

When rods of equal length are placed end-to-end with each rod of the original pair, new pairs of lengths are obtained, but the difference in the lengths is unaffected. Notice the *difference* between Figs. 2.36(*a*) and (*b*).

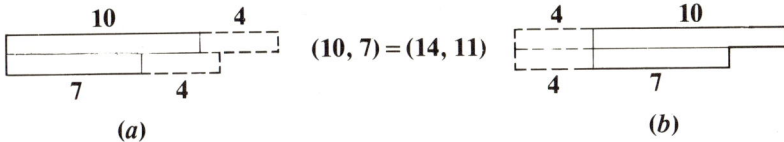

$(10, 7) = (14, 11)$

(*a*)   (*b*)

Fig. 2.36

In (*a*) the difference in length has been translated, whereas in (*b*) it remains in the same position in space relative to the rods. A group of five- to six-year-olds, working on differences was asked to take two rods of the same length and place them end-to-end with each rod in the pair. Some children placed the rods as in (*a*) and others as in (*b*). It was an interesting moment, because the two actions produced such a different outcome in relation to the constancy of the difference in length. The children who had made (*b*) saw that the difference really hadn't changed; it was just as it was before. For the group who had made (*a*), some said at once it hadn't changed and others measured the gap with a rod to check. Alternatively, equal-length rods can be used to cover up part of each rod in the original pair: again, the number pair changes, but the difference is unaltered.

Graphs of Equivalent Pairs

Since pairs of numbers are involved, we can represent them on a graph (Fig. 2.37). Here the first number is shown along the horizontal axis and the second on the vertical. For example, (8, 2) will be in the position shown.

The set of pairs ..., (3, 2), (4, 3), (5, 4), ... have been marked and we can see that they lie on a straight line.

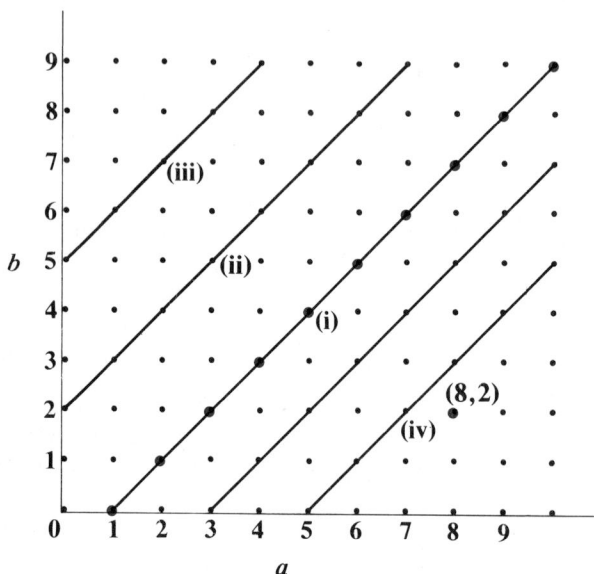

Fig. 2.37

Draw another line parallel to this. And another. And another. Which sets of pairs correspond to each of these lines and what do you notice about them?
For line (iv), we have:

$$(5, 0), (6, 1), (7, 2), (8, 3), (9, 4), \ldots$$

The difference in each case is 5.
And for line (ii) we have:

$$(0, 2), (1, 3), (2, 4), (3, 5), (4, 6), \ldots$$

Are the differences the same? Yes, but if we write them in the subtraction form, we have

$$0 - 2, 1 - 3, 2 - 4, 3 - 5, 4 - 6,$$

each of which is equal to -2.
Which lines join points corresponding to number pairs in which the first number is greater than the second? In which the second is greater than the first? What about the pairs in which the numbers are equal? And what about points on the lines which are not the original lattice points?
The series of parallel lines obtained by varying the difference is a striking visual representation of how all possible pairs of numbers can be partitioned

into families or classes by the size of the difference between them. Every dot on the graph represents a number pair and lies on exactly one of the parallel lines.

In the graphical example above, we started with a set of number pairs having the same difference, marked the corresponding points, and then drew in the straight line joining them. This line has a direction and having noticed this we drew other lines parallel to it and examined the resulting sets of points.

We can now start the opposite way round. Choose a direction, draw several lines in that direction and examine the set of number pairs obtained on each line (Fig. 2.38). *What do you find?*

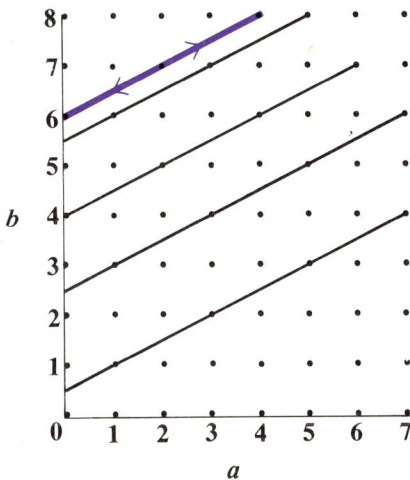

Fig. 2.38

How does the change in direction affect the relation between the number pairs on each line?

Choose the direction again. How are the pairs related now?

Out of all possible directions, why does the first one give the pairs with a constant difference on each line?

Transforming In Order to Subtract

Once we know (i) that there are families of equivalent differences, and (ii) that the transformation of adding or subtracting the same amount from each number in the pair allows us to move around in any family, we can use this knowledge to replace a subtraction by any other equivalent one. If we move with care, we can finish up with an easier one.

$44 - 18 \rightarrow (44 + 2) - (18 + 2) \rightarrow 46 - 20 \rightarrow 26$
$173 - 125 \rightarrow 73 - 25 \rightarrow 78 - 30 \rightarrow 48$
$67 - 24 \rightarrow 43$

$3484 - 1637 \rightarrow 3487 - 1640 \rightarrow 3447 - 1600 \rightarrow 3847 - 2000 \rightarrow 1847$

Make up some awkward subtractions and try this transformation method. Notice whether there are particular changes that you begin to use more frequently. Using this method, what is the smallest number of steps you can take, in your head, to find the answer to 59 374 − 36 587?

Although we have used the word 'method' to describe this way of working, it contains within it complete freedom to make individual choices as far as the transformations are concerned. It allows us to make use of what we know.

A particular example of this transformation underlies the 'equal additions' algorithm, but it is well disguised since 10 is added to the units in one number and 'paid back' to the tens in the other.

$$\begin{array}{cc} 8 & {}^{1}3 \\ {}_{1}5 & 7 \\ \hline 2 & 6 \end{array}$$

$$83 - 57 = (80 + 3) - (50 + 7) = (80 + 13) \quad - \quad (60 + 7).$$
$$\uparrow \qquad\qquad \uparrow$$
$$10 + 3 \quad\quad 10 + 50$$

Equivalent Fractions

Locate the points on a line segment, labelled 0 at one end and 1 at the other, which correspond to the number labels $\frac{1}{2}, \frac{3}{4}, \frac{4}{5}, \frac{2}{8}, \frac{6}{8}, \frac{3}{6}, \frac{1}{4}, \frac{30}{40}, \frac{12}{15}, \frac{7}{8}$.

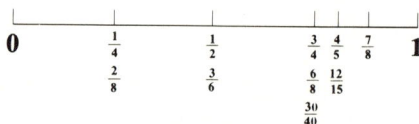

Fig. 2.39

It is clear that there are not as many points to label as there are labels (Fig. 239). Each of the marked points could be labelled in many more ways—

indeed, in infinitely many more ways (even without introducing, say, decimal notation). We can say that all the labels that could be attached to one point are equivalent and form an (infinite) equivalence class. More informally, we can say that each point has infinitely many different fractional names (for they are, though equivalent, manifestly different: they sound different and look different).

Do the endpoints of the segment have infinitely many different names too?

The class of all the fractional names attached to one point is called a *rational number*. The rational number corresponding to a particular class is usually written in exactly the same way as the fraction in the class which is 'in lowest terms'. So, apart from context, we cannot say whether the sign $\frac{1}{2}$ refers to the rational number $\frac{1}{2}$ (that is, the class $\frac{1}{2}$, $\frac{2}{4}$, $\frac{3}{6}$, ...) or the single fraction $\frac{1}{2}$. (And generally this uncertainty has no practical effect since when it comes to operating arithmetically with them, rational numbers and fractions behave in the same way.)

Suppose we label the points of a square lattice with fractions instead of the customary co-ordinates, writing a/b instead of (b, a) (Fig. 2.40). Then

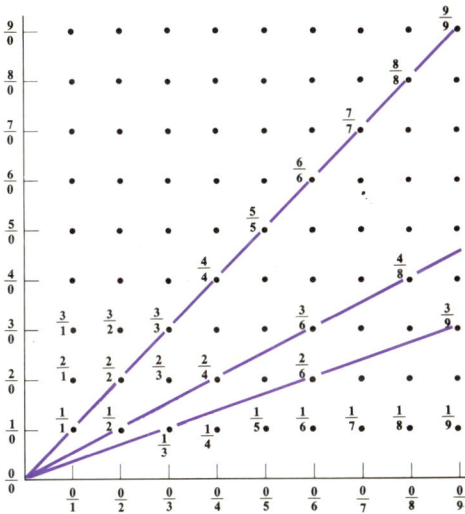

Fig. 2.40

we see, for example, that the fractions $\frac{1}{1}$, $\frac{2}{2}$, $\frac{3}{3}$ $\frac{4}{4}$, $\frac{5}{5}$, ... lie on a straight line; so do $\frac{1}{2}$, $\frac{2}{4}$, $\frac{3}{6}$, $\frac{4}{8}$ and so do $\frac{1}{3}$, $\frac{2}{6}$, $\frac{3}{9}$. These lines pick out sets of equivalent fractions.

Would the lines, if extended, pass through other points with equivalent labels? How do you know?

We could say that just as each lattice point *represents* a fraction, each marked line *represents* a rational number.

What significance could you give to the fact that each of the marked lines passes through $\frac{0}{0}$? Does every line through $\frac{0}{0}$ represent a rational number? Can you use the geometry of the lattice to find the sum of any two fractions? Or the product?

The above two situations, illuminating though they may be, are not adequate foundations for an awareness of the existence of equivalent fractions. The second, in particular, uses an existing awareness of the equivalence classes to *give* some of the lines through $\frac{0}{0}$ a particular significance.

We find very few acknowledgments in everyday usage to the existence of equivalent fraction names. Two quarter-pound packets of tea are equivalent to a half-pound packet (although not necessarily the same price), and two quarters of an hour in succession are equivalent to half an hour. But one hardly ever refers to two-quarters of a pound of tea, and no one ever says two-quarters of an hour. And such equivalences as three-quarters of a cake and six-eighths of a cake, or half a pound and eight-sixteenths of a pound, belong exclusively to the classroom. The everyday colloquial world manages, in fact, to get along very well without any significant use of equivalent fractions, and if we want to teach them we need to find a good reason – and that reason exists only within mathematics.

If we have introduced the notion of a fraction as an operator through, say, folding a piece of paper ('Find three-eighths of this piece of paper.') or using rods ('Find two-thirds of the blue rod.'), we may take the answer and the original quantity and immediately seek confirmatory feedback by asking, '*What* fraction is this of that?' This puts into circulation a new form of question that is now available for use in its own right.

'What fraction is this piece of paper of the original sheet?'

'What fraction is this pink rod of the dark green?' etc.

Consider the question, 'What fraction is the tan rod of the orange and red train?' It asks for the fractional operator that will produce a length equivalent to the tan rod when it is applied to the orange–red train (Fig. 2.41).

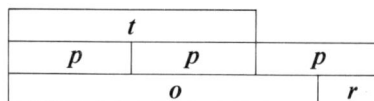

Fig. 2.41

The answer may be '$\frac{2}{3}$', since each pink rod is $\frac{1}{3}$ of the train, and the tan rod is equivalent to two of these. But we see that there is no particular reason for this choice of answer, other than having noticed that both of the lengths mentioned in the question can be made with pink rods. Can they not equally well be made (both of them) with red rods? Or with white rods? Yes; and so we may find the equally good answers, '$\frac{4}{6}$' and '$\frac{8}{12}$'.

Since three different fractions acting on the train produce the same length, the evidence suggests we should acknowledge the validity of each one by saying that we have found three different names for the same operator, or that the three fractions are equivalent. The phenomenon is, in fact, a consequence of the way we give names to fractional operators, although it is also influenced by the particular lengths involved. With another choice, say the black instead of the tan, and the blue rod instead of the train, the question would not have elicited multiple answers.

However, this situation only introduces the awareness that equivalent fractions exist; it does not give the whole equivalence class, nor does there seem any way in which it can be stretched to do so. How *could* the above question turn up the answer '$\frac{6}{9}$', for instance?

But before we take a new breath and embark on plugging this gap, let us remark how the transformation of the fractional names into equivalent ones is intimately related to the transformation of the pink rods into red rods and into whites, that is, to transformations in the rods which are used to compare the two given lengths.

To get much further requires a shift of viewpoint. Instead of thinking of a fraction as an operator that acts on one quantity to give another, let us think of a fraction as the name of the relationship *between the two quantities. It may not seem much of a shift – and it wouldn't make sense if it weren't directly related to the earlier experience – but it achieves the crucial step: it replaces the perception by the mind of two distinct, though connected, quantities by the perception of a single thing, their relationship. It is only when this stage is achieved that fractions are free to become autonomous entities, capable of existing alone and unqualified by the effect of their actions on any particular quantities. The full extension of the equivalence classes is now accessible.*

Let us say that a red rod and a light-green rod placed side-by-side model the fraction $\frac{2}{3}$ (because – temporarily shifting the viewpoint back again – the red rod is equivalent to $\frac{2}{3}$ of the light green) (Fig. 2.42).

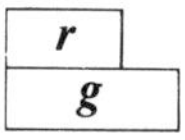

Fig. 2.42

It is clear that other pairs of rods could model the same fraction, for example, pink/dark-green and dark-green/blue.

We can now enjoy the full fruits of the double transformational mobility present in the situation we have created:

(i) that the relationship between a pair of lengths has more than one fractional name;

(ii) that any one fractional name can be represented by more than one pair of lengths.

Say we begin with red/light-green representing $\frac{2}{3}$. Then the relationship between *two* reds and *two* light greens is also $\frac{2}{3}$, as is the relationship between *three* reds and *three* light greens, as is the relationship . . .

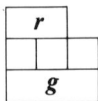

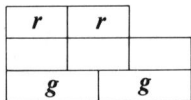

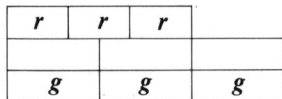

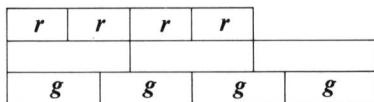

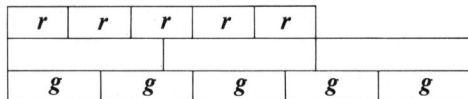

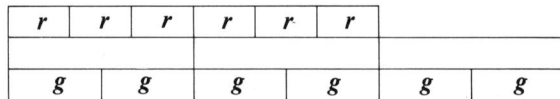

Fig. 2.43

In Fig. 2.43, an intermediate row of rods confirms that the relationship between the lengths of the first row and the third row is $\frac{2}{3}$ in each case. There is absolutely no reason to stop this sequence of models at any particular stage. It is, in principle, an endless sequence.

But we can shift viewpoint again. If we imagine that in *each* case the name of the relationship is determined by an intermediate row of *white*

rods, then the successive names become

$$\frac{2}{3}, \frac{4}{6}, \frac{6}{9}, \frac{8}{12}, \frac{10}{15}, \frac{12}{18}$$

or, expressing the fact that every length is made of reds or light greens only,

$$\frac{2}{3}, \frac{2 \times 2}{2 \times 3}, \frac{3 \times 2}{3 \times 3}, \frac{4 \times 2}{4 \times 3}, \frac{5 \times 2}{5 \times 3}, \frac{6 \times 2}{6 \times 3}.$$

The continuation of the sequence will generate as much of the equivalence class as we may need.

The reader is invited to consider the development of equivalence classes through the model provided by paper folding, or any other approach, and to decide how far such models can give the full equivalence class structure.

The reader is also asked to express the facts about equivalent fractions in terms of transformational rules, and show how to use them in the transformation of the addition or subtraction of 'unlike' fractions into the addition or subtraction of 'like' fractions.

Miscellany

Consider the meanings we can attach to the lines in Figs. 2.44, 2.45 and 2.46.

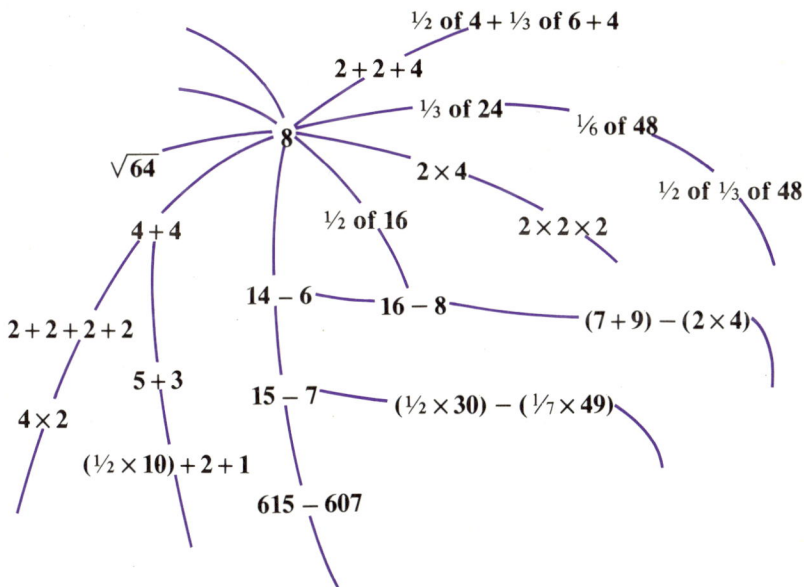

Fig. 2.44

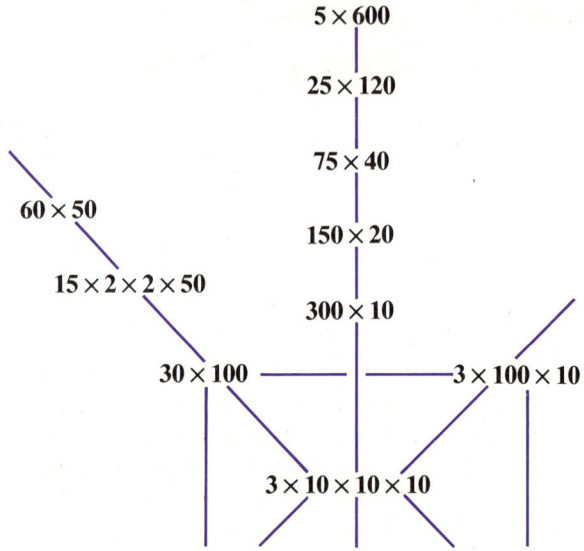

Fig. 2.45

Fig. 2.46

A six-year-old was working through some subtractions based on 36:

$$36 - 12, 36 - 21, 36 - 18 \text{ etc.}$$

She was asked how she did some of them, and for $36 - 18$ she said:
'I know that 18 is half of 36!'

$$10 = \tfrac{1}{2} \times \tfrac{1}{2} \times \tfrac{1}{2} \times 80 = \tfrac{1}{3} \times 30 = 4 + 7 - 1 = \sqrt{100}$$
$$= \sqrt[3]{8} + (\tfrac{1}{2} \times 4 \times \tfrac{1}{2} \times 8 \times \tfrac{1}{2} \times 2) = \tfrac{1}{4} \times 40$$
$$= \tfrac{9}{20} \times 2 \times \tfrac{1}{3} \times 30 + \tfrac{1}{2} \times \tfrac{1}{2} \times \tfrac{1}{2} \times \tfrac{1}{2} \times 16$$
$$= 18 - \tfrac{1}{2} \times (10 + 6 \times 1) = \sqrt[3]{64} + 8 \times (\tfrac{1}{2} \times \tfrac{1}{3} \times 6)$$
$$= 6 \times \tfrac{1}{2} \times 2 + \tfrac{4}{7} \times \tfrac{1}{2} \times 10 \times \tfrac{1}{3} \times 12 = \tfrac{1}{6} \times 60.$$

(Part of a free composition from a six-year-old boy, quoted in *Mathematics and children*, M. Goutard, Educational Explorers, 1964.)

Children use the transformations available to them and an example such as the one above shows the build-up from a simple expression to a more complex being easily achieved because the inventor is free to choose what he will according to what he knows. Such expressions looked at the other way round – from the complex to the simple – present a very different story.

$$5 = 2 + 3 = (\tfrac{1}{2} \text{ of } 4) + 3 = (\tfrac{1}{2} \text{ of } 4) + 9 - (\tfrac{2}{3} \text{ of } 9)$$
$$= (\tfrac{1}{2} \text{ of } 4) + (3 \times 3) - (\tfrac{2}{3} \text{ of } 9).$$

Compare with $\qquad (\tfrac{1}{2} \text{ of } 4) + (3 \times 3) - (\tfrac{2}{3} \text{ of } 9) = \square$.

Start with one expression equivalent to 27,

$$27 = 9 + 9 + 9.$$

We can transform this and produce from it a group of expressions related in some way to it, for example:

$27 - 9 = \square$	$18 + (\tfrac{1}{2} \times 18) = \square$
$\tfrac{1}{3} \times 27 = \square$	$\square + 18 = 27$
$27 = \tfrac{2}{3} \times 27 + \square$	$\tfrac{4}{3} \times 27 = 27 + \square$
$3 \times \square = 27$	$\square - 9 = 27$
$\tfrac{1}{2} \times 18 = \square$	$\tfrac{3}{2} \times 18 = 18 + \square$

The questions are not numbered since any one of them may provide a starting point and different children are likely to find different tracks through them.

Choose other simple equivalent expressions and invent corresponding sets of questions.

Using only the four operations and four threes try to make equivalent expressions for 1, 2, 3, ...

$$1 = (3 + 3) \div (3 + 3)$$
$$2 = (3 \div 3) + (3 \div 3)$$
$$3 = 3^3 \div (3 \times 3)$$
$$4 =$$
$$5 =$$

If *four* threes is difficult, relax the rule a little and try any number of threes.

Make equivalent expressions for 1, 2, 3, ... using only $\boxed{2, 3, 5, + -}$
The signs in the box can appear any number of times.
For example,

$$1 = 3 - 2$$
$$2 = 5 - 3$$
$$3 = 5 - 2$$
$$4 = 5 + 2 - 3$$
$$5 =$$
$$6 =$$
$$\ldots$$

Try the following:

$$\boxed{3, 4, 5, \times, -} \qquad \boxed{2, 5, 6, \div, +}$$

$$\boxed{2, 3, 4, +, -} \qquad \boxed{5, 7, 8, -}$$

According to the choice in the box, the game can be made too easy, and therefore not a challenge, or it can be impossible to generate certain integers. It is worth making up sets of signs which can be used, and checking to see what kind of game each produces.

If you know that $36 \times 48 = 1728$ what else do you know?

Transformations to Get New Numbers

We have looked at several examples of transformations which enable us to travel around an equivalence class and it is clear that transformations of this kind are extremely powerful. However, if we can combine them with transformations which enable us to leap from one equivalence class to another, then we are in an even stronger position with respect to the exploration of number relations. The example given on p. 18 illustrates these two kinds of transformations.

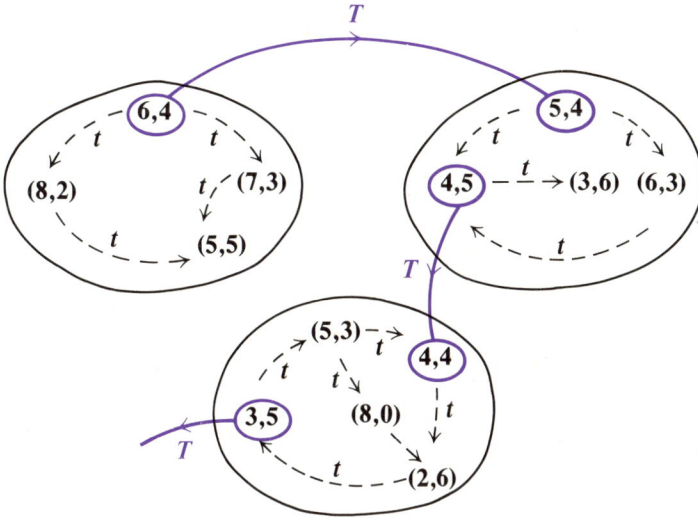

Fig. 2.47

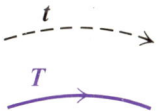

 : add to one number in the pair what is subtracted from the other.

 : change one of the numbers in the pair by one.

In the example, as we saw before, the sum is unaltered under t, but changed by T.

A similar diagram can be drawn using products (Fig. 2.48) where, for instance,

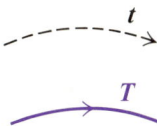

 : doubling one number in the pair and halving the other.

 : doubling (or halving) one number in the pair.

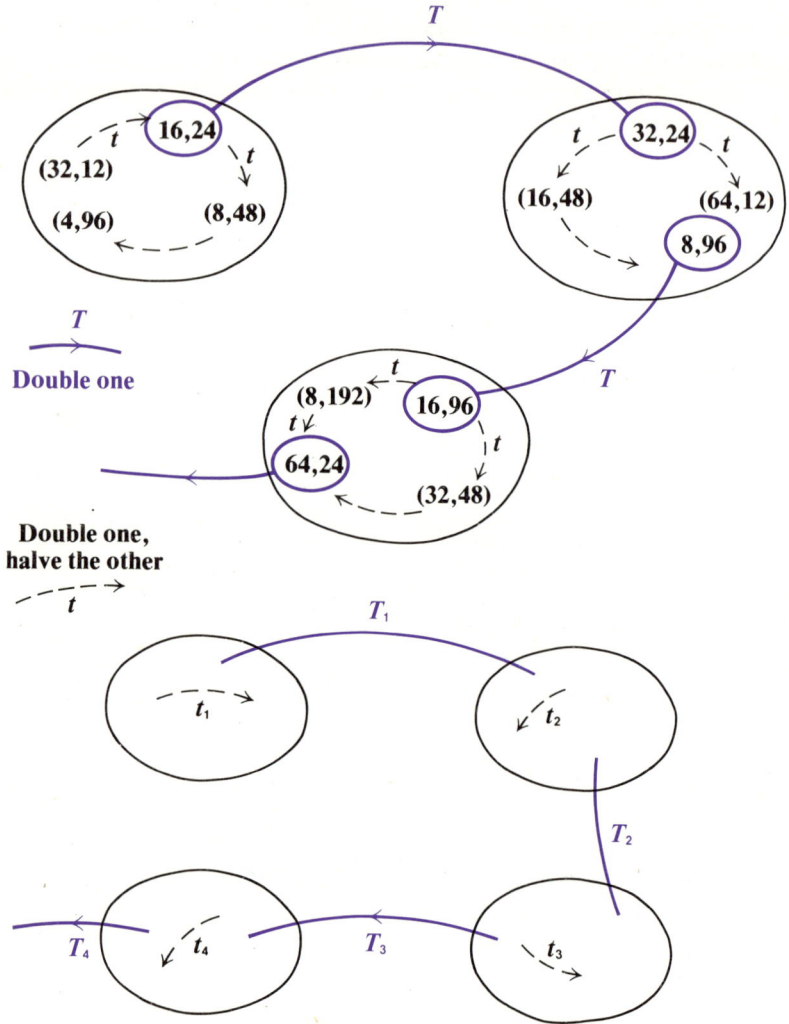

Fig. 2.48

Doubling is a transformation which children find fairly easy, and also the opposite transformation, halving, provided the two are studied together. The one is implied by the other:

But we notice that doubling and halving will not on their own generally give all *the pairs of factors with a particular product. Unless the transformation is altered to* multiply one number and divide the other number by the same, *the generation of all pairs is not possible. This transformation can certainly be considered by the children and similar arrow games played, but it will no longer have the same ease and accessibility of doubling and halving.*

An Exercise in Doubling

1	3	5	7	9	11	13	15	17	·	·	·
2	6	10	14	18	22	26	30	34	·	·	·
4	12	20	28	36	44	52	60	68	·	·	·
8	24	40	56	72	88	104	120	136	·	·	·
16	48	80	112	144	176	208	240	272	·	·	·
32	96	160	224	288	352	416	480	544	·	·	·
64	192	320	448	576	704	832	960	1088	·	·	·
·	·	·	·	·	·	·	·	·	·	·	·

The table can be built up mainly by the children. The number of entries is arbitrary – the table continues to the right and below. There is a different impact if it is begun from the first row or the first column. If it is begun from the first column we can ask, 'What is the smallest whole number not yet used?' and the answer will start the second column. If it is repeated it will each time give the next start of the adjacent column. 'Why are the first numbers the successive odd numbers?'

Perhaps the 'complete' table contains every whole number. *Does it?* Each whole number eventually appears once and once only. *How could we know that?* The answer may become clear once we are able to locate any given number in a particular place.

How shall we launch an investigation into the properties of the table? We can ask a general question – 'What do you notice?' – and start from that. This kind of beginning carries some moral obligation to go where the answers lead. If it is only a gesture to a free response, and then the teacher directs attention to what he wants to be noticed, he can hardly avoid conveying the impression that the children failed *to observe something. There is so much in this table that he can start the investigation without fearing that he will exhaust it.*

1. It is like a multiplication table: the product of any number in the top row and one in the first column gives the entry in the corresponding row and column.

2. The numbers along the rows increase by the same amount each time. What is the amount of increase for any given row?

3. The numbers down the columns increase by doubling each time.

4. If you multiply any two numbers in the top row you get another number in the top row, and if you multiply any two numbers in the first column you get another number in the first column. Does this work for any other row or column?

5. How can you predict where a number which has not already appeared will turn up? Where is 1728, for instance? (Where will a half of 1728 be, and a half of 864, and a half of 432, and so on?) Does the information from this halving process tell us which row and which column it is in? Could you predict the position of any number? 1 000 000, say?

6. We know where the product of one number from each of the top row and the first column is. Can we find out where the product of *any* two numbers in the table will be? (It must be somewhere, since we know the table contains all the whole numbers.)

7. Take any two numbers in different rows and different columns – say 96 and 28. Then since we double numbers by going down the columns and halve them by going up, the product of 96 and 28 must be equal to the product of 48 and 56, or 192 and 14. Can you find all the pairs of numbers multiplying to the same answer as (96, 28) from the table? Would you always be able to?

8. Would it make any sense to extend the table upwards or backwards?

Doubling and Halving

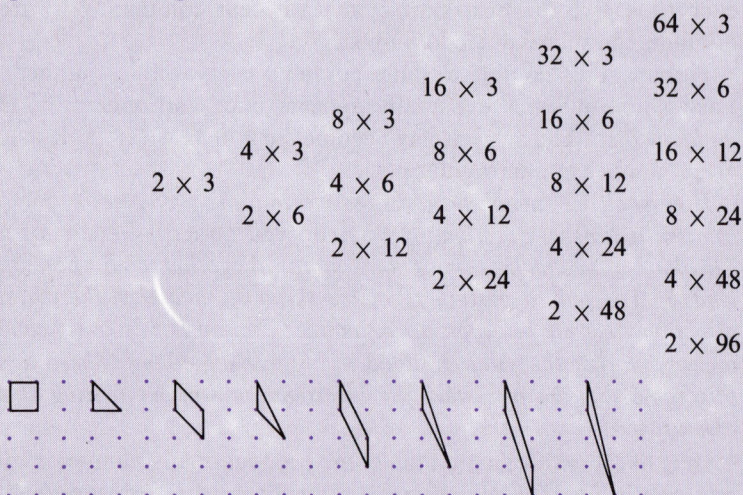

						64×3
					32×3	
			16×3			32×6
		8×3		16×6		
	4×3		8×6			16×12
2×3		4×6		8×12		
	2×6		4×12			8×24
		2×12		4×24		
			2×24			4×48
				2×48		
						2×96

$$1 + \tfrac{1}{2} + \tfrac{1}{4} + \tfrac{1}{8} + \tfrac{1}{16} + \tfrac{1}{32} + \cdots$$

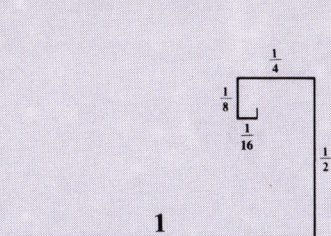

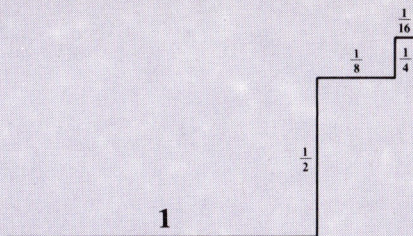

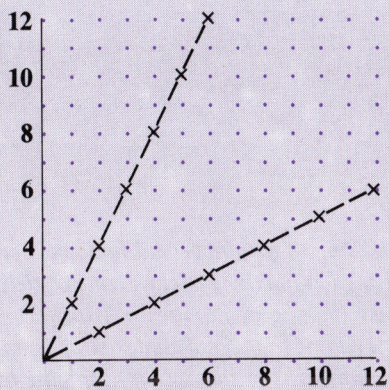

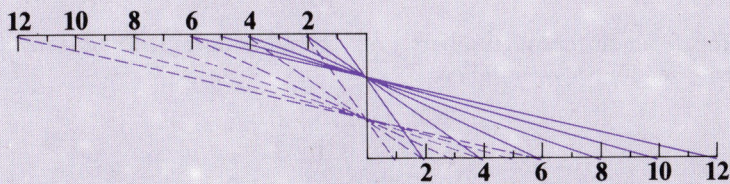

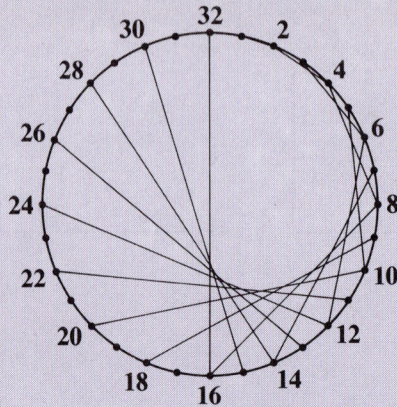

Repeated Operations

The facility of being able to do something to a number and find another one is basic to arithmetic. Doubling and halving is something that we can do fairly easily and there are many consequences. By looking at families of transformations, more and more properties of numbers can be found and made use of. Sometimes these families become new forms of number. For instance multiplying by 2 followed by dividing by 3 can become a single object called a fraction or in other circumstances a rational number.

Addition Sequences

Starting from different numbers and simply adding 3, for instance, can generate sequences of numbers:

$$5 \rightarrow 8 \rightarrow 11 \rightarrow 14 \rightarrow 17 \rightarrow$$
$$3 \rightarrow 6 \rightarrow 9 \rightarrow 12 \rightarrow$$
$$14 \rightarrow 17 \rightarrow 20 \rightarrow 23 \rightarrow$$
$$10 \rightarrow 13 \rightarrow 16 \rightarrow 19 \rightarrow 22 \rightarrow$$

We may see that if we start with other numbers the sequences turn up again at some point. For instance $9 \rightarrow 12 \rightarrow 15 \rightarrow 18 \rightarrow \ldots$ is in the second sequence above. The third sequence is in the first. We can ask how many different sequences are there? What are the smallest starting numbers? The first one could have started at 2, the second at 0, the third is like the first and the fourth could have started at 1. Any others? It looks as though, given the transformation 'add 3' and starting with the numbers 0, 1, 2, that we can generate *all* the whole numbers.

If we take the transformation 'add 7,' then we don't generate all the whole numbers until we have seven sequences beginning with 0, 1, 2, 3, 4, 5, 6.

By adding different numbers the whole numbers are split into as many sequences as the size of the added number.

In any one of the sequences from one number you can find any other number by adding the generating number or subtracting it as many times as necessary.

How do you get from one sequence to another?

Grid Patterns with Two Operations

Add 2 : add 5

$1 \xrightarrow{+2} 3 \to 5 \to 7 \quad 9 \quad 11 \quad 13 \quad 15 \quad 17 \quad 19 \quad 21 \quad . \quad . \quad .$
+5↓　　↓
6　　8　　10　　12　14　16　18　20　22　24　.　.　.　.
↓　　↓
11　　13　　15　　17　19　21　23　25　27　.　.　.　.　.
.　.　.　.　.　.　.　.　.
.　.　.　.　.　.　.　.　.

Sequences are generated this time but they are not independent. Numbers appear in different places. *What patterns can you see? Can you explain them? How many times will 27 happen? Are all numbers going to happen?*

Some haven't appeared yet: 2 and 4. *Are these the only ones? How many times will 59 happen?*

If I think about going from 1 to 59 with adding 2 or adding 5 then I can go on different routes.

Or I can think about adding 58, which is what all the routes eventually do. 58 in 5s and 2s

2	5
29	0
24	2
19	4
14	6
9	8
4	10

Does this check with the grid?
Try a similar grid for 'add 3' and 'add 7'.
What happens with 'add 4' and 'add 8'?
Can you account for the difference?

Multiplying

Earlier, a doubling table was made and we could see that every column was headed by an odd number (p. 73). Unlike adding a number where we found a limited number of sequences, doubling seems to need a never-ending number of them. *Is it the same for trebling?*

1	2	4	5	7	8	10	.	.	.
3	6	12	15	21	24	30	.	.	.
9	18	36	45	63	72	.	.	.	.
27	54	108	135	.	.				

. . . . . .

. . . . . .

. . . . . .

Remember a column can be started by the smallest number that has not yet appeared.
What happens if we try to make a grid out of two multiplications, say, multiply by 2 and multiply by 3?
Can you get from 1 to 108?
*   1 to 192?*
What differences are there in the patterns here from those found with two additions earlier?
Do all the numbers appear?
Do any appear more than once?
How many routes to get to 108 from 1?
What about making a grid which starts with the smallest number which hasn't appeared in the first grid?

```
1  →  2  →  4  →  8  →  16 → . . .
↓     ↓     ↓     ↓     ↓
3  →  6  → 12  → 24  →  48 → . . .
↓     ↓     ↓     ↓     ↓
9  → 18  → 36  → 72  → 144 → . . .
↓     ↓     ↓     ↓     ↓
.     .     .     .     .
```

.   .   .   .   .

.   .   .   .   .

5?

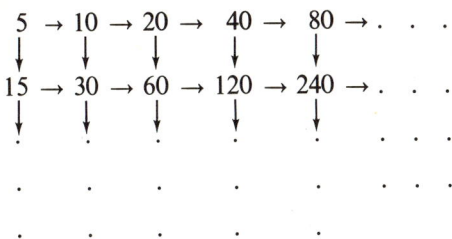

7?

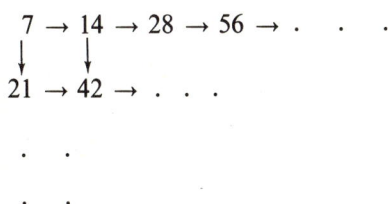

The first few that occur are prime numbers.
Will they always be? Consider the ways in which you could show whether this is so or not. (See also p. 92.)
What meaning can you give to $\downarrow \rightarrow$?
Is it the same as $\overset{\rightarrow}{}\downarrow$?
Is $\overset{\rightarrow}{\downarrow}\rightarrow$ the same as $\overset{\downarrow}{\rightarrow}\rightarrow$?

Mixed operations

Can you make a grid if we have two mixed actions like 'add 3' and 'multiply by 2' starting with 1? Using combinations of these two, find ways of going from 1 to 28. Does the order matter?

Fig. 2.49 shows a schema. Can you sort this out into a neater picture? Can you trace out different ways of getting from 1 to 28? I have found fourteen different ones (Fig. 2.50).
What numbers do not occur?
It involves two of the sequences we found earlier when we 'added 3'. Why not the third?
Using 'multiply by 3' and 'add 2' the journey from 3 to 35 is different. (Fig. 2.51). How?

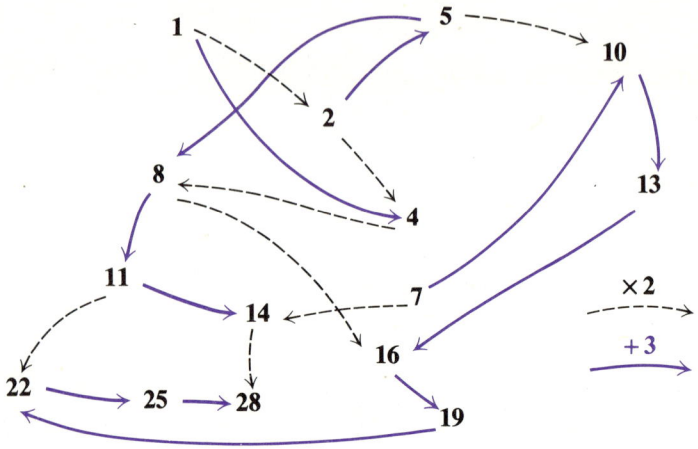

Fig. 2.49

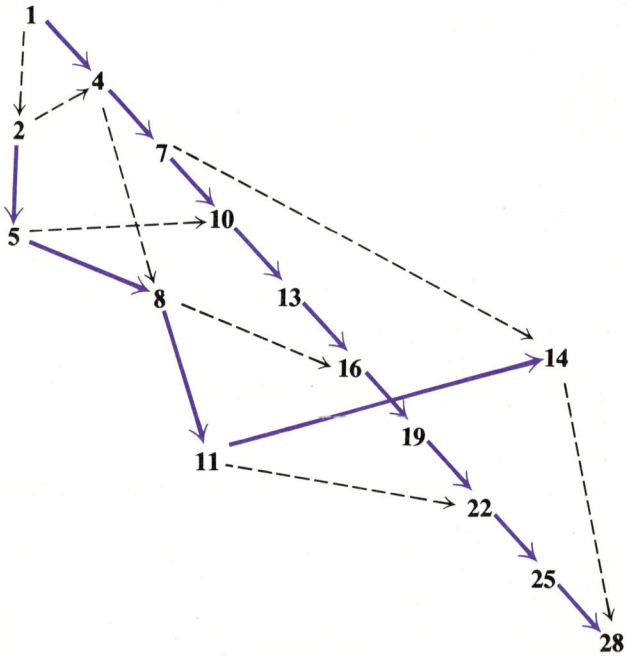

Fig. 2.50

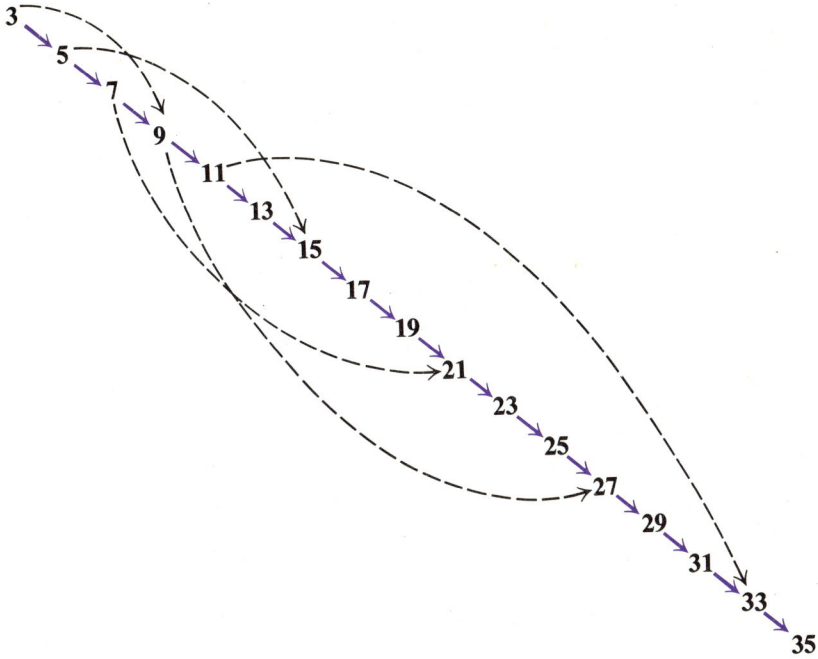

Fig. 2.51

No even numbers appear in Fig. 2.51 at all. And if you try to get from 2 to 35 using these two operations you can't! Why not?
What happens with three actions?
Fig. 2.52, overleaf, gives an example.

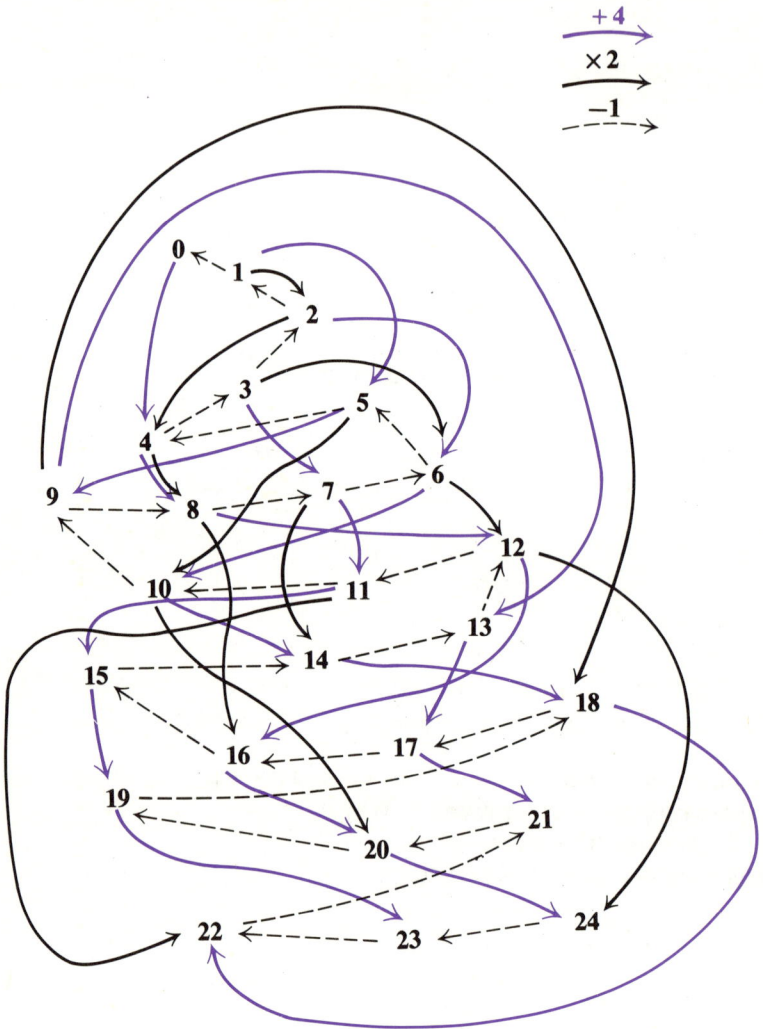

Fig. 2.52

Some notes on getting from 1 to 23 are given in the following scheme.

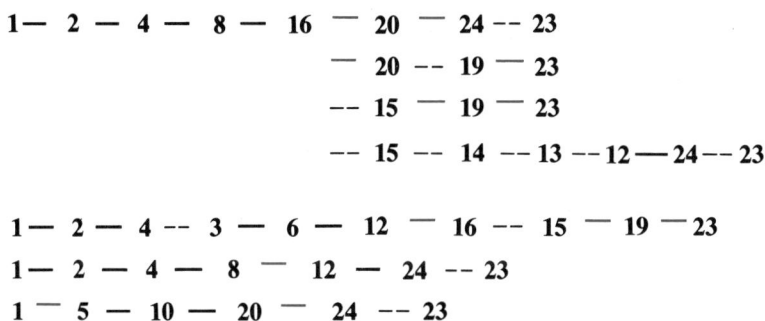

1— 2 — 4 — 8 — 16 ⎺ 20 ⎺ 24 -- 23
                                ⎺ 20 -- 19 ⎺ 23
                                    -- 15 ⎺ 19 ⎺ 23
                                    -- 15 -- 14 -- 13 -- 12 — 24 -- 23

1— 2 — 4 -- 3 — 6 — 12 ⎺ 16 -- 15 ⎺ 19 ⎺ 23
1— 2 — 4 — 8 ⎺ 12 — 24 -- 23
1 ⎺ 5 — 10 — 20 ⎺ 24 -- 23

Fig. 2.53

There is a lot to explore!
Can you get from 1 to 23 without using $\xrightarrow{-1}$?

If a broken arrow always follows a blue arrow, does this become the example in Figs. 2.49 and 2.50?
There is more in Fig. 2.53 because all the numbers up to 24 were entered and the maximum number of arrows drawn connecting the numbers written.
If we started with 1, how does 3 get in?
Here is something else. Start with 1 and use the operations shown in Fig. 2.54.
Look at the consequences of taking the three operations in turn and starting with 1 (Fig. 2.55).
Can you explain why some are the same?
Try other sequences of operations.
Try other number bases.

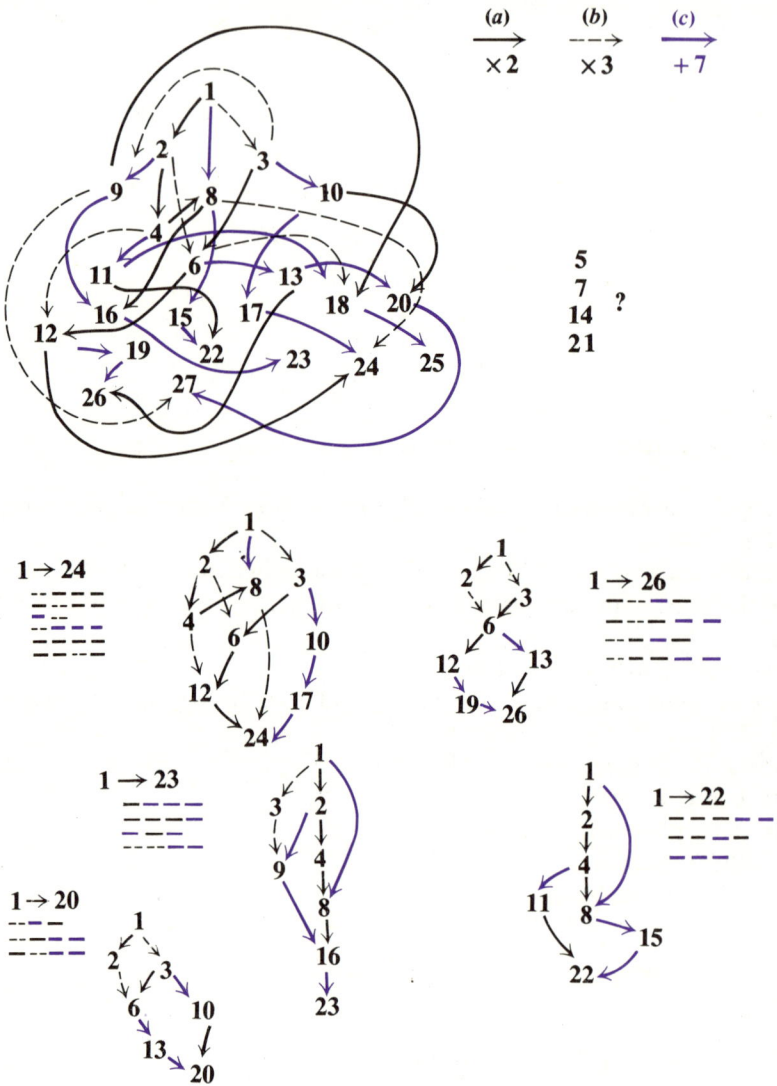

Fig. 2.54

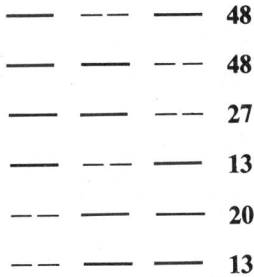

— —— — **48**

— — —— **48**

— — —— **27**

— —— — **13**

—— — — **20**

—— — — **13**

Fig. 2.55

When we use numbers our aim is to become familiar with them. They must become easy to move, alter, relate, apply. We are not expecting to have difficulties. Here we are looking at ways of relating numbers so that this familiarity can begin. The use of coloured arrows to set up relations and to explore possibilities is not made extensively enough. The reliance on formal methods of setting out number relations in the first stages may well reduce the chances of children increasing their familiarity with number.

Indeed it has been found possible to wipe out early familiarity, at say five or six years, by improving strictly formal procedures as a learning process. This is probably the main fault. It is one thing to recognise the efficiency of a procedure or an algorithm. It is quite another to use the form of the procedure as a complete teaching method.

The six-year-old who couldn't divide 2 into 64 but knew there were 32 twos in 64 is a potential victim of this approach. By thinking about change and transformations we can develop a control of the methods we use at different stages. Formal procedures use particular transformations. These particular ones belong to larger families, familiarity with which makes the formalising process obvious. As we shall see in the next chapter the word 'understanding' can be dangerously ambiguous. I have no hesitation in allowing its use when someone *understands* how a process happens. It seems clear that this is the meaning at this point – it will be another matter when he wishes to know what makes the process work. This will be understanding of something different (not necessarily 'deeper' – a word which can lead to invidious comparisons).

Through our thinking of mathematical activity, transformations of all kinds can be our basic support tool.

Argument

Elsewhere in this book, as in the majority of books about the teaching of elementary mathematics, there are signs that place value is a matter for worry because it is considered to be a difficult 'concept' for children to grasp; (I put the quotation marks since I have doubts that the word is the right one to use, but as it is the one everyone else tends to use in this kind of assertion, I write it to aid recognition.) I would like to suggest for quiet consideration that it is, in fact, a far less difficult phenomenon to come to terms with than many of the other things that children take in their stride — getting hold of the colloquial grammar of their native language, for instance. To express it more bluntly, if place value is a bugbear and a bugaboo, then it is probably nothing more than the heavy weight of teachers' anxieties bearing down on it that has made it so. After all, if children are exposed to one-tenth of the extant recommendations for giving them 'preconceptual experience leading up to the idea of place value', or one-twentieth of the assorted abacuses, place value games and structured materials that fill the catalogues, one can't be surprised if they get a little anxious and off-colour too at the prospect of having to conquer something that requires such a vast machinery. Thank God many children know how to preserve sanity by biding their time.

Let us start with a general principle. What we really need to ensure is that children can handle the numeration system comfortably and efficiently and know enough about how it works to be able to work it. Are we, in fact, by fussing about place value, asking them to be more sophisticated and self-conscious about it than *we* are when we use it?

To handle the numeration system requires:

(i) knowing the correspondence between spoken and written numerals;

(ii) knowing the sequence of numerals; not only being able to count from 'one', but also being able to count on or back from any point in the sequence;

(iii) knowing that exactly the same structure makes it possible to count on or back in tens, hundreds, thousands, millions, etc., without learning anything new except a few irregular names;

(iv) knowing the association between a numeral and the cardinal ('how many') number it represents so that some information about the magnitude of a number can be drawn from seeing or hearing the numeral instead of looking at a set containing that number of objects. (Note that this information covers a spectrum, from considerable detail and precision for small numbers to almost none for large ones.)

(v) knowing the standard and non-standard manipulations that enable one to operate vicariously on numbers by operating on the numerals instead.

It is item (iv) that mistakenly leads teachers to restrict children's acquaintance with numerals to the 'small' ones. If item (v) can be distanced from the others, as it always is, why do we not feel free to teach *any* of the items on its own? This would at once enable us to teach (i) and (ii) for *all* numerals without worrying that the connection with cardinality hadn't yet been made — and give children access to the complete spoken, written and sequential structures in a way that is quite impossible if they are kept messing around with the numerals 1–10 or 1–20 for ages. To say of *this* activity that it is wrong 'because they don't know what they are saying' is as irrelevant as the same comment would be if applied to learning nursery rhymes or nonsense songs or the Lord's Prayer.

If we indulged in this separatist approach with some abandon, we might be surprised to find that the *sounds* of the numerals contain a great deal of 'place value information' in a way that the written numerals do not. Attention to what numerals *sound like* would prevent us mystifying children by always pointing at what they *look like* where there is nothing to see.

Working these proposals out in detail is not my purpose here, but rather to get readers worrying about why they are worrying about place value.

On a slightly technical point, I would just add that the above five-stage analysis implies an important distinction between numerals and the numbers they represent. This distinction certainly exists, as a moment's thought about 'other bases' and Roman numerals will show. But it is also true that in practice it seems as if we progressively invest numerals with more and more properties until they are, for most of our purposes, identifiable with the numbers they stand for. It is wearisome pedantry to insist on a careful acknowledgment of the distinction every time numerals are used.

3

Multiplication Tables, and All That

If we want to know how to teach children any mathematical skill, an obvious source of evidence is our own functioning in that skill. By looking intently at our own way of working we can bring into consciousness all the elements that may have become automatic and habitual, and from this evidence begin to make inferences about the demands that the skill must make on someone who doesn't yet have it. Naturally we may find that we do not ourselves operate the skill in the most efficient way – as may emerge when we discuss our observations with someone else – but it is hard to deny that such an inspection must bring us closer to the problem of acquiring the skill than an uncritical adoption of the folklore of the classroom. It may be that the folklore enshrines the correct techniques for passing on the skill, but who could be sure without checking it? And what better criterion can we use than our own experience?

Suppose we find that our own facility in multiplying any number by a power of ten rests entirely on our grasp of a transformation which changes the given word or sign into the answer (for example, 'fifty-seven' becomes 'five thousand seven hundred' and '57' becomes '5700' when we are instructed to multiply by 100), then it is self-evident that the transformational rules contain all that is necessary to meet the demands of this particular skill. The rules are, one might say, operational definitions of the particular skill – that of giving the correct word or sign in response to the request to multiply a number by any power of ten. If anyone has the rules and applies them correctly, the skill is completely mastered: the cleverest mathematician could not do the same job any better. To look for deeper significance in this process is to pursue a chimera.

If anyone now says that these rules bypass the concept of place value, or that they don't necessarily entail any understanding of the magnitudes of the numbers involved, the response can only be to agree. So we shouldn't teach multiplication by a power of ten this way, even though it infallibly gives the right answer?

Before we can find a secure base from which to answer questions of this. kind we first need to appreciate the inconsistent position it is easy to find ourselves in. It is not uncommon to find that time is spent in classrooms trying to communicate to young children an understanding of multiplication, particularly through an extensive study of repeated additions, and that this is then followed by hours of repetition designed to commit a small number of multiplication facts to memory. The peculiar characteristic of this situation is that the latter activity tends to get bolstered by appeals to reason and 'understanding' whenever the children fail to memorise their products, whereas the desired behaviour appears to be an automatic and mindless response to a stimulus. One can imagine a child saying to himself, 'If you want me to be able to say "63" when you say "7 times 9" and snap your fingers, why didn't you make it clear to me that this was all I had to learn? And, if, on the other hand, you want me to know the "meaning" of "7 times 9" so that I can relate it to "6 times 9", or "7 times 10", or "7 times 18", why do you make me keep repeating utterances like a parrot?'

How do we remember a friend's telephone number? The name of his eldest daughter? The date of the beginning of the Second World War? The chemical formula for hydrochloric acid? Wordsworth's 'On Westminster Bridge'? We only have to check with our experience to see that memorising has almost no relation to understanding the thing memorised. We remember some things because we use them so frequently that we don't have to make any effort to retain them, but when we deliberately set out to memorise, we find a device, or a mnemonic, or an association, that will help to do the job of triggering our memory. Whether we 'understand' what we have memorised is another, separate question.

If we want children to be able to give a quick response to the question 'What is 9 times 8?' then we can show them how, by holding their hands together, palms up, in front of themselves and bending down the eighth finger, they can 'see' the digits of the answer in the two sets of fingers still extended. All 'What is 9 times?' questions can be answered in the same way. With this device it is not necessary to take time 'climbing up' the '9 times' table until the appropriate place is reached. What is more, the device dynamically links one configuration of the fingers to another in an obvious way, so that memorisation is that much easier.

Consider the first ten 'times' tables. Does anyone need to set about memorising the '1 times' table? Or the '10 times' table? (Orally the only problem is the irregularity of some word formations – *six* times ten is *sixty*, but *three* times ten is *not* threety; there is no corresponding problem in writing the answers.) Suppose that the children have been shown how to double numbers quickly and easily. Then they already know the '2 times' table. By doubling they can get the '4 times' table from the '2 times' table, and the '8 times' table by doubling again. Once they know the '3 times' table they are given a bonus of the '6 times' table by doubling. The '9 times' table, as we have seen, presents no problems. Therefore only the '3 times' and '7 times' tables may need to be learned the hard way.

This analysis shows that it isn't necessary to expand large quantities of emotional energy trying to prove that the usual way of rote-teaching tables is bad for the children. It stands condemned, judged by its *own* criterion of instant efficiency, because it is clumsy and long-winded. Children taught tables by the method outlined above would have less to commit to memory, and fewer stages to recreate when they forgot.

The question 'To teach tables or not to teach tables?' is more complex than it seems and the argument between those in favour of teaching tables and those against is usually an ideological struggle rather than an attempt to deal with the problem. There are at least three contextual aspects that must be taken into account.

1. What awarenesses and what degree of fluency in multiplication do we want children to acquire?

2. What choice of methods do we have for achieving them?

3. What is the present state of the game for these particular children?

Each of these aspects is complex in itself. The first may look like a local and exclusively mathematical question, but answers to it are bound to be influenced by criteria relating to educational aims and practical policies. A school teacher concerned with younger children may not particularly value fluency, but what if this is the main component measured by examinations that her pupils must take, or expected by the teachers in schools her pupils will pass on to? By the time all the complexities have been allowed for, who can expect a straight '*Yes*' or '*No*' to the question about teaching tables, valid for all circumstances?

An advance that we can make, however, is to take the question of fluency or facility in multiplication and study it in its own right, detached from what is only one very special technique for producing it.

There are necessarily two elements involved in having facility in any mathematical skill. One is *know-how* – that is, awareness of what has to be done to perform the skill; the other is *fluency* – that is, having the know-how at one's fingertips, being able to apply it with reasonable rapidity and efficiency. The two elements have to be taken together, since anyone who thinks of multiplication as repeated addition, and can add, can be said to have a know-how. He can do 57×31 as $31 + 31 + 31 + \ldots$ But this know-how would never translate into efficiency. The standard 'long multiplication' algorithm is a know-how, and a better one, since it can produce the answers to very complicated multiplications in a very short time. It is rather a blunt instrument, though, since it is not at all sensitive to any differences in the multiplications one may encounter. It would be foolish to use it for, say, 4000×2000 and even unnecessarily lengthy for an example like 399×23 (which is $9200 - 23 = 9177$), or even 68×72 (which is $70^2 - 2^2 = 4896$). In fact we can see emerging here the potential value of a kitbag of know-hows rather than one all-purpose tool. This brings in its train a further demand, if we are to have all-round facility, that we should be fluent in the *choice* of know-hows. The person who has a fairly wide range of multiplicative know-hows *and* can use his inspection of a particular example to trigger his selection of the best one to use, will end up with a great deal of facility.

We know, by looking at our own way with learning a new skill, that fluency is a pay-off of practice. Without practice a skill does not become integrated into our competence. The familiar phrase used above, 'at one's fingertips', is a powerful metaphor indicating the situation of a skill 'at hand' ready to be picked up and used as an extension of the self.

It is important here to draw a distinction between practice and repetition. Practice necessarily entails the intention of the person practising – it is a personal activity undertaken in order to become more proficient. In fact practice is *never* repetition for the practiser since he is engaged in overcoming difficulties and constantly changing himself to meet the demands of the skill. As soon as the skill is acquired he stops this particular activity, unless it is one that gives him pleasure or benefit in itself, or unless he is forced to continue by some insensitive person.

Is multiplication, then, only a skill? Is it only an ability to handle fluently a range of techniques or know-hows? To say 'No', which is clearly the right answer, may not be very helpful without some further insight into the relation between skill and understanding. It is first of all obvious that one does not necessarily imply the other – skill doesn't inevitably lead to understanding, nor understanding to skill – even though there are extreme schools of pedagogical practice which act as if they did. (The analogy of driving a car may be a suitable counter-example.) Getting a skill is a short-term activity requiring an intensive application of the self to a set of specific problems. It may subsequently require 'brushing up', but it never changes its essential nature once it has been acquired. Understanding, on the other hand, requires a more diffuse attention over a long period – diffuse, because understanding necessarily involves taking in the whole complexity of an area, relating it to others, being sensitive to shades of meaning and distinctions in usage; long term, because the whole field cannot be scanned at once, and at any moment a jarring element may be met which leads to a recasting of awareness. With some generosity in the interpretation of the adjectives, we can say that the acquisition of a skill is permanent, but understanding is always temporary; skills are local, but understanding is global.

It is unlikely to be profitable for teachers to take understanding as an objective – if for no other reason than that it would be an arbitrary decision to say what understanding, or, rather, whose understanding should be taken as the goal. What is appropriate for them to do is to keep constantly in mind those elements in a situation which understanding must take account of and draw the children's attention to them now and again.

Many teachers, by methods of their own choosing and devising, put in much time trying to get children to memorise products. What then?

Certainly the availability of products makes one's progress through later stages of a mathematics course much easier and happier; it may even signal the difference between success and failure since it has freed the mind from anxiety and any further need to re-do these calculations. It is necessary for a teacher to be aware of the shifting balance between the relaxation in the approach to a study in new areas which comes from having products, or any other set of facts, readily available, and the imprisonment which too great a concern for memory work can bring. If, for example, too much attention is given to the memorisation of products up to 10 × 10 as essentially isolated bits of memory, then the power to transform what is known to reach something new may recede. One may not be ready and able to find something known which will give an unknown, like, say 16 × 12.

Diagrams for Factors

This is an account of a lesson in which a knowledge of products was used.

My class of girls ages 9–11 shared in the exploration which resulted in the 2-D and 3-D type diagrams shown below. First we selected triples of three different numerals from the set (1, 2, 3, 4, 5, 6, 7, 8, 9) that would give 'hundreds' numbers divisible by 9. ('Add the digits' rule.) We found (126, 135, 189, 234, 279, 369, 378, 459, 468, 567). We saw that each triple would make six numbers and gave ourselves the task of finding the prime factors.

'What does it mean', I asked, 'to find all the factors?' And I offered to show a way of putting it on a diagram. (See Figs. 3.1 and 3.2)

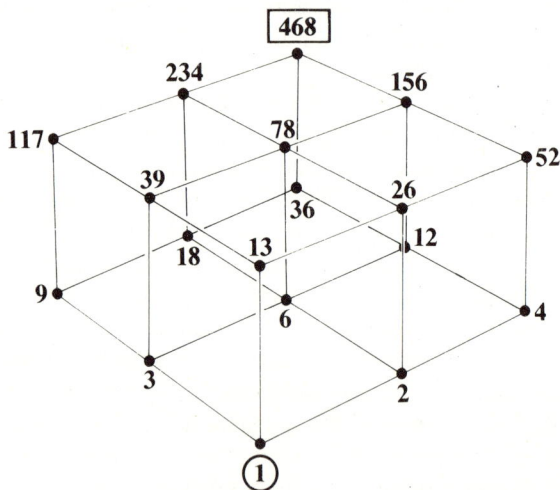

Fig. 3.1

Example

	468	486	648

$$
\begin{array}{ccc}
468 & 486 & 648 \\
2 \cdot 234 & 2 \cdot 243 & 2 \cdot 324 \\
2^2 \cdot 117 & 2 \cdot 3^2 \cdot 27 & 2^2 \cdot 162 \\
2^2 \cdot 3^2 \cdot 13 & 2 \cdot 3^5 & 2^3 \cdot 81 \\
& & 2^3 \cdot 3^4
\end{array}
$$

3-D   2-D   2-D

$$
\begin{array}{ccc}
684 & 846 & 864 \\
2 \cdot 342 & 2 \cdot 423 & 2 \cdot 432 \\
2^2 \cdot 171 & 2 \cdot 3^2 \cdot 47 & 2^2 \cdot 216 \\
2^2 \cdot 3^2 \cdot 19 & & 2^3 \cdot 108 \\
& & 2^4 \cdot 54 \\
& & \quad\quad 6 \\
& & 2^5 \cdot 3^3 \quad 9
\end{array}
$$

3-D   3-D   2-D

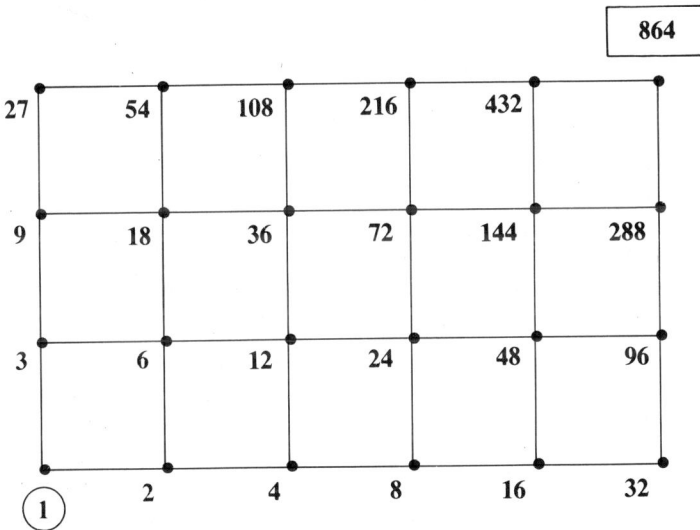

Fig. 3.2

The idea caught on. They showed each other how to make the diagrams. They marked in chosen routes from 1 to the end. They became very confident about multiplications, and enjoyed the discovery of several ways of aiming at each of the larger factors.

The reader may enjoy making diagrams from the other four permutations of 4, 6, 8. It was with this in mind that the factors have been set out.

The set of triples for numbers divisible by 9 is given so that anyone who feels enthusiastic has a safe starting point. The children will need to have some method for splitting a number into its prime factors, and a list of primes up to about 109.

The word 'safe' refers to the fact that there are a few three-digit numbers that factorise into four different primes, for example, $2 \times 3 \times 7 \times 11 = 462$. Although a satisfactory diagram is possible to show this, it is very difficult to draw. If you want to avoid this trap, do not use 462, nor 546, 798, 858, 924 and 966. There are fourteen others (less than a thousand) which have both 2 and 5 as factors and so have the last figure zero.

Computation

Routine computation procedures, such as the 'four rules' of number were created so that the arithmetic of everyday life could be done with the minimum of fuss and bother. They relieve the arithmetician from the need to make decisions about how to do his sums, or even how to set them down. He is able to work with efficiency, 'programmed' to perform the computations he needs. Unlike the computer, though, he can forget his programs if he does not need to use the techniques regularly. Children are particularly likely to lose the edge of their computational skills if they do not meet situations in which they fairly regularly need to use them. In some recently published books the need to compute occurs only spasmodically and when it does children often take themselves by surprise by having to confess that they have 'forgotten how to do it'.

The ability to compute quickly and accurately is clearly a useful skill to possess when it is likely that tasks will be met which require its use. It is often thought desirable that children should have the techniques at their fingertips pending the time when they need them. This time probably comes when they begin to use their arithmetic as a 'tool' subject in other fields of learning. A problem involving quantity in mathematics or science, for instance, may be regarded as virtually solved when the answer can be expressed as a piece of arithmetic. At this stage the thinking is over and one can now turn to a calculating machine which will carry out the computation automatically. In the absence of a machine the answer needs to be worked out on paper or in one's head.

Not long ago children spent part of every day of most of their school lives working towards this pattern of skill to the exclusion of all else in mathematics. They spent their time concentrating exclusively on the learning and practice of the 'four rules' of number, measurement and money. The assumption was that it would take them many years to achieve good standards of arithmetical skill. We take the view that such a skill can be acquired by the time it is needed with relative ease, virtually as a by-product of some important mathematical activity that should be taking place in the earlier years. The mathematics we have in mind, as the sections so far have indicated, is associated with number and the operations on number which take us 'behind the scenes' of the conventional procedures and reveal the underlying transformations.

The need is to make the construction of arithmetical procedures a problem area for children. Telling them how to do their sums, or so to structure their learning that they are inevitably led to a set of algorithms of which the teacher approves, short-circuits a rich field of mathematical experience. Decision-making, creating problem-solving strategies, and the refining of home-made algorithms, are integral parts of mathematics and it is precisely in these areas that children will gain experience if they are allowed to generate their own computational procedures.

Numbers can produce numbers. When numbers are acted on in certain precisely-defined ways – as, for instance, when we 'add' two numbers together – they will produce another precisely-determined number. Calculation and computation are names given to the general processes of turning numbers into other numbers by the application of well-defined operations. We exclude from these terms any processes with a chance element – for example, throwing a pair of dice in order to produce the total of their spots. Even here the totalling of the spots *after* the throw is determined, and is therefore a calculation, but it is not possible to predict the total from the data of the number of dice to be thrown.

Computational procedures are programmed instructions for arriving at the correct output when numbers are fed in. The machine analogy reminds us how many examples of machines there are for carrying out computations automatically: slide rules, desk calculators, adding machines, ready reckoners, nomograms, Napier's bones, logarithm tables, computers and so on. The analogy reminds us of the importance of predictability – given the same input and the same set of instructions, everyone will arrive at the same output. But we further see the economic generality – a machine will accept *any* numbers from a particular universe as input. The universe of a machine is usually large, but always finite; logarithm tables, for instance, are restricted to inputs of numbers expressible with 3, or 4, or 7 etc., decimal digits.

One can argue that since machines exist, they should do all the computations and leave people to do what only people can do. But any machine is an extension of its operator, not a substitute for him; it will only do what it is told, and it has to be given the right message. More important, though, is the fact that an understanding of the characteristics that make 'universal' calculating procedures possible takes one close to the nature of mathematics itself.

The essential nature of a computational procedure is that it is a set of rules for breaking down or transforming a calculation into a set of calculations whose answers are already known.

For instance, finding the answer to

$$
\begin{array}{r}
248 \\
+\ 375 \\
\underline{197} \\
\end{array}
$$

involves no more than finding the sum of each of three component additions $7 + 5 + 8, 90 + 70 + 40, 100 + 300 + 200$ together with the addition of the three totals: $20 + 200 + 600$, giving 820. In fact, the procedure makes use of our place-value notation, so that these component additions become $7 + 5 + 8, 9 + 7 + 4, 1 + 3 + 2$ and the final sum is obtained by combining these totals, modified by 'carrying figures'. Although at each stage in this sum, there are many choices of direction that could be taken to produce the result, one fixed path which defines the procedure is taken.

Again, finding the answer to

$$
\begin{array}{r}
473 \\
\times\ \ 24 \\
\hline
\end{array}
$$

using a standard procedure involves a set of component multiplications together with a final addition and, once again, the place-value notation allows $4 \times 3, 4 \times 70, 4 \times 400$, for example, to be replaced by $4 \times 3, 4 \times 7$, 4×4.

Many Ways

What are the component calculations for 'the standard subtraction procedures'? If we release the above addition problem from the shackles of its traditional format and present it to a child in the form:

$$
248 + 375 + 197 = \qquad ,
$$

then we invite him to make up his own mind about how he is to arrive at an answer. (It isn't the written format alone that must offer the invitation, since a teacher may still take it away by demanding that the units must be dealt with first, then the tens and then the hundreds.)

1. A nine-year-old invented three ways of doing it:
   (i) $248 + 375 + 197 = 648 + 75 + 97 = 648 + 72 + 100$
   $= 748 + 72 \qquad = 750 + 70 = 800 + 20 = 820;$
   (ii) $248 + 375 + 197 = 223 + 400 + 197 = 220 + 400 + 200$
   $= 820;$

(iii) $248 + 375 + 197 = 250 + 370 + 200 = 450 + 370$
$= 750 + 70 \ = 820.$

2. One of the challenges in the class at the time was to work out computations 'in as few jumps as possible'. The particular addition sum was 'done in three' by one girl.

$$248 + 375 + 197 = 448 + 372 = 820.$$

3. Another challenge to this third-year junior class was:
'Can you continue the story:

$$26 \times 32 = (26 \times 30) + (26 \times 2) = 13 \times 2 \times 32 = \ldots ?'$$

A fairly average child wrote:

$26 \times 32 = 13 \times 2 \times 2 \times 16 = 13 \times 2^2 \times 2^4 = 13 \times 2^6$
$= 104 \times 8 = (100 \times 8) + 32 = (25 \times 32) + 32$
$= \dfrac{32 \times 100}{4} + 32 = (26 \times 15) + (26 \times 15) + (26 \times 2)$
$= 208 \times 4 = 832.$

(This sort of exploration is reminiscent of the 'free composition' work of much younger children, illustrated in Goutard's *Mathematics and children*, pp. 177–80.)

4. A nine-year-old boy worked out a subtraction sum in four different ways:

(i) $657 - 389 = 658 - 390 = 668 - 400 = 268;$
(ii) $657 - 389 = 358 - 90 \ = 308 - 40 = 268;$
(iii) $657 - 389 = 668 - 400 = 268;$
(iv) $657 - 389 = 650 - 382 = 600 - 332 = 300 - 32$
$= 298 - 30 \ = 268.$

He asked his teacher which was the best way and she said, '(iii)'.
'No', he said, 'the fourth way's best because it was the hardest to work out.'

5. Attempts of a nine-year-old at division:

First attempt $89 \div 17 = (89 \div 10) + (89 \div 7)$
$= 8 \text{ r } 9 + 12 \text{ r } 5 = 20 \text{ r } 14.$
Second $89 \div 17 = (89 \div 10) - (89 \div 7)$
$= 8 \text{ r } 9 - 12 \text{ r } 5 = ?$
Third $89 \div 17 = (89 \div 7) - (89 \div 10)$
$= 12 \text{ r } 5 - 8 \text{ r } 9 = 4 \text{ r } ?$

He then used a method that the teacher had shown to the class – repeated equal addition – and got 5 r 4 as an answer.

Fourth $89 \div 17 = 2 + (55 \div 17) = 2 + 2 + (21 \div 17)$
$= 2 + 2 + 1 + (\text{r } 4) = 5 \text{ r } 4.$

What follows happened at home. Jonathan aged nine years asked his father how many seconds there were in a century (probably because he knew it was the sort of question his father liked to hear).

Dad said, 'Work it out.' The strategy that follows is Jonathan's but he was 'jollied along' by Dad from time to time:

$$60 \times 60 \times 24 \times 365 \times 100$$
$$= 3600 \times 24 \times 365 \times 100$$
$$= (72\,000 + 14\,400) \times 365 \times 100$$
$$= 86\,400 \times 365 \times 100$$
$$= 8640\,000 \times 365$$
$$= 864\,000\,000 \times 3 = 2592\,000\,000$$
$$\ \ 86\,400\,000 \times 6 = \ \ 518\,400\,000$$
$$\ \ \ \ \ 8640\,000 \times 5 = \underline{\ \ \ 43\,200\,000}$$
$$3153\,600\,000 \text{ seconds}$$

There is a sequel. His father has just reminded Jonathan, now aged 14 years, of this achievement and asked him if he would work the calculation out again. Would he tackle it in a similar or different way? Jonathan's immediate reply: 'Why can't I work it out on the slide rule?'

Counting Numbers and Addition

Suppose we begin with counting numbers and addition. If we abstract the addition of counting numbers from any situations to which it may relate, we see that as a computational procedure it only requires the ability to count. Addition of counting numbers is 'counting on', in the sense familiar to young children. We can show this by setting up a simple model: in order to add 7 and 5 we set up two imaginary identical machines which can speak or write the counting numbers in the correct sequence and in strict rhythm. Machine *A* is started; as soon as 7 has been spoken or written, machine *B* is started to keep in step with *A* from the next numeral. Then when *B* reaches 5, the simultaneous numeral uttered or recorded by *A* is taken as the result of the addition process. 'Counting on' is the playing of the parts of both machines by oneself.

The procedure of 'counting on' can also be modelled by a 'slide rule' of two equally graduated rulers where the length dimension substitutes for the time dimension (Fig. 3.3).

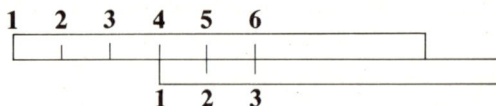

Fig. 3.3

This definition of adding does not refer to the counting *of* anything, and therefore does not involve one–one correspondence, union of disjoint sets, or the like. It can be *applied* to situations where two disjoint sets of discrete objects are united, but this is a demonstration of its usefulness and not of its *meaning*.

The 'counting on' definition is perfectly general and can be used as well with 329 + 276 as with 7 + 5. But we do not normally expect to have to go through the details of the method in either case – in the first case, because it would take too long; and in the second case, because we know the answer already. If it were feasible to memorise the answers to all the additions we were likely to encounter, as we have done for 7 + 5 = 12, no doubt we would endeavour to do that. The speediest computational procedure is to know the answer beforehand. But it is here that the particular structure of our system of counting numbers makes its powerful contribution.

We notice first that if we know the answer to 7 + 5, we also know the answer to 70 + 50, 700 + 500, 7000 + 5000, etc. since our system allows us to count in tens, or hundreds, or thousands, etc. So we can use this extension to modify the 'counting on' definition.

For example, 329 + 276: count on 6 ones from 329, giving 335; then count on 7 tens, giving 405; then count on 2 hundreds, giving finally 605.

Clearly this process requires no more than a mastery of the written (or spoken) notation of counting numbers and an ability to count on from any digit up to 9 any number up to 9. If the additions (countings on) of any two digits not greater than 9 are already memorised, then the required addition becomes just the assembling of component additions which are already available. What is particularly important is that it is the behaviour of the counting number system that makes this possible. It very nearly does all the adding by itself; it is the best calculating machine of them all.

The way that the set of counting numbers is constructed, as displayed in the way we write them, has an effect on the operations that can be performed readily on the numbers. (We need only think of the system of Roman numerals to be aware of the difficulty of doing things with numbers in that system that we take for granted in our own.) We have also established that since addition is not *necessarily* tied to a concrete situation, and since the other operations of subtraction, multiplication and division can be defined in terms of additions, all four operations on counting numbers can be readily introduced as operations on the *signs or sounds* of the counting number system independently of any application these operations may have. It helps to be quite clear that computation is essentially an inbred activity – an intellectual achievement rather than a practical necessity.

The reader is invited to consider the use of two 'counting machines' to model subtraction, multiplication or division.

Show that in the modified 'counting on' method of adding 2 three-digit numbers, the order of the steps is not mathematically significant. Is it psychologically significant? Is it, for instance, easier to perform the transformations mentally in one way rather than another? Always?

The sounds of the numerals carry more place-value information than the corresponding signs. 'Listen' to yourself performing some mental computations and study any effect the imagined sounds have on the steps you take and the confidence you have in them.

Counting and Structure

The following is part of a conversation between two six-year-old boys.

JONNY   The biggest number in the world is a million trillion billion.

JOHN   No it isn't, it's a googol

The adult present is amused by John's reply. Trust a six-year-old to come up with a fanciful name for a fanciful number!

ADULT   What happens if you add one to a googol, John?

JOHN   You can't 'cos it's the biggest number.

He is used to daft adult questions, but decides to be charitable on this occasion. He goes on:

There's a biggest word in the world too and that's the word 'infinity', and you write it like an eight on its side.

(*Long pause*)

ADULT   How do you know all this, John?

JOHN   It's in my new book.

ADULT   What is the name of your new book?

JOHN   *Every child's answer book*, my daddy got it from the newspaper shop.

Later that day Adult paid a visit to the newspaper shop and asked for a copy of *Every child's answer book*. And sure enough on p. 94 . . . (The only mistake that John made was that a googol is described as the biggest *named* number.)

Two years later on a warm May morning Jonny and John are playing in Adult's garden. Adult looks speculatively at John.

ADULT   I know the biggest number in the world.

JOHN   (*rather cross at the interference with his game*) What is it?

ADULT   A googol.

JOHN   No it isn't, numbers go on and on and on. (*He gives Adult a quick quizzical look and resumes his game.*)

Time for lunch. John pauses at the gate and looks up at Adult.

JOHN It isn't a googol, it's a centillion.

ADULT What is?

JOHN The biggest named number. It's ten to the power six hundred and my dad says that means ten multiplied by itself six hundred times.

ADULT Where did you find this out John?

JOHN It's in my *Guinness book of records*.

Adult calls at the newspaper shop and buys himself a copy.

Children are fascinated by the grotesque and the unusual – in fact by anything that is just that much larger than life. It is as though they are seeking ultimate realities in their efforts to make sense of the world they live in. Their interest in large numbers conforms to this characteristic. What is particularly interesting is that when they speculate about such numbers they are dealing with, what is for them, a new sort of reality, namely a reality for which they seem to require no concrete model. They are interested in numbers for their own sake and we could say, with some truth, that they are involved in a purely mathematical speculation.

What prompts a child to speculate about large numbers? What experiences suggest to him that large numbers exist? He is provided with no clues if, at school, he is allowed to work solely with numbers 1–20 when he is very young and 'HTU' sums when he is a bit older. A sharp focus on the properties of small numbers, their operational manipulation and inter-relationships are unhelpful in this context.

Probably he becomes aware of the existence of large numbers through his ability to count. Most of us will remember the pleasure of a young child when he discovers that he can count 'up to a hundred'. If the word 'a thousand' is in his vocabulary this might well suggest to him his next goal – but how to get there! An incident comes to mind when a young child, after a manful but unsuccessful attempt to count up to a thousand – he ran out of a steam – asked his father in a rather petulant voice, 'Is there a number to count bigger than a thousand? 'Yes,' said his dad, 'a million.'

There is a lot for young children to learn about number. Rigid decisions about what they should learn and in what order seem to be out of place – like most adults, few children are neat learners. They impose their own structures on experience and make their own connections in their own time. Perhaps the best we can do in the early stages is to offer them a wealth of varying and seemingly unrelated experiences with a number connotation, provide the associated vocabulary, help them with the means of symbolising on paper when there is need, take a step back and speak when spoken to.

Counting experiences have their place in such a scheme of things. For some children they could provide the beginnings of an insight into the inherent structure of the number system. Certainly structure is implied in the pattern of the counting sounds and probably it is this aural pattern that enables them to count a very long way. Perhaps it is not surprising that children are often able to establish a mastery over the process of counting before they begin to realise what counting is about.

Betty told her teacher that she had 'walked up to a hundred' across the playground – 'I had to stop for a long time when I nearly got there to get all the numbers in.'

The best way to learn how to use a tool is to use it and there is plenty of scope for the more adventurous.

In a reception class the same ritual was observed each day. A child stood on his chair and began counting aloud the number of children present. By the time he got to 'three' all the children had joined in and the final counting word was shouted by everyone with great gusto. On the way out to assembly each child added a Unifix cube to the growing length in the number track and the boy who had started the counting recorded the aggregate on a wall chart. One day two children decided to find out how many children there were altogether in the whole school. With the teachers' co-operation each child in each class was given a Unifix cube to place in a box. The boxes were collected by the two children who promptly tipped their content into one big heap and proceeded to count the cubes one by one, reciting in unison. There were 231 altogether. They then joined the cubes into one long length to see how far it would stretch.

Given challenges that make sense to them and a range of materials to help them with their thinking, their counting ability can give them a satisfying mastery over quite complex situations involving number.

Peter wanted to know if there were more children in Miss Smith's class than his. There were 36 children in his class and 34 in Miss Smith's. He counted up to 36 on the wall number strip and marked this number with a crayon, then counted from 1 again up to 34. He kept his finger on 34 and counted back from 36 to 34 to get his answer.

A six-year-old decided to find out how many wheels there were on all the cars in the school car park. He matched each car with a yellow Cuisenaire rod (yes, a yellow rod). Then changing each rod for four white rods which he arranged in a line and counted.

Tommy is almost seven years old. His workcard told him to find out how many nuts weighed a pound. (The answer was 17.) It then asked him if he could find out about how many nuts would weigh 3 lb, but he was not allowed to weigh again. Tommy put his nuts in a straight line, and counted them up to 17, counting them again took him to 34 and he reached 51 at the end of the third count.

The sort of skill shown by these children is fairly commonplace when conditions favour it. Such mastery as they display is impressive and it is tempting to make optimistic assumptions about their understanding of the numbers they are dealing with which, in fact, might well be misplaced.

Compare the strategy Tommy invented when he was almost seven years old, to find out three lots of seventeen with the methods used by some children who were a year or so older.

(i) $17 + 17 + 17 = 30 + 14 + 7 = 44 + 7 = 51.$
(ii) $17 + 17 + 17 = 20 + 14 + 17 = 20 + 20 + 11 = 40 + 11 = 51.$
(iii) $17 \times 3 = 30 + 21 = 51.$

These older children are operating in ways that owe little to the ability to count, upon which Tommy based his strategy. They are using a new knowledge which gives them manipulative power over the actual numbers themselves. They have acquired some grasp of the structural properties of number, namely notation and place value, and this has enabled them to operate in a new and powerful way.

The fact that some children have difficulty in coming to terms with the ideas of notation and place value is well established and much thought has been given to the means by which they can best be helped. Teaching strategies currently in common use tend to centre around such apparatus as Dienes Multibase Arithmetic Block material, Cuisenaire and the abacus, the idea being that their structural characteristics restrict the range of choice open to a child and prompt him to operate in ways which highlight those properties of number we want him to learn about. It is possible, however, for him to miss the point. Much will depend upon what he thinks is the more important – the answer to a problem or the means of getting there. Apparatus can be used as ritualistically to get answers as any other calculation procedure. Some children will be a long time making the connection.

We might help them by including a set of experiences which highlight the ideas of notation and place value without the added distraction of computation. We return to counting, but this time with an added degree of sophistication.

A good start is made when children begin to appreciate the advantage of grouping in tens.

A class of first-year junior children aged about seven, just up from the infants, are standing by the school railings counting the number of cars passing, traffic is fairly heavy. They are working in twos, one of them calls out as the cars pass and the other records (see Fig. 3.4(a)). When they get back to class they are asked their score, but few pairs can agree, they find it hard to count the marks on their paper without making mistakes. So their teacher shows them a different way of recording (see Fig. 3.4(b)) which, after a bit of practice, they find makes counting much easier: 'Ten, twenty, thirty, forty, fifty, fifty-five, fifty-six, fifty-seven.' Some children take their recording pads home so that they can count cars over the week-end. They get into the habit of drawing a line across the page after ten rows of ten.

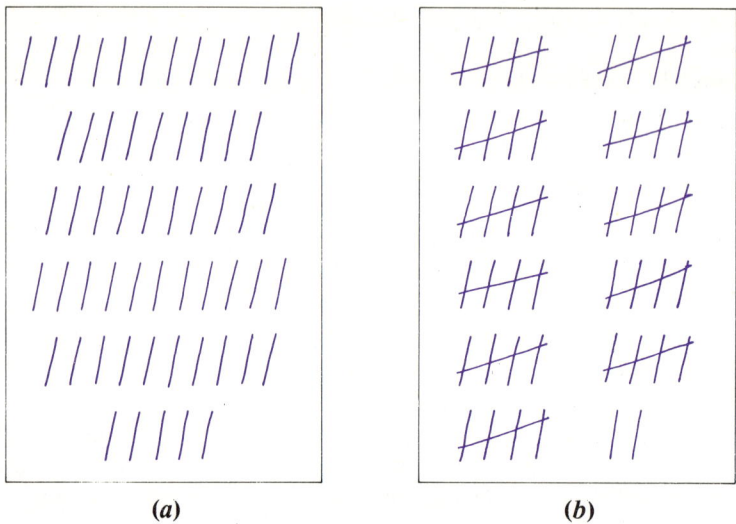

(a)   *(b)*

Fig. 3.4

Part of the exercise is recording the counts in a number of different ways:

(i) as numerals in a written narrative account,
(ii) as Cuisenaire trains, using as many orange rods as possible,
(iii) as Unifix lengths in the number track, each length of ten cubes in a different colour,
(iv) with pebbles grouped in tens and ones.

Some further suggestions for recording larger counts follow.

Units	*Tens*	*Hundreds*
(i) Buttons	10 buttons on a safety pin	A ring of 10 safety pins with 10 buttons on each
(ii) Peas	10 peas in a foil dish	10 dishes (of 10 peas each) in a cream carton
(iii) $\frac{1}{4}$ length wooden 'smoker's' spills – or matchsticks	Thin rubber band round bundle of 10 spills or matchsticks	Thick rubber band round 10 bundles of spills or matchsticks

When children are around six or seven years of age there tends to be a flurry of such structured counting and recording experiences and one gets the feeling of something starting which is well worth developing:

The teacher suggested a way of counting cars without having to write anything down except the final score. One boy is to count the cars on his fingers and each time he uses them all up he shouts, 'Ten!'. His friend is to count the tens on his fingers. Later that week the teacher noticed several groups of three children working away at the railings well before school was due to start. They had come early to catch the end of the rush-hour so that they could count past a hundred!

A pebble abacus is useful at this stage. It is best made out of a piece of hardboard about 40 cm × 30 cm. Flange the edges on three sides with thin wooden strip, which can also be used to partition the board. The top is left unflanged to facilitate removal of pebbles (see Fig. 3.5). Two

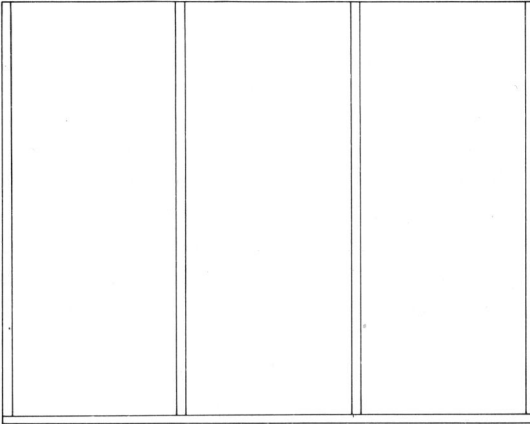

Fig. 3.5

children can work this abacus together to count, say, children going into assembly. One matches each child entering the hall with a pebble which he places in the 'ones' column. Each time he completes a count of ten his friend removes the pebbles and places one pebble in the 'tens' column.

After experience with a pebble abacus eight-year-old children were given bead abacuses to use (with three rows of ten beads). The following day one of them complained, 'This abacus is no good, it only counts up to nine hundred and ninety-nine.' Later in the month the teacher was asked if he would make an abacus which would 'count up to a million'.

'Yes', he said, 'if you will tell me how many rows of beads to put on it.'

It occurred to some children that they could count cars using the Dienes material and took the 'Base 5' box to the school railings to do so. Later they returned for the 'Base 2' box to see if they could manipulate the wood fast enough to keep up with the flow of traffic.

Dienes makes a point of suggesting that children are more likely to become aware of the open-ended nature of his Multibase Arithmetic Block material if they are allowed to extend the sequence implicit in the shapes of the wood available to them. He even provides names for the new pieces: 'Long Block', 'Flat Block', 'Block Block' etc. The following incident took place about the time that the children were considering extending Dienes in this way.

A class of second-year juniors (early in the year – about eight years old) were introduced to a large zinc bath full of small pebbles and the question was posed – how many pebbles are there? Guesses ranged from a few hundred to several million. The class was told that they would have to count the pebbles themselves if they wanted to know who was nearest. One day they decided they were ready. Teacher was given a piece of chalk and told to stand by the blackboard. Each child took a pile of pebbles, counted them, told the teacher to write the answer on the board, and then took another handful. It took a long time to count the pebbles in this way and by the time it was finished the blackboard was covered in figures. The children sat down and waited. 'Well', asked the teacher, 'how many are there?' 'It's on the board', they said. 'Where?', asked the teacher. 'All you've got to do is to add up those numbers', they replied. The teacher pointed out that it was their job to do the counting, not his. So after play the figures on the board were divided into groups of three and the numbers in each group were added together by a child. Once more the board was covered in figures, fewer this time, but the numbers were larger. The process of adding was manfully repeated again and again until one large number was eventually arrived at. 'That took you a long time', said the teacher. 'I think there must be a quicker way. Tell me if you think of one.' Some children lost interest at this point, but not all. Eventually, under the direction of one or two of the more earnest, the bath of pebbles was taken into a corner of the playground. The pebbles were arranged in piles of ten and each ten piles were put into a jam-jar. The jam-jars were then arranged in rows of ten. In the end there were ten rows of ten jam-jars, two jam-jars, three piles of ten pebbles and two separate pebbles. 'That's ten thousand, two hundred and thirty-two', said one bright spark. Most of the other children took his word for it. It was one of these who asked 'Can we do it again one day?'

In this last section of this chapter we take up a number of points connected with various computational procedures, not with a view to an exhaustive discussion: simply to raise questions.

What am I Finding Out?

Practically, and at an early age, there are two distinct actions that are symbolised indiscriminately as ' $\div$ '.

Suppose I am working with a group of 8 children and we have 40 sweets (*a*) I want to give equal numbers of sweets to each child. They can be distributed one-by-one and when I have discovered the answer empirically I can write $8 \times 5 = 40$.

I can also describe the situation by the sentence: $\frac{1}{8} \times 40 = 5$. $40 \div 8 = 5$ would mean, '40 sweets shared among 8 children give them 5 each'.

(*b*) I decide to give parcels of 5 sweets : will all 8 children get a parcel? The answer can be found out by removing as many sets of 5 sweets as possible and counting the number of heaps. This can be symbolised in the form: $40 \div 5 = 8$. I can also write: $5 \times 8 = 40$ or $\frac{40}{5} = 8$.

Algebraically, the two different situations are seen to be equivalent. If c is the number of children, p the number sweets in a parcel and s the total number of sweets I have, then I can write

(*a*) as $c \times p = s$ or $s \div c = p$ or $\frac{1}{c} \times s = p$ or $\frac{s}{c} = p$,

(*b*) as $p \times c = s$ or $s \div p = c$ or $\frac{s}{p} = c$,

and all these expressions are interchangeable. Division is seen to have several writings and to be the operation that 'undoes' multiplication. We say that division and multiplication are a pair of inverse operations, that is,

$$8 \times 5 = 5 \times 8 = 40; \quad 40 \div 8 = 5, \quad 40 \div 5 = 8,$$
$$\tfrac{1}{5} \text{ of } 40 = 8, \quad \tfrac{1}{8} \text{ of } 40 = 5.$$

From the practical method of solving (*b*), division is also clearly repeated subtraction.

For example, if I need to know how many 13s there are in 100 I can keep subtracting 13 (see Fig. 3.6) and then count how many times I have removed a 13.

```
                   100
        1          13 –
                  ─────
                    87
        2          13 –
                  ─────
                    74
        3          13 –
                  ─────
                    61
        4          13 –        Fig. 3.6
                  ─────
                    48
        5          13 –
                  ─────
                    35
        6          13 –
                  ─────
                    22
        7          13 –
                  ─────
                     9
```

Fortunately this method does not have much appeal, since most people do not enjoy doing subtraction. To save trouble, we learned products instead of repeatedly adding a number to itself again and again every time we wanted this snippet of information. Because division is the inverse of multiplication we can use the products we know to take away chunks instead of removing the number in question one at a time.

The problem now is: 'How many in a chunk?' Perhaps at first it doesn't really matter. Suppose I think of $5 \times 13 = 65$ and then see what is left. $100 - 65 = 35$.
I can take a 13 off; $35 - 13 = 22$, and now another; $22 - 13 = 9$.
So $5 + 1 + 1 = 7$; answer $100 \div 13 = 7$ rem 9.
In any case I can check the result by multiplying: $13 \times 7 = 91, 91 + 9 = 100$.
If we are directly concerned with the product numbers and their factors, there is no problem. $63 \div 9 = 7$ and $63 \div 7 = 9$ are direct deductions from $7 \times 9 = 63$. Any number a little larger only needs to be transformed by addition: $66 \div 9$ means $63 \div 9 + 3$ not used, since $66 = 63 + 3$. The answer is written 7 rem 3.

Before dealing with numbers in the hundreds it is helpful to do some multiplying by 10, 20, 30, ... and to link this extended idea on to the products the children have learnt. For example, what is

$$90 \times 7 \quad \text{and} \quad 70 \times 9?$$

Then

$$630 \div 9 = ?, \text{ etc.}$$

We also have to be able to decompose numbers into two or more parts, the larger of which we conceive as directly useful for our purpose. For example, for

$$684 \div 9 \text{ we need } 684 = 630 + 54,$$

from which

$$630 \div 9 = 70$$
$$54 \div 9 = \underline{6}$$

therefore

$$684 \div 9 = 76.$$

An Approach to the Long Division Algorithm

Let us assume $11 \times 12 = 132$ as a starting point.
Is it clear that $132 \div 11 = 12$ and $132 \div 12 = 11$ are, in a sense, the same thing?

So, $133 \div 11 = 132 \div 11$ and an odd 1, viz. 12 rem 1.

$134 \div 11 = 12$ rem 2		$134 = 132 + 2$
$135 \div 11 = 12$ rem 3		$135 = 132 + 3$
$136 \div 11 = 12$ rem 4		$136 = 132 + 4$
$137 \div 11 = 12$ rem 5		$137 = 132 + 5$
$138 \div 11 = 12$ rem 6		$138 = 132 + 6$
$139 \div 11 = 12$ rem 7		$139 = 132 + 7$
$140 \div 11 = 12$ rem 8		$140 = 132 + 8$
$141 \div 11 = 12$ rem 9		$141 = 132 + 9$
$142 \div 11 = 12$ rem 10		$142 = 132 + 10$
$143 \div 11 = ?$		

Everyone agrees that $143 \div 11 = 13$ and that $11 \times 13 = 143$.

Problem. Could we find the answer to $143 \div 11$ from the information $11 \times 10 = 110$?

Well, $110 + 33 = 143$. Is this a help?

We could try dividing these two bits of 143 separately and add the results: $143 \div 11 = (110 \div 11) + (33 \div 11) = 10 + 3 = 13$. It works!

Good. We can write down what we have just done in another form:

```
11 ) 143
     110 ... 11 × 10
     ───
      33
      33 ... 11 ×  3
      ──        ───
      . .        13
```

'But why ten times?'

I point out that ten is an easy number to multiply by.

We decide to experiment with a larger number, someone suggests 543. Have we enough information to work out $543 \div 11$?

First way
```
11 ) 543
     110   10
     ───
     433
     110   10
     ───
     323
     110   10
     ───
     213
     110   10
     ───
     103
      99    9
      ──
       4
```

We could refine the method by taking fewer 'bites'.

Second way
```
11 ) 543
     440   40
     ───
     103
      99    9
      ──
       4
```

I remind them that the transformation we have used is $440 + 99 + 4 = 543$.

Answer 49 rem 4

'Which do they prefer?' They agree with the second way but have the confidence to admit that they wouldn't have known it would be 40.

'Why not?' I ask for 11 × 20, 11 × 30, 11 × 40 etc. and they see that it is, after all, easy to know.

Now they want one to try for themselves, but I hold them back to show the way to check, and how to check is really almost the same as the method already used.

$$\frac{49 \times 11 + 4}{40 \times 11 = 440}$$
$$9 \times 11 = \ \ 99$$
$$\text{rem} \quad \underline{\quad 4}$$
$$543$$

or could be
$$49 \times 10 = 490$$
$$49 \times \ \ 1 = \ \ 49$$
$$\text{rem} \quad \underline{\quad 4}$$
$$543$$

For that lesson we stick to division by 11, but towards the end, getting bold, someone suggests a number in the thousands, 2345. I invite them to have a try on their own in the dinner hour.

N.B. *When experimenting with 'approaches' I have sometimes been thwarted by parents, or older children, showing the established method prematurely. Hence I now avoid setting homeworks at early stages of an important new topic that I am developing in an unconventional way.*

This class was pretty keen. By a combined effort they had got the idea of 100. A girl volunteered and did this for us on the blackboard:

```
11)2345
   1100      100
   ────
   1245
   1100      100
   ────
    145
    110       10
   ────
     35
     33        3
   ────      ───
      2      213
```

But on seeing it stuck up there, even those who had helped her in the dinner hour, wanted to know why the two hundreds hadn't been combined. Someone else put this right:

```
11)2345
   2200      200
   ────
    145
    110       10
   ────
     35
     33        3
   ────      ───
      2      213
```

and wrote triumphantly: 'Answer 213 rem 2'.

A third child did the check which recapitulates the transformation used:

$$200 \times 11 = 2200$$
$$10 \times 11 = 110$$
$$3 \times 11 = 33$$
$$\text{rem} \qquad \underline{\quad 2}$$
$$2345$$

There is always a danger, having had an initial success, that one takes the next stages too quickly for some – or, alternatively, too slowly for others! It seemed a good idea to give some more practice with multiplying by 10, 20, 30, ... and by 100, 200, 300, ... I happened to suggest that the prime numbers greater than 11 should be operated on in this way. It seemed an idea for getting a variety of divisors rather than the iteration 12, 13, 14, 15, ... which I suspected they would otherwise have offered.

After checking that they could make a 'table' and knew what to do for tens and hundreds, I wrote my own choice out in full so that we could discuss it.

		Units	Tens	Hundreds
Table of 37	1	37	370	3 700
	2	74	740	7 400
	3	111	1110	11 100
	4	148	1480	14 800
	5	185	1850	18 500
	6	222	2220	22 200
	7	259	2590	25 900
	8	296	2960	29 600
	9	333	3330	33 300

We compared methods of forming the unit column: adding on 37, combining lines, doubling and trebling, etc. Nearly everyone thought that the tens and hundreds columns were unnecessary.

I got the example, one digit at a time, from five children, writing from the units end and asking for the last figure to be 1, 2, or 3.

$$
\begin{array}{r|r}
37)25134 & \\
\underline{22200} & 600 \\
2934 & \\
\underline{2590} & 70 \\
344 & \\
\underline{333} & \underline{\quad 9} \\
11 & 679 \\
\end{array}
$$

Check

			or		
679 × 30	20 370			4600 × 37	22 200
679 × 7	4 753			70 × 37	2 590
rem	11			9 × 37	333
	25 134			rem	11
					25 134

We also discussed the merits of the two checks.

Although it seems only a short step from this to the traditional method, in fact we have avoided some complications:

$$\begin{array}{r} 6 \\ 37\overline{)25124} \\ \underline{222} \end{array}$$

Do the children know, without anxious thought, which of the digits of 25 134 represents 'hundred'? If not, some work on numeration is needed. Are they happy to leave 6 isolated, on top of the 1, in faith that it will eventually be the hundreds of the 679? Would they even be aware, when first writing it, that it does represent 600?

Some teachers would argue that this awareness is not necessary: that correct placing will automatically give the answer. I can only plead that this kind of awareness is going to be valuable when we are repeating the same technique, later, with decimal numbers.

Breaking Open the Procedure for Long Multiplication

How are the answers obtained?

36	36	36	36	36
×23	×23	×23	×23	×23
108	432	360	288	72
720	396	360	288	720
828	828	108	144	36
		828	72	828
			36	
			828	

Only one aspect of the usual procedure has been changed. The 'rule' of partitioning the multiplier into 'so many tens + so many units' has been relaxed and any partition of the number used (Fig. 3.7). Knowing that choices of this kind are available enables us to break away from the usual routine if we wish. The characteristics of individual numbers may suggest certain partitions as being more appropriate than others. The commutative property offers a second relaxation. We can work with 36 as multiplier and this presents its own set of partitions.

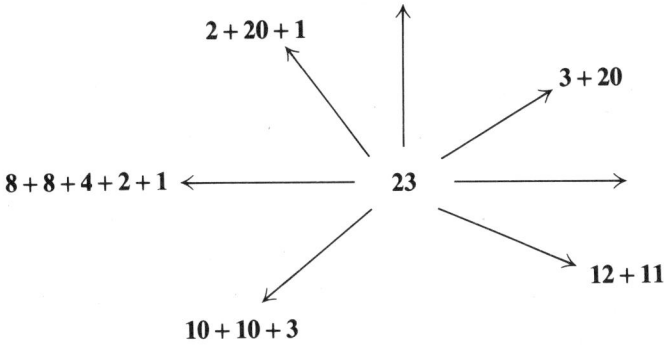

Fig. 3.7

```
   48          34           73
  ×19         ×28          ×96
  ───         ────         ────
  960        1020         7300
   48          68          292
  ───         ───         ────
  912         952         7008
```

What is happening here?

Since we know that any number can be expressed as an infinite number of subtractions, this knowledge can be used within the multiplication. We also know that numbers excluding primes can be expressed as products (Fig. 3.8).

```
    54        54         54          54
   ×24       ×24        ×24         ×24
   ───       ────       ────        ────
   108       216        648         162
   216      1296       1296         324
   432                             1296
  1296
```

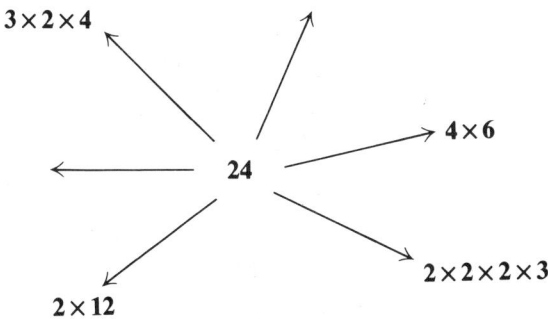

Fig. 3.8

Some choices give a quick answer; others are rather cumbersome. If we know of the possibilities, then we are in a position to choose. What transformations have been used in these examples?

	(i)	38	(ii)	43	(iii)	98	(iv)	63
		×77		×36		×34		×49
		266		258		3400		6300
		2660		1548		68		3150
		2926				3332		63
								3087

What has just happened is called 'breaking open the procedure for long multiplication'. It probably had to be called that in order to show people who are familiar with the technique that it has an underlying structure. On the other hand a five-year-old who had been able to count and do simple calculations from the age of three was constructing a table of products – a multiplication table – a table of 'ofs'. She was clearly using a variety of methods to fill in the blank squares – the table went up to 15 × 15. She counted on, sometimes across a row, sometimes down a column, she filled in the tens column and row quickly. She clearly used previous results to fill in new blanks sometimes using commutativity, sometimes not.

At one point she said: 'Look! I can use the answers I've already got to make the ones I want.' On this occasion it was using 4 of 6 = 24 to get 8 of 6 = 48 by doubling the first answer. On another occasion 7 of 13 came through 7 of 10 and 7 of 3 – half known, half checked. Though this child had a skill with numbers well beyond most five-year-old's attainment, what was revealed was the wide variety of methods that she used.

It does point to a very important notion referred to earlier that a computational procedure is a set of rules for transforming a calculation into a set of calculations whose answers are already known.

b

a of b	1	2	3	4	5	6	7	8	9	10
1	1	2	3	4	5	6	7	8	9	10
2	2	4	6	8	10	12	14	16	18	20
3	3	6	9	12	15	18	21	24	27	30
4	4	8	12	16	20	24	28	32	36	40
5	5	10	15	20	25	30	35	40	45	50
6	6	12	18	24	30	36	42	48	54	60
7	7	14	21	28	35	42	49	56	63	70
8	8	16	24	32	40	48	56	64	72	80
9	9	18	27	36	45	54	63	72	81	90
10	10	20	30	40	50	60	70	80	90	100

(The label a runs down the left side of the rows.)

Fig. 3.9

Consider the table of products (Fig. 3.9). These are the building bricks for long multiplication and we can, with a knowledge of these products, carry out any multiplication of larger numbers. The difficulty in learning long multiplication is that multiplying 23 and 34 gives you a number for which you have no check. The calculation has launched you into the hundreds, amongst whose numbers you will recognise only a few. We do depend on recognising numbers to get a feeling of being right.

But inside the table can be found the structure of long multiplication and it can be explained with the confidence that all the answers are known.

8 of 6 can be built out of
3 of 6 and 5 of 6.

So we can make a picture

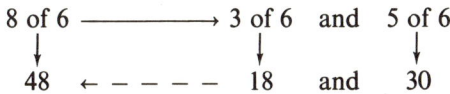

$$8 \text{ of } 6 \longrightarrow 3 \text{ of } 6 \quad \text{and} \quad 5 \text{ of } 6$$
$$\downarrow \qquad\qquad\qquad \downarrow \qquad\qquad\quad \downarrow$$
$$48 \leftarrow - - - - \ 18 \quad \text{and} \quad 30$$

or it goes into

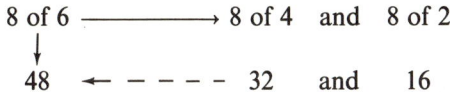

$$8 \text{ of } 6 \longrightarrow 8 \text{ of } 4 \quad \text{and} \quad 8 \text{ of } 2$$
$$\downarrow$$
$$48 \leftarrow - - - - \ 32 \quad \text{and} \quad 16$$

All this uses products already in the table.

9 of 7 can change into 4 of 7 and 5 of 7.

And these can change into

4 of 3 and 4 of 4, and 5 of 3 and 5 of 4.

More clearly, perhaps:

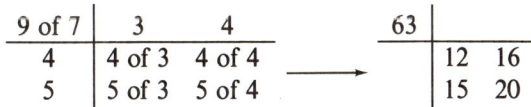

9 of 7	3	4		63	
4	4 of 3	4 of 4	$\longrightarrow$	12	16
5	5 of 3	5 of 4		15	20

All five numbers in the right-hand diagram can be found in the table of products as well as the sub-totals 28, 35 or 27, 36.

Once this combination of partitioning and product recognition has been explored, then long multiplication as a specific technique need not be a mysterious process.

Don't Talk Nonsense

Let us consider '43 subtract 27', not at present in the light of the situations this might represent, but as a 'sum' susceptible of treatment by several methods. Below we give extracts from a discussion with student teachers who, faced with the problem of teaching subtraction, were trying to look more closely at their own thinking.

$$43$$
$$- \ \underline{27}$$

1. *How do you do this?*
'Seven from three you can't, so seven up to ten is three and ...'
Where is the ten?
'Oh, you *say* that. It isn't anywhere really.'
Really? Well go on, and tell me later.
'Seven up to ten is three and three is six; and two is less than three' [*or some said 'three is less than four'*] 'so you take that away and it's 16.'
So if you say 'two is less than three' you've really ...
'Yes, taken a ten from the top line; and I took a ten from the bottom – no, I mean I put a ten on the bottom'.
So?
What was happening?

2. Others said, 'I don't do that. I borrow ten.'
Show me.

$$43$$ 'Seven from three, you can't, so borrow ten and say
$$-27$$ seven from 13. That's six. Now pay it back.'

How?
'Here'⟋   43 (pointing)
      $$-\underline{27}$$
        6
Is that where you borrowed it from?
'No. OH! Here' ⟋43   'Two from 5 is – No! *That's* not right!
       $$\frac{-27}{6}$$ You *do* pay it back here⟍   43
                                $$\underline{-27}$$

        But I *did* borrow it from the top. . .'

Can we find a set of transformations which would correspond to what was being said and show how the method did preserve the difference?

$$43 - 27 \rightarrow (43 + 10) - (10 + 27) \rightarrow (40 + 13) - (30 + 7)$$
$$\rightarrow (40 - 30) + 6 \rightarrow 16$$

3. 'I don't do that either, I say "Seven from three won't go", so I take ten from here →43 and say "Seven from thirteen is six",
     $$\underline{27}$$

and then I've taken ten so it's two from three is one and it's sixteen.'
Does this description correspond to

$$43 - 27 \to (30 + 13) - (20 + 7) \to 30 - 20 + 6 \to 10 + 6 \to 16?$$

The question 'How do you do this?' suggests that we describe an action and in that sense a transformation sequence such as that above is irrelevant as an answer. Once we have committed a technique of action to memory, any question of understanding is irrelevant if our purpose is simply to arrive at an answer. I am quite at ease with my 'action' for subtracting and if I were asked to justify what I was doing, I would step away from the action and look for some description in terms of transformations. Of course, I might justify it by saying that it works! Too often the request for help in coping with a technique is confused by turning it into a starting point for a discovery process. Slogans like 'Children should discover things for themselves' inhibit teachers at points when it is probably more important to give direct information. The apocryphal story of the child who in exasperation demanded of his teacher, 'What are six sevens – and please don't ask me what I think', has probably been experienced in many forms recently.

When we can calculate quickly and with little analytic thinking we probably use a complex of transformations which are highly idiosyncratic but which ensure, for us, the desired end-point.

A boy was asked to 'Find the value of x for $3x + 4 = 16$, and show your working'. He wrote

$$3x + 4 = 16 = 16 - 4 = 12 \div 3 = 4.$$

When discussing this some teachers have become enraged. What he has written is clearly nonsense, they say. How can $16 = 16 - 4$ etc. But we can all look at this line and if we understand what

$$3x + 4 = 16$$

was about in the first place, we have no doubt about what has been written. And if you read the sequence, substituting 'gives' for 'equals' for the last three '$=$' signs, something like the process gone through by someone who really understands the first statement is felt.

The correct procedure, someone will say, is

$$\begin{aligned} 3x + 4 &= 16, \\ 3x &= 16 - 4, \\ 3x &= 12, \\ x &= 12 \div 3, \\ x &= 4. \end{aligned}$$

But that wasn't my working – and that's what I was asked to show. . . .

Division of Fractions

$\frac{3}{4} \times \frac{4}{3} = ?$

$\frac{21}{17} \times \frac{17}{21} = ?$

etc.

$\frac{5}{7} \times \frac{3}{4} \times \frac{4}{3} = ?$

$\frac{19}{8} \times \frac{21}{17} \times \frac{17}{21} = ?$

etc.

Since $2 \times 3 \times 5 = 30,$

then $2 \times 3 = 30 \div 5.$

Since $11 \times 7 \times 10 = 770,$

then $11 \times 7 = ?$ etc.

Since $\frac{5}{7} \times \frac{3}{4} \times \frac{4}{3} = \frac{5}{7}$

then $\frac{5}{7} \times \frac{3}{4} = \frac{5}{7} \div \frac{4}{3}$

Since $\frac{19}{8} \times \frac{21}{17} \times \frac{17}{21} = \frac{19}{8}$

then $\frac{19}{8} \times \frac{21}{17} = ?$

etc.

$? = \frac{21}{3} \div \frac{6}{5}$

$? = \frac{107}{100} \div \frac{4}{15}$

etc.

How can you change a division of fractions into an equivalent multiplication of fractions?

Which Infinity?

The unimaginably large, the poet's infinity, the distance of the farthest star, the number of grains of sand in the world . . .

But note *Archimedes*, who reckoned the grains, and *Pascal*, who reminded us that the infinitely large is infinitely beyond the largest we can ever conceive . . .

hands forever circling a clock

multiple reflections in two mirrors

counting on, and on, and on

a snake swallowing its tail

Chinese boxes

a picture of a man holding a packet, and on it a picture of a man holding
   a packet, and on it . . .

the cycles of the days, the seasons, the years, . . .

a competition entry: 'The prize-winner in this week's competition was A. B.
   who sent us the following entry: ''The prize-winner in this week's
   competition was A. B. who . . .'''

the moments filling an hour and the points filling a line

                                   . . . and so on
                                   . . . and so on

Infinity as a class (*all*)

the word 'triangle' and the symbol standing for '*all* triangles'

Infinity as indifference (*any*)

'If I can carry out this operation on these elements, then I can equally well
   carry it out on those' — adding *any* two numbers, bisecting *any* line segment

Infinity as a definition

'An infinite set is one which is equinumerous with a proper subset of itself'
(*Dedekind*)

4

Measurement

We have become so used to thinking of measuring in terms of numbers that it is difficult for us to think about experiences of measuring that do not involve numbers and which do not even need anyone else to be involved. The general use of measuring instruments in forms accessible to quite young children draws our attention. The complexity of the world we occupy has demanded standardisation and agreement about common measures. The drive for metrication is characteristically a manifestation of one current need to have a technologically common base for handling data of an incredibly diverse nature. The history of the development of measuring is important and the work to which we introduce children is vital for their survival in the present environment.

Yet this picture is a distortion. It holds up to the light those matters that give us cause for worry: complexity of multipliers in different units, problems of communication between different technologies, the facility that numerical methods gives and so on.

Simultaneously we are still individual human beings with many of the problems and difficulties that have always faced people. We have to eat, clothe and shelter ourselves. We have to walk and run; avoid and fit the spaces we meet and occupy. To do these things with ease we depend on our perception and kinaesthetic sense; that is, on our awareness of our physical senses and capabilities.

An attempt to jump across a stream is not usually accompanied by thoughts like, 'I must fetch my measuring rod in order to know whether I can jump across or not.' If we talk of measuring in this circumstance it will be personal. 'He estimated the distance and leapt as hard as he could.' Even this does not mean that he said to himself that it was twelve feet or fifteen feet – it simply means that he related what he could see of the banks of the stream to what he felt he was capable of mastering. It is only later when such jumping becomes formalised into an athletic activity that numbers are used – and then only for competitive purposes.

Just as we learn to control the complexities of talking, we also learn to control the complexities that our bodies meet in physical space. Measuring may be a formalised activity with many ramifications, and this is what we feel we should teach as part of mathematics. But at other times of the day we work with children in many other ways. There is movement, dance and physical activity; there is the handling of materials of all kinds. Throughout this there is a steady growth of personal awareness of self and space.

A girl learning to sew gradually finds that she makes assessments of regularity in stitching; she also learns of the appropriateness of different stitches in different circumstances. The ability to control the space occupied by a lump of plasticene which can be distorted, stretched, compressed, gives a feeling of possibilities and limitations.

One can go on thinking of such situations:
climbing on frames, fences, trees . . .
running so far and then walking . . .
eating so much . . .

(Someone once said that infinity was first met as the chocolate pudding one could not finish.)

As these multifarious activities are experienced and skills develop, there is an increase in the need for occasional greater precision; times when the estimates do not work, even though these will be rare.

Some thirteen-year-old girls once decided to make model rooms out of cardboard boxes that had arrived in school. In one afternoon curtains, fireplaces, tables, chairs and people were made. They were produced rapidly using scissors, paint, pencils, card, glue; but there was not a ruler to be seen. I had the feeling that if the task had been conceived as one in which proportions were to be calculated and measurements with rulers to be made, then in the same period about half a fireplace would have been finished. It does not seem reasonable to introduce measurement as a formal skill without first thinking clearly just what is being formalised. And then to remember that such formality is only of use in particular situations.

It is the failure to relate effectively the important, though particular, skill of formal measurement to the vast world of controlled action in which we normally live that leads to the distortion referred to earlier. Our present experiencing of measurement in the formal sense is not straightforward. Anyone who learns to cook now will usually be introduced to it through the medium of measures of a variety of kinds: actual weight, capacity in cups or teaspoons or tablespoons, pinches, and the mysterious 'add to taste'. Some of these are easy to control, others not. The scales will give me my 4 oz of sugar but nothing but experience, or someone helping, will let me know what a knob of butter is.

Measuring in its formal sense happens when we want to be more certain about repeating something that we have already experienced than we could be if we relied on our unaided senses. In this way it can be an aid, but if extended it can be a tyrant. What is the area of balance between these two states? It is important to see that this statement about measuring as it happens refers to 'when *we want* to be more certain about repeating something'. This implies a personal feeling about past experience. What are the conditions under which such feelings can be given full rein against the times when 'to wish to repeat' is a way of avoiding risks and uncertainties which could be exciting and challenging?

One of the consequences of the distortion of accepting formal systems of measurement is that it is possible for a philosopher to say that something is only meaningful if it can be measured, and not be howled down. To teach children how to measure in the abstract seems to have the consequence of teaching them that measuring is, in itself, a respectable activity for its own sake, and not one which has validity only in relation to the wishes of the people involved with respect to tasks or actions undertaken. To teach techniques of measurement without discussing purpose and motive can be dangerously arid. A more fruitful approach to thinking about measuring depends on the notion of *compatibility* rather than that of *comparison*. The latter is certainly a characteristic of our more sophisticated measuring technique but does not seem appropriate for the direct 'measuring up to' notions that pervade this discussion. Before arriving at formal repeatable standard procedures with abstract measures like inches or metres, a series of possibilities could be described.

IDIOSYNCRATIC

The immediate relating of one's self to an action.

Assessment in this case is immediate and only concerns one's self. It will be concerned with what action one chooses in order to deal with a situation.

SIMPLE TRANSITIVE

An extension of the 'idiosyncratic' through the recognition that a situation has characteristics one feels one has met before. This implies an ability to hold an image from the past.

OBJECTIVE TRANSITIVE

When part of what has been experienced is preserved in order to deal with the same thing again: a stick for lengths, a cup, conscious use of body-size, spanners, etc.

SELF-OBJECTIVE

The possibility of carrying out an action with objects, that are deliberately constructed or found variously usable: bricks, stones, yarns, timber, etc.

This list is a precursor of lists of standard objects and of standard measurements. It covers everything that people will use in an everyday sense. By including things like spanners it acknowledges the simple use of objects which themselves depend on more complex social arrangements. This use is in no way different from the use of simple objects like sticks which do not exist, like screwdrivers, only as a consequence of increased complexity. This is a vital feature of the awareness of measure in its total sense, because it frees us from the presumption that because an object like a spanner only exists because of a complex technology it must in some way be humanly different. The argument here denies the thesis that man develops from primitive to sophisticated and accepts that man is simultaneously as primitive (immediate) or as sophisticated (indirect) as the particular environment allows him to be.

Up to this point standards are local, confined to particular activities and are dependent on convenience. References to histories of measurement show that local standards developed in terms of particular crafts or trades. ('Local' means confined and does not necessarily have a geographical sense though this is sometimes the case.)

Number is associated with measuring in connection with the 'self-objective' situations in the first place. The repeatability of an object can be controlled by reference to a counting system. The ability to repeat is an important element of control and the use of number to control repetition is no exception. In other words a number becomes more efficient in its ability to control when it itself uses repeatability for its own structure. The fact that fingers can be used again and again to count as the numbers get larger is often referred to as modularity.

Though the use of the symbols 1, 2, 3, 4, 5, 6, 7, 8, 9, 0 governs the repeatability that gives a very flexible control system, it has become so embedded in habitual actions that when 'modular arithmetic' came on the scene it hardly occurred to anyone that this topic is really at the root of the ability to control numbers and counting.

Modularity of Numeration

I remember finding it very intriguing once I had been able to grasp that what I was involved in was modular arithmetic. Having first met the idea through a rather obscure medium, a university lecture on congruence and residues, and not being moved in any way except perhaps to despair when I couldn't do the problems, it was pleasurable to feel the control when I met it in a more relaxed way.

But as a simple diversion it seemed out of the mainstream of what I thought mathematics was about; it seemed to be a little bit of number theory. I introduced it into my teaching as an accessible example of an arithmetic with similar rules but with different consequences from 'real arithmetic'. The algebraic properties were useful in that very quickly children could work with another algebra beside the one to which they had become accustomed. Then modular arithmetic started turning up in textbooks often linked (confusingly?) with number bases which in turn were often linked (again confusingly?) with multiplying factors when handling units of measurement (inches $\times$ 12 $\rightarrow$ feet; feet $\times$ 3 $\rightarrow$ yards.)

I was asked recently what was the use of 'modular arithmetic'. By the time I was asked this I had recognised quite a lot of ordinary situations that had something of the 'modular arithmetic' feel about them. So much so that my answer to the question was not to discuss 'useful applications' at first but to point out that modularity in counting and ordering was more fundamental a control of our environment than ordinary arithmetic. More than this it is the very modular property that has allowed us to develop the sophisticated handling of all our current number systems in arithmetic.

The fundamental characteristic of number control is that of recognising a successor. The notion of 'following on' is pervasive in our experience of living and has an intense localised value wherever we recognise a necessary ordering of events either of those we control or of those which happen to us. It is important to see that the use of the word 'localised' allows the 'following on' notion to be used without any presumption of a universal ordering of all events. Too many things happen to us simultaneously, and with no simple connection, for it to be of universal application.

In watching an athletics meeting we can be aware of exact sequences of events in different parts of the arena, all with their different rules of succession. The simultaneity of these is random except when two of the sequences impinge (the 1500 metres cannot be staged simultaneously with the 400 metre hurdles). To watch an athletics match from the stand can be very confusing to a spectator ignorant of such things, simply because of the necessary simultaneity of the different events. Yet each event is inexorable in its obedience to the sequence. The complexity of the sequence of jumps allowed in the high-jump and the mapping of the consequences of the competitors' actions into a final placing is very different from the manner in which the 800 metres is run and judged.

Most of the time the recognisable actions we take are limited in their immediacy. Journeys have beginnings and ends, so do meals, rests, periods of work. The beginnings and ends are not always easy to identify but it is those that we recognise that I am talking about and not those which we do not. Re-cognition means to know again. If this sounds odd, think that it is possible to conceive of having a new experience which we will only recognise after it has happened. The actual happening in this case cannot be recognised, only felt (cognised?). But when paying attention to those that we do recognise we find that we link them to notions of period, repeatability or repetition.

It appears almost basic that we subject ourselves to points of repetition or period in order to know where we are. How far this is a necessary state of being and how far we should attempt to subdue periodicity in order to be more aware of other possibilities is an open question, but periodicity of events is characteristic of most societies and seems basic to survival. Seasons of growth and the consequent availability of food; the survival of materials and the need to re-furbish shelter; sexual awareness and the generation of new beings, all have basic periodicities. Further, what seem to be necessary practices in religious ritual have similar characteristics with respect to festivals and rites and have practical outcomes in hours, days, weeks, months, years, which govern closely the way we organise our actions. The awkwardness of the placement of Easter is a consequence of the conflict between two incompatible periodic systems.

One can have a picture of a stream of living punctuated and controlled by points of repetition.

So it seems, in the control of events, besides the fundamental awareness of succession, we impose (some would say we inherit naturally) periodicities or modular repetition.

This awareness is fundamental to our ability to deal with issues of measurement. The ability to limit experiencing by recognising repetition is basic to the ability to communicate 'measure' to another person.

What is our experience of counting and numbers? We are very well acquainted with numbers that seem to be able to go on forever. Our ability to speak and write numbers makes us feel that they could get bigger and bigger. On the other hand, it is very difficult for us to imagine large numbers of objects. We continually surprise ourselves when faced with large numbers. 'I didn't realise how many there were until . . . ' So if we look into our everyday lives we find that we cope by splitting our counting into sequences small enough to 'feel'. Days of the week, months of the year, measures of quantity (four or five gallons of petrol for a car rather than thirty or fifty pints).

(The week, it is said, probably originated in terms of the amount of food that could be worked for, and eaten, before the next market day.)

But in various ways, as a consequence of a large variety of technical needs more and more sophisticated methods of dealing with number arose and have been developed.

Consider systems of numeration. An arrangement for counting implies a unique beginning and a unique succession. In terms of repeatability we can agree to start again and so have 1st, 2nd, 3rd, 4th, last, 1st, 2nd, 3rd, 4th, last, 1st . . . Thus with market days 1st after market, 2nd after market, 3rd, 4th and then it is market day again.

Many stories of the Creation describe finite sequences from the beginning to a time of rest.

For many other purposes besides those which require repetition we have small finite numbering situations to handle. The daily order for four pints of milk is such as not to allow a steady build up of milk in the house but at the same time to allow for sufficient milk to be available for the needs of the house. The fact that the house consumes around 150 gallons of milk a year is merely interesting.

To symbolise counting requires a set of arbitrary characters with a unique beginning and an assigned order. The alphabet is an example. The collection of letters which we use in order to write contains 26 characters. The order in which we list them is irrelevant to their use as written symbols. To 'know your letters', as the many alphabetic books suggest, is only a side issue to the act of knowing how they can be used to make words. A child can and does spell without knowing the alphabet. But there happens to be an order and its definiteness is most likely connected with the former use of letters as numerals. Indeed the main use of an alphabet is to order words in a dictionary, index, catalogue or directory, where information on a finite set of objects is required to be efficiently accessible. The assigned successor relation between the letters, having started with A, is as much evidence of the skill of counting as that found in the signs 1, 2, 3, 4, 5 . . .

But what happens when we need to extend the symbols to count or organise large quantities? The alphabet is probably one of the longest sequences of arbitrary symbols with a well-defined succession. Its application in a dictionary extends this sequence in two dimensions depending on the agreed spelling of words. Again, 'agreed spelling' is another example of defined succession. Rules of spelling are attempts to find common features between the different methods of assigning order to the letters in any particular set of words.

If we look at any numeration system associated with any depth of usage we can see that the extension of the uniqueness of succession is not achieved by going on inventing new symbols, but by using a form of repetition. The word *modular* is an adjective derived from *module*, which can be thought of as meaning the basic string of numerals. The module of repetition is the base of the numeration system. Different cultures have from time to time adopted different sizes of module.

The consequence for us is the adoption of the symbols 1, 2, 3, 4, 5, 6, 7, 8, 9 as the basic module. In our written symbol-form, signs are strung together one-dimensionally to create two, three, four, etc. figure numerals, for example, 3215.

A similar thing happens when we speak the numerals. But the recycling of the module in the next numerals 10, 11, 12, 13, 14, 15, 16, 17, 18, 19 follows an unusual sound-pattern, almost as if each pair of digits were reversed. It is possibly significant that we have inherited this particular form of symbolic expression from an Arabic system probably using a right to left orthography. If we had invented it ourselves it could well have been that the spoken numerals named ten, eleven, twelve, thirteen, fourteen, fifteen, sixteen, seventeen, eighteen, nineteen, would have been written 01, 11, 21, 31, 41, 51, 61, 71, 81, 91. Note the order of the spoken words for the underlined numerals.

We still sometimes say five-and-twenty past seven when telling the time. Our ability to control calculations with these numbers is dependent on our control of the properties of the modular set together with the ability to cope with the passage from one position (called place) to another in the combined forms of the larger numerals.

The spoken English numeration system uses a base of nine numerals and deals with placing in a different way from the Arabic sign system. Thus four hundred and six uses three signs and a conjuction. Two of the signs ('four' and 'six') are from the original module and one ('hundred') is the additional sign needed to show that the 'four' refers to a different position in the sequence in the counting sense. Nothing is said about the absence of tens. The fact that there are inconsistencies in the numeral names up to a hundred is evidence of the growth of such a system from simpler structural beginnings. I mean by this that 'eleven' and 'twelve', being very different sounding words from 'thir-teen', 'four-teen', etc., suggest a different history.

We use the modular notion when we see that by learning a set of multiplication tables involving numbers up to nine, we are in business with the rest of the set of numbers so long as we have a means of denoting the extension at each point when the module runs out. Thus we have *hundred, thousand, million* in the spoken form but symbolically (more efficiently?) 100, 1000, 1000 000, by the use of the cipher (0) to identify a place system in a set of signs. This latter allows us to write the name for an enormous number such as 15 745 032 495 724 039 810 025 926 and, indeed, we can say it as 'one, five, seven, four, five etc.' without any need to have a number for the new points of extension. In this particular number we would only need to have 'trillion' meaning a 'billion billion' to be able to say it in words.

The importance this has for children learning arithmetic is that a distinction is clearly drawn between, on the one hand, coming to know what the numerals for 'higher numbers' may indicate, and, on the other, the structure of the formation of the numerals from the basic numeral characters.

Thus in making a progression in a syllabus from 'the numbers up to ten', 'the numbers up to twenty', to 'the numbers up to a hundred', allowance is being made for the increasing difficulty in conceiving the size and possibilities of the larger numbers. On the other hand the modular form of numeration allows a grasp of 10, 20, 30, 40, . . . , 90 to be made very shortly after 1, 2, 3, 4, 5, . . . , 9. The fact is that '2 and 3 make 5' is virtually the same as '20 and 30 make 50' even though from the point of view of quantitative comparison they are very different.

The experience of handling bundles of ten in order to give meaning to the names of bigger numbers may lead to an understanding of the quantitative relationship but does not necessarily help with the mystery of the change in the meaning of the symbol 1 when it appears in the second place.

Thus:

Action *A*:   1111111111   11111   The two actions, *A* of bundling a group of sticks with another lot next door, and *B* of

Action *B*:   15   writing the characters 1 and 5 in close proximity, do not relate particularly easily to the perception.

It seems that the modularity associated with how we name numbers allows an ease of handling number names. This means that handling $1, 2, 3, \ldots, 9$ and possibly 10 can be associated quickly with handling $10, 20, 30, 40, \ldots, 90$ and possibly 100. In one sense it is the same thing. But alongside this is the notion of numbers representing an increase in quantity as they go on. In this case $10, 20, 30, \ldots$ represent quite different things from $1, 2, 3, \ldots$ The modular equivalence is made to generate a continued sequence of representation of quantity and in some way a method of indicating the difference between the two modules (apart from their names) has to be established in order that they can be also seen as a continued sequence.

$$1 \quad 2 \quad 3 \quad 4 \quad 5 \quad 6 \quad 7 \quad 8 \quad 9 \quad (10)$$
$$(10) \quad 20 \quad 30 \quad 40 \quad 50 \quad 60 \quad 70 \quad 80 \quad 90 \quad (100)$$
$$\Longrightarrow 1 \ 2 \ 3 \ 4 \ 5 \ 6 \ 7 \ 8 \ 9 \ (10) \ 20 \ 30 \ 40 \ 50 \ 60 \ 70 \ 80 \ 90 \ (100)$$

The problem is one of introducing the module again after (10) but now in the first place. The numeral 11 becomes crucial and after that 101. It is almost as if 11 has to be recognised as the 'stop' which prevents the two modules $1, 2, 3, \ldots, 9$, and $10, 20, 30, 40, \ldots, 90$ from sliding apart altogether. We often speak of our number base as 'ten' but it should be noted that as soon as we write 10 we have begun the module again in the second place and are preparing for a repetition in the first (units) place. We never actually place one more in with the nine – we start again. Eleven is hence the first point when we see the modules developing together.

The 'problem of zero' is that it is treated as a numeral, but it does not belong to the base module. It is significant that '.' is the Arab sign for 0. This makes it easier to see the new start 1. (instead of 10), followed by 11 with the beginning of the repeat of the module in the first position.

Number and Measure

The history of the relation of number symbolisation to various human activities in terms of the effect of the concrete characteristics of any particular activity is not well known. Stories are told, for instance, about furrows, oxen and furlongs, and whereas there is no doubt some truth in these, the inevitably wide variety of idiosyncratic usage is hardly recorded. When it is, it tends to be recorded in a way which suggests that such primitive methods are in some way of lesser status than our present sophisticated procedures.

This is dangerous for it allows us to forget that measurement is more complex than a simple standardised procedure. It has led recently to a wholesale condemnation of our non-standard systems of measure in favour of metrication.

In the face of a metric system one is compelled to ask questions about non-metric systems. It seems mindless merely to accept another system without questioning the virtues of the systems that have survived. Rationalisation does not necessarily imply being rational.

Looking at those systems based on halves, quarters, eighths, sixteenths, it seems that as far as lengths are concerned there is some connection with the ease of halving. If halving can be done by eye then it is not surprising that a consequent numerical structure grew up based on this very ability. The estimation of a fraction between two marked points is best done by using a binary (halving) procedure.

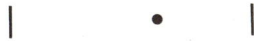

$$| \qquad \bullet \qquad |$$

Fig. 4.1

Make an estimate to the nearest eighth of the position of the dot with respect to the two marks (Fig. 4.1). Compare this with making an estimate in tenths.

Another halving situation is that produced by the balance scales. These scales can be used to divide a quantity into two halves by weight. The division can continue to quarters, eighths and so on. This act in itself would be sufficient means to share and agree on shares between two people.

It lends itself also to the numerical notion that by taking a small weight as standard and preparing one that is double, and another, and another, in sequence, a very efficient system of weights is formed:

$$1 \quad 2 \quad 4 \quad 8 \quad 16.$$

Using just one of each it is possible to weigh any multiple of the unit weight up to 31. Each multiple will be given by a unique set of weights: thus, for instance, 5 is $1 + 4$, 23 is $1 + 2 + 4 + 16$.

For this purpose this set of numbers is the most efficient. Compare the metric system in which it is necessary to have five weights (presuming 10 to be included) as before:

$$1 \quad 2 \quad 2 \quad 5 \quad 10 \quad \text{(the weights are divisors of 10).}$$

But now we can only weigh up to 20 and we have to repeat one of the weights. Here is a direct conflict between efficiency in counting (using fingers and bases of 5 or 10) and efficiency in measuring.

There is thus no case for telling measurement stories from the past as if old-fashioned things were inefficient. The kind of inefficiency that has led to the increased use of the metric system has nothing to do with appropriateness for purpose. It has been mainly to do with the pressing need for ease of exchange between one set of measures and another. If in the future we invented methods which made such conversion simple then we could return to a time when the measures we used were idiosyncratic and appropriate for their purpose.

There is no doubt about the versatility of a measurement system closely linked with a constant method of numeration, but as we show later this tends to be proportionately more helpful as the purposes grow more sophisticated.

Value

The relationship between measurement and purpose is not easy to describe. It is not sufficient simply to say that we need to measure in order to carry out certain skilful operations. The use of measurements in cooking hints at the temporary nature of the measurements in respect of the greater insight consequent on increased experience.

Standards of measure may be seen as methods of projecting ourselves with confidence into regions in which we would otherwise have no faith in ourselves or others. They can always be discarded when our confidence is adequate to the tasks involved. Perhaps measuring is a support for a lack of faith.

If this is a valid thing to say, it means that we must look closely at the way we encourage a belief in measuring as a virtue in itself.

A standard measure is one with which people will agree. A shopkeeper sells material in terms of a standard yard or metre and we accept the brass rod clamped to the counter. Why do we accept that rather than him?

As trading became more complex and more people, living at greater distances from each other, were bartering, then standard measures grew as the ability to trust diminished.

The belief in fair shares depends essentially on a lack of trust between those concerned to share. Mary Boole contrasts sharing sweets with sharing a daffodil bulb. The one is susceptible to arithmetic; the second can be shared by growing it and all having the flower. To submit it to Solomon's decision is to miss reflecting on the irony of his judgment.

But how could science have developed without the ability to measure? No simple answer can be given for there is a real sense in which a scientist or group of scientists or technologists is still, despite the sophistication, actually working in the spirit of the individualised or local measures described earlier. These are an aid to information; to be discarded when necessary; to be reinforced when confidence disappears. On the other hand, scientists have entered the publicity game so that they barter their successes in public. And in this sense measure may be used to convince where trust is lacking.

Clearly if children are growing into an untrustworthy world it is vital that they learn the ways in which we attempt to limit the effects of a lack of trust.

The question for teachers concerned with mathematics is that the sophisticated development of measurement systems is so complicated that it appears sufficient in itself. It is not easy to see the ethical nature of the situations in which an expert acquaintance with measuring is used. But we measure and classify people and this is even held in esteem. Indeed it is hard for children to grow up now without being affected by the measurement systems that are applied to people. What, then, is our task if we begin to see that the objectification of measure through facility with number may be an unwitting invitation to be morally degraded?

A solution to this lies in a greater recognition of the relative nature of measuring in its connections with surprise. This implies a separation of our awareness of the complexity of what it is to which we are attempting to relate, from the awareness of what it is possible to communicate (to make common) by means of a measurement.

So long as we do not need to communicate there is no need for any but the individualised or local awareness of measuring. As soon as we need to make connections with people who are at a distance too great to be in touch with what is locally possible, then we attempt to express something of what we know. We attempt to put a measure on the object of our concern. Number is an easy vehicle for communication but it does not mean that we have hence communicated what we know. It is important to develop skills in this, but it is also important to know the limitations.

The ease with which someone can say he is measuring the gas consumption in his house may take us away from the more precise statement that the dials on his meter show numbers to which he agrees as a basis for payment. It is not pedantic to make this separation when one also knows that a psychologist may use the same kind of language to say that he is measuring intelligence. One has to ask him also for a more precise statement about the agreements involved.

How Long is a Piece of String?

When we actually use a piece of string we usually have a particular task in mind. A piece of string can then be just one of three things: too short, just right or too long. There will be a direct idiosyncratic judgment whose correctness will be judged by attempting the task.

It may be that similar tasks have been undertaken before so that in a *simple transitive* (see p. 122) sense we look for a piece of string compatible with what we already know. A shoe lace, for instance.

There may be a need to carry out a sequence of similar tasks, like tying up balloons or threading a loom. In which case one may have an *objective transitive* method by using a stick or a known appropriate piece of string as a guide.

In none of these activities will number be necessary to come to any conclusion about the appropriateness of the string for the task. Yet I anticipate that most people will say that a piece of string possesses a length which is measurable. There is a confusion in this between, on the one hand, *length* as reminding us of a particular physical quality of extension and, on the other, *length* as defined by our ability to put a measure on it.

We have already seen that the latter can be satisfied for a great many tasks without using number. We can probably agree that a particular piece of string will be long enough for a large variety of tasks, which seems to say that the piece of string has as many lengths as tasks it is used for.

But the attachment of numbers to measures is so strong because, it seems, of the abstract force of mathematics, that we believe the string to have an actual length. Some mathematicians would say it has a 'real number' for its length.

This is unfortunate for the concept of 'real number' is one of the most sophisticated of mathematical notions and has very little to do with what is ordinarily called real. Or at least the connections can be made but when they are, they turn out to be not unlike the idea that the length of a piece of string is the set of all tasks for which it is long enough.

Measuring: Instruments and Tasks

As our needs become more complex we need not only to be aware of the beginnings of measure and its relation to number but also of the development of devices.

Using a Ruler

All mesuring *instruments*, the ruler being no exception, are devices for transforming measuring into counting. That is only a rough description since measuring *is* a sort of counting. But we know that when we are counting a collection of objects we will eventually exhaust the whole of the collection by going on long enough, that we will not have missed any out, and that there will not be any left uncounted. We may have 117 objects. We can't have 116-and-a-bit objects or 117-and-a-bit objects. But in measuring a length we *can* arrive at 116-and-a-bit centimetres. The usual way to make the distinction between the two situations is to talk of *continuous* and *discrete* quantities, and to say that length is a continuous quantity whereas the number of objects in a collection is a discrete quantity. Definitions get difficult, and in fact it is probably best to give an operational definition – a discrete quantity is one that can be counted. With this terminology we can say: length is a continuous quantity, but measuring a length is the act of finding a discrete, and therefore countable, quantity that is *as equivalent as possible* to the given one. In finding the length of the segment *AB* we may lay a ruler marked in centimetres against it (Fig. 4.2). This enables us to

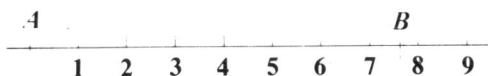

.4   B

1   2   3   4   5   6   7   8   9

Fig. 4.2

say that the length of *AB* is roughly the same as the length of seven discrete, countable centimetre lengths placed end-to-end. We just read '7' from the marks on the ruler, perhaps, but this is only a convenient shorthand for what we have just said.

What do we mean by 'roughly'? If we took *one more* centimetre length we would overshoot the end *B*. We know that the length of *AB* is more than 7 cm but less than 8 cm. If we feel that we could get closer we would use the word 'roughly'; but some tasks may make us feel that 7 cm is a good enough statement. We can, if we wish, use some smaller discrete objects obtained by subdividing a centimetre length and count those in exactly the same way as we counted the centimetre lengths earlier. We may find that the 'extra bit' is 'roughly' equivalent to six of these. We may now say that the 'length' of *AB* is 7 cm 6 mm.

But this is clearly not really the length of *AB*, but the length of a countable equivalent. It may be better to say that the length of *AB* is more than 7 cm 6 mm but less that 7 cm 7 mm; then at least it is apparent just what we *have* found out about the length of *AB*.

With an ordinary ruler this will be as far as we can go. Should the purpose of measuring demand a smaller unit then we should have to use a different instrument.

We could have done this by counting in millimetres, although this would have been much more tedious and liable to error. There would be no difference to the general argument to say that we could have counted 76 mm before overshooting the end *B*.

If we write 76 mm $<$ length of *AB* $<$ 77 mm, we can say that 76 mm is a *lower bound* to the length of *AB*, and 77 mm is an *upper bound*. What is the relation between the two bounds, and why is it reasonably satisfactory in many cases to use only the lower bound when asked to find a length?

Measuring an Area

Some of the same points apply; others do not. One can rarely 'straighten out' an irregular area as one can straighten out a wiggly piece of string. Some very special cases *are* amenable to transformation (especially if the areas arise from shapes made in restricted conditions, as on squared paper, or spotty paper, or on a geoboard, for instance).

But if we consider the non-transformable shapes, what does the process of measuring involve? It has to involve a transformation of the problem if not a transformation of the shape involved: we have to find a *countable* area that is as equivalent as possible to the one we want to measure. The usual method is that of superimposing the shape on a square grid, for example, by putting a leaf on a sheet of squared paper and drawing round the edge of the leaf. It may often be better to put the grid, marked on tracing paper or cellulose acetate sheet, on top of the shape. In this latter case it is easier to alter the relative positions of the shape and the grid. In measuring a line with a ruler we know where to place the ruler, but in measuring an area with a grid, where should we put the grid? It is usually assumed that it doesn't matter, but how do we know that? Perhaps shifting the grid, or twisting it through an angle, will entirely change the count (Fig. 4.3). Anyway,

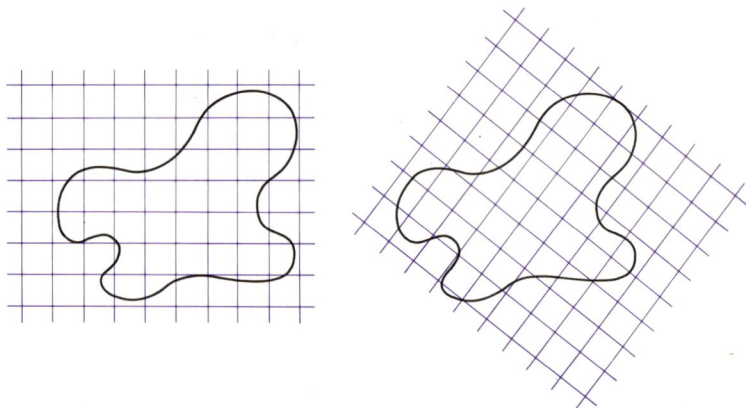

Fig. 4.3

having selected some position for the grid, one has a countable area which is more or less equivalent to the area one wants to find. The usual procedure is to count all the whole squares inside the perimeter of the shape. But the situation is now not at all like that of measuring the line segment. Would adding *one more* whole square to the total overshoot the area of the shape? Probably not – and in any case, it is difficult to tell. So it is almost certainly impossible to say that we now have the *best* lower bound to the area in the chosen square units.

Again, the usual procedure is to make some allowance for all the *parts* of squares that are within the perimeter of the shape. In fact there is one suggested rule at this point which instructs that each part square should be counted as if it were a half square. It could be said that the difference between the scientist and the mathematician on an issue like this emerges sharply. The 'scientist' will say, 'By using this rule of thumb I am nearer to the actual area than I am if I count just whole squares.' The 'mathematician' will say, 'In most cases your rule will make you better off, but not always, and I can give you an example to show that your rule will give you a worse estimate that the first one.' (*Can you invent such an example?*) 'But, what is more important, your rule has closed the door to any further improvement. You've finished your estimation now; there is nothing you can do, and you've lost control of the situation. What *I* want is to find a method which will show me how to get as good an estimate as I may need, depending on the purpose for which I need it. I want to go on in stages until it is as good as I want it to be, and in such a way that I know just how good it is.'

So the 'mathematician' will probably say, 'What we have learned about measuring lines is that we can get lower and upper bounds to the length, and that these can always in principle be improved – that is, brought closer together. Let's apply the same general idea to measuring area.' (See Fig. 4.4).

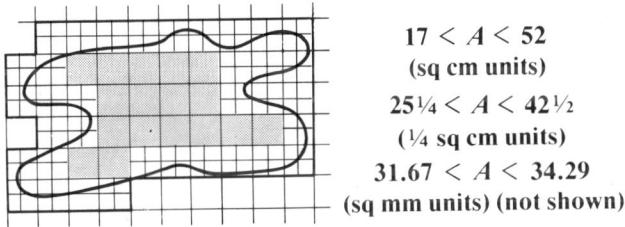

$$17 < A < 52$$
(sq cm units)
$$25\tfrac{1}{4} < A < 42\tfrac{1}{2}$$
(¼ sq cm units)
$$31.67 < A < 34.29$$
(sq mm units) (not shown)

Fig. 4.4

In practical measuring situations we shall arrive at an equivalent length which will be of use, or an equivalent area appropriate to our task. It can be seen that for a surface there can be a set of numbers any of which could be thought of as the area. We can always add another 'better' number but indeed we obviously choose for use the one that serves our practical purpose.

How do these ideas carry through in measuring other quantities such as mass, capacity, temperature, etc.? Think about the function of some other measuring instruments from this point of view.

Postscript on Measuring

What is the relationship between the activity of measuring and computations involving measures? It's quite easy to see that computation with measures is either nothing to do with measuring at all (as in *all* textbook and work-sheet examples where the data are provided – this is only attaching labels to numbers and it doesn't matter what the labels mean; you only have to know that you can substitute ten of *those* for one of *those*), or is the application of what one already knows about numbers to the counting numbers that turn up in actual measuring situations (e.g. you can find the perimeter of a rectangular room by measuring half way round and then using your knowledge of doubling *numbers*). In neither case does one learn anything about the behaviour of numbers *from* the measuring situation (or the fake measuring situation); this has got to be fed in from elsewhere.

Measuring is an *activity*, and it requires the use of oneself as well as any instruments that may be appropriate. Like a computer, a measuring instrument is obedient to the will of its instructor; it doesn't do anything on its own. One tends to think exclusively of the external aspect of the activity whereas for the child the internal aspect is paramount. There are all those stories of children doing 'peculiar' things in measuring situations to show that an instrument alone is not enough.

Take the problem of deciding which of two masses is the greater. It's not enough to say I lift them one at a time, or hold one in each hand. I've got to be aware of what happens inside me. If I lift one at a time I have to be able to retain for comparison an impression of all the muscular movements I had to make in lifting the first. If after lifting them I don't know which is the greater, it's not because I did the wrong thing but because I wasn't *aware* of what my muscles had to do. If I hold one in each hand I still need an awareness of the muscular activity in both arms before I can say which is the greater mass. Of course pre-school experience has given this awareness to many children, but for others no one has ever called their attention to what they know. It's this the teacher should be doing, not giving lots of experiences which have already been experienced.

Now if I know the action of myself in weighing, I can see that a scalepan or a balance is only an extension of myself. In fact it is probably *me* who has to lift the things to be weighed into the pan – so cannot I know what the machine 'takes over' from me? In this way I can transfer my experience of myself to a vicarious experience of what the machine is having to do.

Measuring for measuring's sake is a very trivial activity; but measuring to know more about myself and the instruments in my world, now that is worth spending some time on.

Time

1. You know a lot about distances and directions without having to measure. For example
   - you know how to throw a ball for someone to catch
   - you know how loud to speak for someone to hear you
   - you know where to look to see who called out to you in the street
   - you know how to walk about so that you don't bump into the furniture.

   Give examples to show that you know at least some things about time without having to measure them.

2. Use your pulse or your breathing to compare the durations of some pairs of events. For example
   - two consecutive television commercials
   - two friends holding their breath as long as they can

   Which do you think is the more relaible way to compare durations? Why do you think so?

   Does your pulse rate vary at different times of the day? After different kinds of activity? What about your breathing rate?

   Can you hold your breath?
   Can you 'hold your pulse'?

3. How well can you estimate a duration of one minute without using a watch or a clock? Does it make any difference whether you are concentrating on estimating, or whether you are doing something else at the same time? Do your estimates improve with practice? Is it harder to estimate five minutes?

   Write a set of instructions for someone who wants to become a good estimator of short periods of time.

4. Look around you with the eyes of a stranger. Make a note of everything you can find that gives you some clue about the time of day, or the time of year.

   Close your eyes. Is any evidence left? Put your fingers in your ears. Is any evidence left?

   Repeat the experiment in several different places until you feel you are better able to pick up clues.

5. Make a collection of pictures from newspapers or magazines and look at them carefully to see whether they tell you anything at all about the time — say, the time of day, or the time of year, the date, the historical period, etc.

   Choose a set of your pictures and exchange them with the set of a friend. Write down any things they tell you about time and then get together with your friend and compare what you found in each picture.

6. When a bicycle is moving quickly enough it is impossible to see the separate spokes of the wheels — they appear to blur and merge together. When a drummer plays a roll of the side-drum the sounds blur together and it is not possible to hear the individual strokes of the stick on the drum. Would you say your eye or your ear is better able to notice very short durations of time? If you are not sure, can you devise some experiments which will tell you the answer?

5

Changing Definitions of Mathematics

One of the problems of the teacher in the current atmosphere of changes in mathematics teaching is the uncertainty about the nature of the beast. The confusion is marked when teaching younger children where much of the traditional arithmetic appears to be neglected, and a number of topics have taken its place. The doubts and insecurities of the teacher are emphasised even more when changes in teaching methods occur, which, while they claim to help the children understand mathematics better, do not generally help the teacher understand the mathematics that the children are capable of, nor recognise it when it does occur.

A natural reaction of the teacher in such a position is to ask the mathematician, 'What is mathematics?' which seems a fair enough question. After all, if we know what mathematics is, we can recognise it when it appears, encourage those activities which will lead to mathematics, and discourage those that don't. The answer to such a question should provide a definition that will give the teacher some degree of security, some reference point from which to view the activities of the classroom.

The trouble with the mathematician is that he never seems to give a straight answer, or if it appears to be a straight answer, it is not in any form the teacher can use. Typical of such replies nowadays is, 'Mathematics is what mathematicians do', which may mean something to a mathematician, but only increases the mystique for an outsider, because it is a definition or justification internal to mathematics itself, without any immediately recognisable reference points or interpretations in the general experience of the enquirer.

Mathematicians have, in fact, been doing many different kinds of things throughout history. St Augustine's tirade against the mathematicians in A.D. 400, 'The good Christian should beware of mathematicians and all those who make empty prophecies. The danger already exists that mathematicians have a covenant with the devil to darken the spirit and to confine man in the bonds of Hell', and the Roman code against mathematicians and evil-doers that 'to learn the art of geometry and to practise in public an art as damnable as mathematics, are forbidden' are because in that culture the soothsayers who forecast events by the positions of the stars, and by the magical properties of numbers, were called mathematicians. In fact,

139

until about the eighteenth century, astronomy, astrology, numerology and computation were often practised by the same 'mathematician'. One fundamental and enduring aspect of mathematics was that it helped people to construct and justify their theories about the nature of the universe. Cosmological stories developed into astronomical theories which became part of the modular system by which man dealt with time – the calendar. The myths also developed into religious beliefs which had their own cycles, sometimes associated with the seasons of the year, but often depending on mystic number patterns. It was in general rare, until relatively recently, to have the astronomical and religious calendars coinciding. All this indicates that mathematics had a very large *functional* part to play, not only in the transactions of daily life, but also in the regulation of that life into manageable parts – man's attempt to come to terms with the continuum of time and space.

By the time of Archimedes, in the third century B.C., mathematics had already several recognised branches, even falling into divisions of 'pure' and 'applied' mathematics. *Arithmetic* was not, as with us, practical calculation, but the study of the theory and nature of numbers, while the word *logistic* was reserved for calculations which included not only the ordinary arithmetical operations, but also elementary algebraic problems. *Harmonics* and *music* were then applications of arithmetic.

Geometry, the study of surfaces and non-comparable (that is, non-rational) numbers, and *stereometry*, the study of solids, were applied in *geodesy*, the division of land and the measurement of the surfaces and volumes of other bodies, and in *optics* and *machines*.

Sphaeric, the pure geometry of the sphere, was theoretical astronomy and applied as *phaenomena*, or observational astronomy.

Theoretical or 'pure' mathematics had, until the eighteenth century, very clear relevance for the philosophical, religious and mystic interpretation of the world. Some early definitions of mathematics recognise this, and we have Philolaus, an astronomer of the fifth century B.C., saying, 'Everything which is known to us has a number, for it is not possible either to perceive or to know anything at all without number.'

A century later, the students of Plato stress the importance of mathematics to the understanding of the real nature of things: 'It is essential to learn mathematics, whose primary and most important discipline is the science of numbers, considered in their own right apart from bodies. The aim of this science is the generation of Odd and Even, and their relation to the nature of other things. Whoever has studied this will tackle the next discipline which is, quite absurdly called "geometry", and which is, properly speaking, the science by which numbers not in themselves comparable are made comparable by relating them to the category of surfaces.'

The distinction between theoretical mathematics and calculation became quite marked, and it could be argued that, on the whole, these two aspects developed separately. The religious, the astrologers, and other seekers of pure knowledge were interested in the theoretical side, while the devices for practical calculation, or the 'folklore' of mathematics were kept alive by the merchants, traders and shopkeepers of different cultures.

The responsibility for transmitting and developing knowledge lay with those who had the leisure or the special position to collect and review ideas from many sources. Usually, but not always, they had a religious background, largely because such an atmosphere encouraged certain attitudes toward learning. The outstanding mathematicians of history were often those who were able to bridge the gap between the mystic–theoretical applications of mathematics, and the developing techniques in the folklore of the merchants.

The economic needs of growing societies demanded more general mathematical education and the first book to be written to this end was Fibonacci's *Liber abaci* of 1202, which could be regarded as the first popular mathematics textbook, introducing the Hindu–Arabic notation to Europe, and a series of problems, one of which concerned the famous Fibonacci series. About this time, in England, Roger Bacon recognised a special importance for mathematical knowledge: 'Mathematics is the gate and key of the sciences ... Neglect of mathematics works injury to all knowledge, since he who is ignorant of it cannot know the other sciences or the things of the world. And what is worse, men who are thus ignorant are unable to perceive their own ignorance and so do not seek a remedy.'

The economic growth of England gave rise to an interest in the usefulness of mathematics and Robert Recorde in one of his textbooks called *The profit of Arithmeticke* says, 'For if numbering be so common (as you grant it to be) that no man can do anything alone, and much lesse talk or bargain with other, but he shall still have to do with number: this proveth not number to be contemptible and vile, but rather right excellent and of high reputation, sith it is the ground of all men's affairs, in that without it no tale can be told, no communication without it can be continued, no bargaining without it can be duly ended, or no businesse that man hath, justly completed.'

Philosophical problems of long standing about the nature of motion began to have more pressing significance with the invention of the cannon and the subsequent recruitment of mathematicians into the current technology of artillery and fortification. The most famous of these was Leonardo who, typical of his class, was an artist–designer and observational scientist with an all-round fund of knowledge.

The appreciation of motion in time brought about attempts to deal with the continuous and the discrete. The invention of the new mathematics and the new astronomy, the calculus and gravitation theory of the late seventeenth century, is probably the point where the separate roles of the astronomer, technologist and mathematician began to be distinguished. The precision of the calculations required to forecast astronomical events and to navigate the surface of the earth, still shows the necessary functional aspects of mathematics, and the ability to deal with infinitely small quantities in an abstract way is reflected in the arguments and controversies that were vigorously taken up about the true nature of mathematical activity. Since mathematics itself was changing and growing, not only in its own established techniques, but in new fields arising from new problem areas, a certain redefinition of territory was taking place. Nevertheless, this redefinition was not always reflected in what mathematicians said when they felt pressed to define the nature of their activity. For instance, in the eighteenth century, we have a typical definition by the French mathematician D'Alembert: 'Mathematics is the science which concerns itself with the properties of magnitude, insofar as this can be measured and calculated.' This hardly indicates that D'Alembert's work was very different from that of Archimedes, yet we can see, with the advantages of hindsight, that his own mathematics was preoccupied with questions which would have meant almost nothing to mathematicians of earlier generations.

Later, in the early nineteenth century, Auguste Comte makes an official definition of mathematics in his encyclopaedia: 'The exact definition of this science consists in saying that one is concerned throughout to compare magnitudes according to the exact relations that exist between them.' Here is an important change, in that relations are stressed rather than properties. But the more one collects similar attempts to put mathematics in a nutshell, the more one feels that mathematics escapes, laughing.

Most contemporary definitions of mathematics derive from one or other of the main views of mathematics put forward early in this century. With the growth and increasing complexity of mathematical techniques, Hilbert recognises the existence of unifying ideas as important: 'Mathematical science is in my opinion an indivisible whole, an organism whose vitality is conditioned upon the connection of its parts. For with all the variety of mathematical knowledge, we are still clearly conscious of the similarity of the logical devices, the *relationship* of the *ideas* in mathematics as a whole and the numerous analogies in its different departments. We also notice that, the farther a mathematical theory is developed, the more harmoniously and uniformly does its construction proceed, and unsuspected relations are disclosed between hitherto separated branches of the science. So it happens that, with the extension of mathematics, its organic character is not lost but manifests itself the more clearly.' Russell, on the other hand, suggests that the logical relations are the true essence of mathematics: 'We start, in pure mathematics, from certain rules of inference, by which we can infer that *if* one proposition is true, then so is some other proposition. These rules of inference constitute the major part of the principles of formal logic. We then take any hypothesis that seems amusing, and deduce its consequences. If our hypothesis is true about *anything*, and not about some one or more particular things, then our deductions constitute mathematics. Thus mathematics may be defined as the subject in which we never know what we are talking about, nor whether what we are saying is true.'

As the mathematics itself becomes more abstract, as mathematicians concern themselves more with fundamental unifying ideas and logical relations, the descriptions of what it is about become consequently more internal to itself, more general, and of less real meaning and use to the outsider.

For example, Bourbaki claims that mathematics is an intellectual exercise and has meaning in the real world only by 'accident' when he says, 'Mathematics manifests itself as a reservoir of abstract forms – the mathematical structures – and it turns out that certain aspects of experimental reality model themselves on some of these forms.' And Sawyer, with, 'Mathematics is the study of all possible patterns', provides an all-embracing definition which is fine for a quick answer – but what, pray, is a pattern?

The search for a definition of mathematics based on the results achieved and the body of knowledge accumulated is obviously doomed to failure. Mathematics can mean and has meant many different things to many different people at different times. The nature and content of mathematics is an element of the culture of a people and liable to change with time. Any definition of mathematics is a personal statement fixed in time, and different 'mathematicians' and 'non-mathematicians' can produce equally valid and meaningful 'definitions' depending upon their own concept of what mathematics is, and what is important in it. This is not really surprising when one considers that other intellectual activities run into similar problems (can we define art or music?), and even an apparently simple concept such as 'transport' will have different aspects when regarded by different people.

'What is mathematics?' is a naive question. There are no tablets inscribed.

But if the mathematician cannot, or refuses, to answer, what hope is there for the teacher? One way of helping may be to *shift the focus of enquiry* away from the results, the body of knowledge, the abstract structures, to the *kind of activity* that seem to produce these results called mathematics. The relevance of modern mathematics for the teacher of young children was perhaps first expressed early this century by Mary Boole: 'All the modern higher mathematics is based on a calculus of operations, on laws of thought. All mathematics, from the first, was so in reality; but the evolvers of the modern higher calculus have known that it is so. Therefore elementary teachers who, at the present day, persist in thinking about algebra and arithmetic as dealing with laws of number, and about geometry as dealing with laws of surface and solid content, are doing the best that in them lies to put their pupils on the wrong track for reaching in the future any true understanding of the higher algebras. Algebras deal not with laws of number, but with such laws of human thinking machinery as have been discovered in the course of investigation on numbers. Plane geometry deals with such laws of thought as were discovered by men intent on finding out how to measure surface; and solid geometry with such additional laws of thought as were discovered when men began to extend geometry into three dimensions.'

We may not agree that the actual *laws* of thought have been discovered, but while the *content* of mathematics may be wide and general, the *kinds of activities* which result in recognisable mathematics may be fairly well defined. These activities may at least be constant long enough to be of use to teachers and provide a meaningful point of reference. A statement of belief to this effect was made in our previous book: 'Mathematics is the creation of human minds. A new piece of mathematics can be fashioned to do a job in the same way that, say, a new building can be designed . . . Mathematics is made by men and has all the fallibility and uncertainty that this implies. It does not exist outside the human mind, and it takes its qualities from the minds of the men who created it. Because mathematics is made by men and exists only in their minds, it must be made or re-made in the mind of each person who learns it. In this sense mathematics can only be learnt by being created. We do not believe that a clear distinction can be drawn between the activities of the mathematician inventing new mathematics and the child learning mathematics which is new to him. The child has different resources and different experiences, but both are involved in creative acts. We want to stress that the mathematics a child knows is, in a real sense, his possession, because by a personal act he has created it . . .'

'Mathematics is now applied to a very wide range of situations and is not confined, as it once was, to the mechanics of the physical world. Completely new fields of mathematical applications have sprung up, some only a few years old . . . Much of this work may seem a long way from the classroom and particularly from the primary school classroom. But its significance for the teacher lies in its demonstration of the vast number of things that are worth thinking about in a mathematical way. *Mathematics is not just about number and space; it can be said to happen whenever the mind classifies and creates structures.* This increases tremendously the range of experiences which turn out to be mathematically relevant, and it makes it easier for the teacher to create occasions for his pupils to use mathematics, and to find situations which release mathematical thinking.'*

The task now before us, it would seem, is to list the characteristic mental activities which give rise to mathematics in such a way that the teacher is able to interpret them in the context of his own observation of children, to recognise their occurrence, and to exploit and encourage not only the mental activities themselves but also the kinds of contexts in which they occur.

* Introduction, *Notes on mathematics in primary schools* (1967).

Working at some Mathematics

As a preface to our task, we may be able to demonstrate the activities involved in doing mathematics by following through some pieces of mathematics, to examine the proofs of some theorems, to widen out some concepts, to make some new generalisations, so that not only the results, but the acts of creation *themselves may be appreciated. Of course, it begs too many questions to claim that we can exactly re-create the original thought-processes of the mathematicians involved, but we might uncover certain principles, certain strategies and modes of thought which could be noted in order to help the teacher recognise the beginnings and plan for the active encouragement of mathematical thinking.*

Identifying mathematics as 'purposeful activity' or the 'study of patterns' is not very useful, and while it may be true that some purposeful activity is mathematical activity – being concerned as it is with comparing the pattern in a situation with other patterns stored in the memory – yet it is arguable that when complete or almost complete correspondence exists between the observed and remembered patterns, the resulting activity is of such a low order of thought as to be virtually automatic.

Many people would say that such action – reflex action – while often highly intelligent, is not sufficiently intellectualised to be called mathematics. They would maintain that some element of change in the pattern is essential to mathematics, and no one can doubt that in any higher level of mathematical activity this element of change is fundamental. Of course, if the change of pattern is too great, the action which results may be eccentric, bizarre, or irrational, and may therefore be excluded from the supposedly rational category of mathematics. Only history can justify some of the eccentric changes of pattern which mathematical genius devises.

In general, genius apart, it would seem that together with this change should be linked some 'equivalence' – that a nice balance must be maintained between the invariants and the variants in the two situations if the resultant activity can be called mathematical. Such a 'change', together with such an 'equivalence', forms such an important part of mathematics that it merits a special name: *transformation*.

Here, then, is a suggested ten-point analysis of a typical mathematical experience:

1. Examining a situation sufficiently unfamiliar to pose a problem.

2. Remembering a pattern sufficiently similar to suggest a possibility of solving the problem.

3. Examining the initial situation to separate out the aspects which are intrinsic to the problem and which must therefore transfer to the changed situation.

4. Re-examining the remembered situation to see whether it can accommodate these aspects.

5. Modifying the model to suit, or rejecting it, perhaps in favour of another model.

6. Formulating rules for transforming from one situation to the other, preserving invariant the vital aspects.

7. Transforming from the experiential to the model situation.

8. Finding a solution in the model situation.

9. Transforming the solution back to the original situation.

10. Returning the new enriched pattern to store for use in solving further problems.

The *results* of these activities are the theorems, generalisations and conjectures that constitute what is often regarded as the body of mathematical knowledge, the 'facts' of mathematics. What are too often missed are the methods by which these results are achieved.

By methods here, of course, we do not only mean the calculations, the algebra or the reasoning processes clearly involved, but the hidden intuitive strategies and the facilitating process by which the theorems are discovered.

The two examples used here, one from 'ancient' and one from 'modern' mathematics, are each different in character, each illustrating similar, overlapping characteristics, yet each retaining something particular to the original situation in which it was first suggested.

One common characteristic is that they are both theorems requiring proofs, and it is in the *examination of the proofs* that the pedagogical value of this picture-gallery approach lies.

The Square Root of 121

To take the example from 'modern' mathematics first, consider the statement:

'121 is a perfect square'.

Perhaps there is nothing remarkable about that, for we can see from a multiplication square, or remember from our tables, that $11 \times 11 = 121$.

However, if we consider the meaning of the notation we use to represent the number one hundred and twenty-one, we may be led to the following conjecture:

'perhaps 121 is a perfect square *in any base*'.

Before continuing, it may be interesting for the reader to pause for a moment to consider the kind of knowledge or insight required into the workings of our commonly accepted number system that enables such a conjecture to be made.

The statement may already be obvious, requiring no further explanation. If so, why is it obvious, and on what level? On the other hand, the statement may appear meaningless. In this case, before proceeding further, a certain amount of curiosity about the statement needs to be present, together with what might be described as a trust in the proposer of the conjecture, that there is indeed something to be investigated, and that the conjecture has a relevant connection with the obvious and well-known $11 \times 11 = 121$.

There are a number of approaches to explanations of the statement: '121 is a perfect square in any base'. These explanations may be used to provide proofs at different levels of sophistication, but it is only after the explanation is understood and accepted that a proof in the traditional mathematical sense may be formulated.

Too often we give children proofs when what they are asking for are explanations.

A proof, in the usually accepted sense, can be regarded as a grouping, a synthesis, a distillation, of *experienced explanations*. The important thing about these experienced explanations (at whatever level) for the mathematician is that not only does he use them to furnish proofs or justifications of conjectures which may already be fairly obvious or generally acceptable, but he then goes on to build on these experiences further generalisations, conjectures and proofs. Transformation from the mental or physical experience to the mental or physical model is a continuous and reversible process.

The approaches to explanations that follow are ordered and numbered, but this is not meant to imply any order of difficulty, but only, possibly, a gradual widening of experience.

(*a*) (i) We know $121 = 11 \times 11$, that is, that 121 is a known square number in base ten.

(ii) How do we find square numbers in other bases?

We may now be led to construct multiplication tables for other bases, noting in particular, the square numbers. For example, for base five:

$$
\begin{aligned}
1 \times 1 &= 1 \\
2 \times 2 &= 4 \\
3 \times 3 &= 14 \\
4 \times 4 &= 31 \\
10 \times 10 &= 100 \\
11 \times 11 &= 121 \\
12 \times 12 &= 144 \\
\text{etc.,}
\end{aligned}
$$

and for base seven:

$$
\begin{aligned}
1 \times 1 &= 1 \\
2 \times 2 &= 4 \\
3 \times 3 &= 12 \\
4 \times 4 &= 22 \\
5 \times 5 &= 34 \\
6 \times 6 &= 51 \\
10 \times 10 &= 100 \\
11 \times 11 &= 121 \\
12 \times 12 &= 144 \\
&\text{etc.}
\end{aligned}
$$

From such experiments it would appear that not only do we have $11 \times 11 = 121$ occurring in each list, but that other statements like $10 \times 10 = 100$ and $12 \times 12 = 144$ occur as well. Also, we don't have $11 \times 11 = 121$ in base two, or $12 \times 12 = 144$ in base two, three, or four. Collecting results in this way, we can hazard that:

'121 is a perfect square in any base *greater than two*', and make similar statements about 100 and 144.

(*b*)   (i) Suppose we begin again from $\sqrt{121} = 11$ (base ten) and try to find the square of 121 in another base.

(ii) Rather than derive a general algorithm for finding a square root, we may be led to experiment by converting 121 in different bases to base ten numbers to see what kind of numbers they are.

Suppose, for example, 121 is in base four.

Then

$$121_{\text{four}} = 25_{\text{ten}} \quad \text{and} \quad \sqrt{25} = 5.$$

We could experiment with other bases:

$$
\begin{aligned}
121_{\text{six}} &= 49_{\text{ten}} \quad \text{and} \quad \sqrt{49} = 7, \\
121_{\text{eight}} &= 81_{\text{ten}} \quad \text{and} \quad \sqrt{81} = 9.
\end{aligned}
$$

So we are led to statements like:

81 is a square number in base ten
so 121 is a square number in base eight.

(iii) The ability to make these conversions implies a knowledge of the relationship

$$121 = 1 \times b^2 + 2 \times b + 1 \quad \text{for a number in base } b.$$

(*c*)   (i) A practical experimental approach may be tried using Dienes

Multibase Arithmetic Blocks, or squares and strips cut from card or squared paper.

121 in base ten is 1 flat, 2 longs and 1 unit,

which can be arranged to form a square with sides of 10 + 1 units (Fig. 5.1).

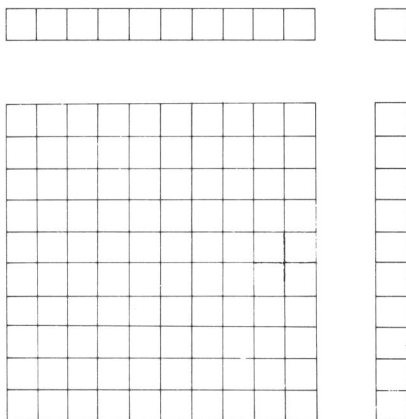

Fig. 5.1

This square can be regarded as:

$$1 \times 10^2 + 2 \times 10 + 1.$$

(ii) If we try this with other bases, we find that

$$b^2 + 2b + 1 \quad \text{(or 1 flat, 2 longs and 1 unit)}$$

can be arranged to form a square of side $b + 1$ units. So we can conclude that 121 is always a square number because the appropriate pieces can always be arranged to form a square.

(iii) If we have the base two set available, we can show that the same relationships are true for base two, because we can still arrange one flat, two longs and one unit to make the next largest square, but in this case the notation 121 is not correct. We would have to write the number as 1001.

(iv) If squared paper is used in this demonstration, we also get the multibase idea coming out, but if the paper is plain, and not marked in any particular way, we can obtain a generalisation of the situation which can be found in some of the 'traditional' geometry texts (Fig. 5.2), namely,

$$(a + b)^2 = a^2 + 2ab + b^2.$$

This result appears originally in Euclid II (4) and can be regarded as a first step in a powerful and widely applicable piece of algebra, the binomial theorem.

(v) Following this train of thought, but returning to the Dienes apparatus, we may be tempted to explore the possibility of building *cubes* in a similar manner to the square-building process explored above.

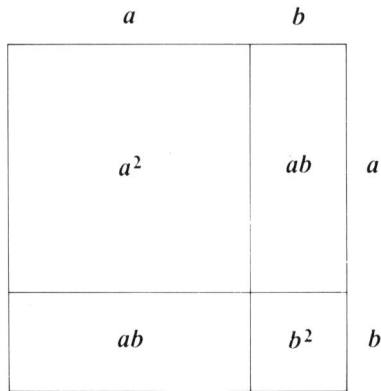

Fig. 5.2

It we take a cube of side b, then we will need three flats, three longs and one unit to build the cube next in size (Fig. 5.3).

By experiment, we are led to the generalisation that 1331 is a perfect cube in any base, which the apparatus clearly demonstrates, but again we have the notational inconsistency in bases three or less.

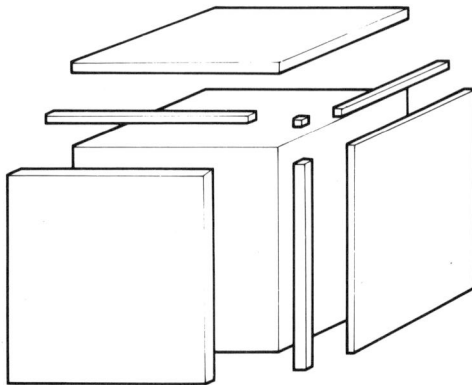

Fig. 5.3

Here we have

$$(b + 1)^3 = 1 \times b^3 + 3 \times b^2 + 3 \times b + 1$$

and we can even take this further by constructing a model out of card to demonstrate

$$(a + b)^3 = a^3 + 3a^2b + 3ab^2 + b^3$$

if we wish.

(vi) If we know the number pattern of Pascal's triangle,

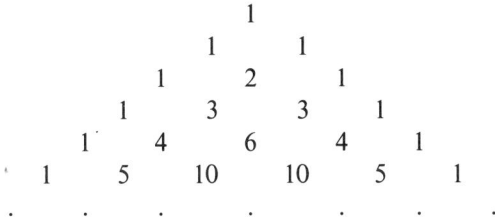

```
              1
          1       1
       1      2      1
     1     3     3      1
   1    4     6     4     1
  1    5    10    10    5     1
  .    .     .     .     .     .     .
```

the conjecture:

'14641 is a perfect fourth power in any base' is available for testing, and we may led to the possibility and consistency of similar statements for other higher powers.

(vii) We are now getting past the stage where physical models might be useful, or even possible. Perhaps by now we have an inner conviction that this kind of pattern is not only possible in any base, but in any power of any base, with appropriate notational adjustments.

(viii) Before leaving practical demonstrations altogether, we can note that Cuisenaire and Colour Factor rods can be used with similar effect. If the Cuisenaire extension material is available, even $(a + b)^3$ may be demonstrated.

(d)   (i) What may be regarded as an algebraic approach is also available and can be developed from the demonstrations above, or arrived at independently.

If we write $11 \times 11 = 121$

as $(10 + 1)(10 + 1) = 100 + 20 + 1$

or $(10 + 1)^2 = 10^2 + 2 \times 10 + 1,$

we can say two things: firstly, it expresses the *meaning of the notation* 121 in base ten and secondly, it is a *particular case* of the expansion $(b + 1)^2 = b^2 + 2b + 1$, where b is any base.

(ii) With this in mind, we can now show that

$$(x + 1)^2 = x^2 + 2x + 1$$

is an algebraic identity and a special case of the general binomial expansion $(x + 1)^n$, and also that $(b + 1)^n$ applied to number systems is an *interpretation* of a general theorem of algebra.

(e) Finally, the use of one of the standard square-root algorithms is another avenue which could be explored. The reader is invited to consider if it would shed any more light on this problem.

The amount of conviction that each of these approaches carries depends very much on the background and previous experience of the reader and the pupil. However, the important factor in appreciating them as mathematics and using them in the classroom is that they be *experienced* and internalised, assimilated and absorbed into the reader's own available and existing map of mathematical structures. Connections with known mathematics must be made so that by a series of transformations the meaning and relevance of the new information may be appreciated and the learner's increase in power realised.

Understanding is a private, personal matter. Each person's route to understanding may well be unique. While at our present state of knowledge we are unable to specify an individual's learning pattern (it may in principle be impossible to do so), we can be sensitive to the type of approach which may be appropriate by assisting the activities at all stages and developing a repertoire of explanations which respect children's curiosity and capitalise on their mental and operational ability at all levels.

One of the crucial problems here is the teacher's own knowledge of the subject matter, the possible and existing mathematical structures; the teacher's own personal map of mathematics, and how flexible and potentially developable this is.

Pythagoras' Theorem

The second illustration, from 'ancient' mathematics, is the theorem of Pythagoras. This may be all too familiar, but even such a well-known piece of mathematics may have a number of explanations and generalisations that are unsuspected when we are faced with a traditional, formal proof.

(*a*) (i) One of the initial presentations of this theorem is the special case of the square tiling made from right-angled triangles shown in Fig. 5.4.

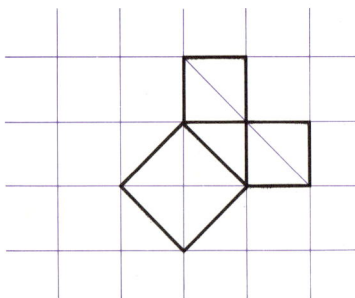

Fig. 5.4

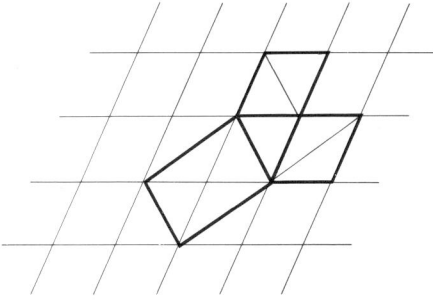

Fig. 5.5

Many mosaic pieces are available in classrooms for younger children, and some of the best have many compatible pieces in various colours, so it is usually not difficult to make a tessellation of *rhombuses* and to consider a similar area relationship there (Fig. 5.5). The two smaller rhombuses can be halved in opposite ways and put together to make a similar figure of double the area.

Having 'squashed' the squares into rhombuses, it does not now seem such a long way to consider what might happen to the area relationship on a tessellation of *parallelograms.*

(ii) Another similar presentation may be on a square geoboard where coloured rubber bands can be used to form the squares or triangles. With this model, it is possible, by a series of physical transformations to move the smaller squares formed by rubber bands so that together they make up the square on the hypotenuse.

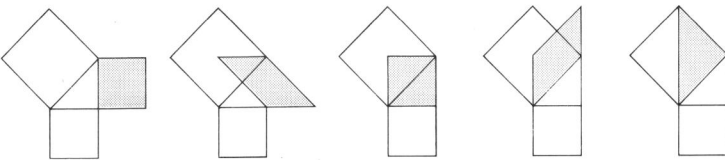

Fig. 5.6

One possible sequence is illustrated in Fig. 5.6, where one of the squares is transformed into a triangle of equal area.

A further extension with this kind of material is to use a trellis of slats or geostrips with rubber bands so that a dynamic picture of squares or rectangles changing to rhombuses or parallelograms can be explored.

(*b*) There are a large number of dissection demonstrations possible, making use of congruent or similar shapes.

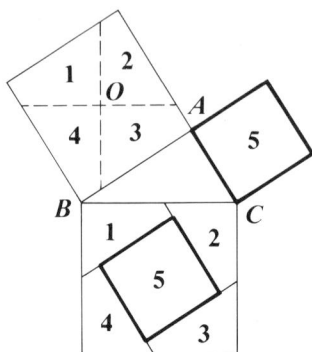

Fig. 5.7

(i) Perigal's dissection (Fig. 5.7): O is the centre of the square on AB and the lines through O are parallel and perpendicular to the side BC of the triangle. The square on AB can then be cut as shown and fitted together with the square on AC onto the longest side BC.

(ii) Loomis' dissection (Fig. 5.8): the lines BX and CZ are perpendicular to the base BC of the triangle. XY is a cut parallel to BC. The pieces are then taken and rearranged as shown on BC.

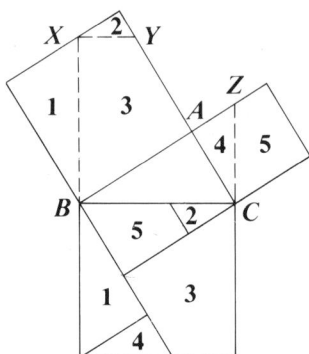

Fig. 5.8

With some ingenuity, patience and elementary notions of symmetry, similarity and congruence of shapes (not necessarily in any formal way), many more dissection demonstrations can be invented and used as proofs and puzzles.

(c) There are a number of visual–intuitive demonstrations like

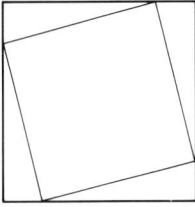

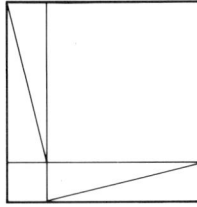

and a very old Chinese version
(ii)

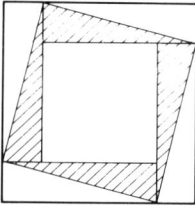

or the proof of Bhaskara, a Hindu mathematician who had the diagram:
(iii)

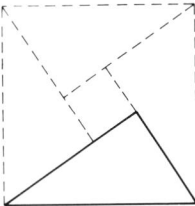

and the single word 'Behold'!.
(iv) These visual proofs can be extended to consider the expansion of
$(a + b)^2$ from the following puzzle of Sir William Rowan Hamilton:

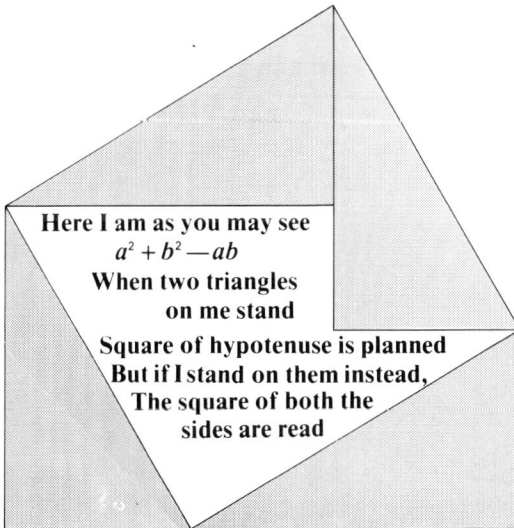

Here I am as you may see
$a^2 + b^2 - ab$
When two triangles
on me stand
Square of hypotenuse is planned
But if I stand on them instead,
The square of both the
sides are read

which, incidentally, links with (*c*) (iv) of the previous theorem (p. 149).

(*d*) Euclid's own demonstration in I (47) is unusually long and difficult to comprehend as a standard proof, but it can be made into a dynamic display by a series of pictures like a film strip (Fig. 5.9).

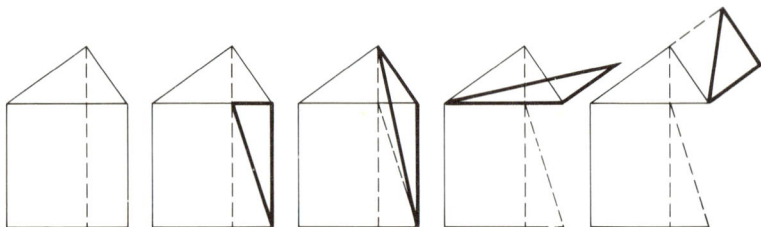

Fig. 5.9

Half the smaller rectangle is transformed by sliding and turning into half the smallest square. Similarly, we can transform half the larger rectangle into half the square on the other side. This connects with (*a*) (ii) above, and enough of these pictures carefully drawn and put together in sequence can make a film strip or flicker book.

(*e*) Extensions of the area relation may also be obtained by considering the area of a triangle half the size of each square, and moving the apex along a line parallel to its base, which is an extension of one side of the square (Fig. 5.10).

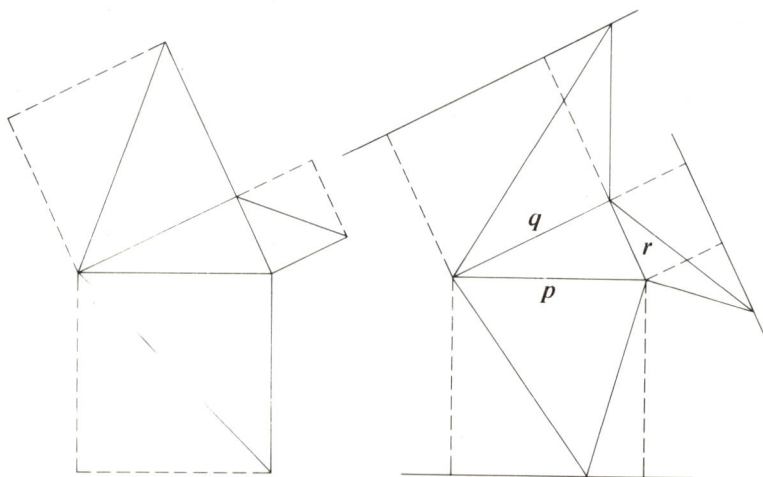

Fig. 5.10

From a simple cutting of the squares to produce a set of three similar right-angled triangles with the same area relationship as that of the squares, we can go on to obtain three non-similar triangles, where

$$\frac{1}{2}p^2 = \frac{1}{2}q^2 + \frac{1}{2}r^2.$$

This is another point where the notation for the algebraic model may produce more than was originally intended, for if we start from

$$p^2 = q^2 + r^2$$

we can, by multiplying by different constants, produce some unexpected results.

If we use $\pi/8$, for example, we get

$$\frac{\pi}{8}p^2 = \frac{\pi}{8}q^2 + \frac{\pi}{8}r^2$$

which says that the area of the semi-circle on the hypotenuse is equal to the sum of the areas of the semi-circles on the other two sides. (The area of the circle radius p is πp^2, so the area of the circle *diameter p* is $\frac{1}{4}\pi p^2$, and the *semi*-circle diameter p is $\frac{1}{8}\pi p^2$.)

Such a suggestive starting point might lead to investigations of a similar relationship for other similar and non-similar figures, and an exploration of area-preserving transformations.

(f) (i) Exploring the area relation by, say, counting squares, we might come up with sets of numbers like

$$9, \quad 16, \quad 25$$
$$36, \quad 64, \quad 100$$
$$25, \quad 144, \quad 169$$

where the third number is the sum of the first two. These can be obtained from the right-angled triangles whose sides are:

$$3, \quad 4, \quad 5$$
$$6, \quad 8, \quad 10$$
$$5, \quad 12, \quad 13$$

The general statement $x^2 + y^2 = z^2$ is known as a Diophantine equation where only integer solutions are allowed.

The triple (3, 4, 5) is a well-known solution to this equation. It is typical of Diophantine equations that they often have an infinite number of solutions. We have two more, but to find them all in this case would really mean to find a formula or procedure that turns them out in some systematic fashion.

Two possibilities might occur here: multiples of triples give further solutions, for example, (6, 8, 10); or new triples can be discovered like (5, 12, 13). Obviously, the latter is more difficult to discover, and the discovery of new triples is a challenging problem. The new triples are called *primitive* solutions.

It may be possible, by experiment, to discover some of the easier solutions:

x	y	z
3	4	5
5	12	13
7	24	25

Noting the odd numbers in the x-column, and that the numbers in the y- and z-columns differ by one, further experiments may lead to:

x	y	z
9	40	41
11	60	61

possibly by noticing that the difference between succeeding numbers in the y- and z-columns increases by four each time.

While this, if we are lucky enough to spot it, will produce new primitives, we have no way of knowing at this stage if we have missed any solutions.

(ii) In order to explore the primitive solutions more deeply, we need to know something about the nature of square numbers.

Since the positive integers are either odd of the form, $2n + 1$, or even of the form $2n$, their squares are correspondingly either odd, $(2n + 1)^2 = 4n^2 + 4n + 1$, or even, $(2n)^2 = 4n^2$. If we look at square numbers in this way, we can see that if we divide any square number by four, there will be a remainder of one if it is odd: $4(n^2 + n) + 1$, and no remainder if it is even: $4n^2$.

Now, if *both* x^2 and y^2 were *odd* (that is, squares of odd integers), we would have, say:

$$[4(n^2 + n) + 1] + [4(m^2 + m) + 1] = z^2,$$

$$4[(n^2 + n) + (m^2 + m)] + 2 = z^2.$$

that is, z^2 would have a remainder of two when divided by four.

If, on the other hand, both x^2 and y^2 are *even* (that is, squares of even numbers), we would have:

$$4n^2 + 4m^2 = z^2$$

or

$$4(n^2 + m^2) = z^2.$$

This now means that z would be even, that z^2 would be divisible by four, and the solution would not be primitive.

So now we have the only possibility: x must be odd and y even, or vice versa.

Suppose x is odd and y is even. This means we can write

$$x^2 + 4n^2 = z^2,$$

where x, n and z have no common factor.

From this, $\qquad 4n^2 = z^2 - x^2$

or $\qquad\qquad 4n^2 = (z + x)(z - x).$

And since both z and x are odd, $(z + x)$ and $(z - x)$ are even.

So we can put $\qquad z + x = 2s \qquad\qquad\qquad\qquad$ (1)

and $\qquad\qquad z - x = 2r, \qquad\qquad\qquad\qquad$ (2)

that is, $\qquad\qquad 4n^2 = 2s \cdot 2r$

or $\qquad\qquad\qquad n^2 = s \cdot r$

Now if we add (1) and (2) we get $z = r + s$ and if we subtract (2) from (1) we get $x = s - r$.

This means that if r and s had a common factor, z and x would have it also; but this is not the case, and the equation $n^2 = s \cdot r$ requires that r and s are *each* perfect squares.

Say, $\qquad\qquad r = p^2$ and $s = q^2$.

Then $\qquad\qquad n^2 = p^2 \cdot q^2 \quad$ and $\quad n = p \cdot q,$

and we have the conditions on x, y and z namely:

$$x = q^2 - p^2,$$
$$y = 2pq,$$
$$z = q^2 + p^2.$$

(iii) What we have done is to show that *if* x, y and z are a primitive solution *then* they must have this form. Having shown this, we are now in a position to write down *all* the possible primitive solutions by choosing integer values for p and q.

The restrictions on p and q can be seen from the relations above:

(1)   Since x must be positive, $q > p$.
(2) p and q must have no common factor.
(3) p and q must not both be odd.

If the restrictions (2) and (3) are relaxed, we still get Pythagorean triples, but they are not primitive.

For example, if $p = 2$, $q = 3$,

$$x = 3^2 - 2^2 = 5,$$
$$y = 2 \cdot 3 \cdot 2 = 12,$$
$$z = 3^2 + 2^2 = 13.$$

The triple (5, 12, 13) has no common factor and is a primitive. But if $p = 2$, $q = 4$, dropping restriction (2), we get

$$x = 4^2 - 2^2 = 12,$$
$$y = 2 \cdot 4 \cdot 2 = 16,$$
$$z = 4^2 + 2^2 = 20.$$

The triple (12, 16, 20) has a common factor of 4. It is a multiple of (3, 4, 5) by 2^2, since p and q have a common factor of 2 in this case.

Dropping restriction (3), we could have $p = 3$, $q = 5$ and so

$$x = 5^2 - 3^2 = 16,$$
$$y = 2 \cdot 5 \cdot 3 = 30,$$
$$z = 5^2 + 3^2 = 34.$$

The triple (16, 30, 34) is a multiple of (8, 15, 17) by 2.

(iv) Thus, from a knowledge of the nature of square numbers, assisted by a suggestive notation which preserves the odd and even nature of squares and emphasises the common factors; we have succeeded in deducing the necessary and sufficient conditions for Pythagorean triples, and hence a procedure that produces them in a systematic fashion.

Tables of Pythagorean triples have been discovered on clay tablets dating back to about 1700 B.C. The Babylonians who calculated them and systematically wrote them out had a method for finding them which was not much different from that above, but obviously lacked our convenient notation. While their methods of calculation of the triples might appear more cumbersome to us, exactly the same principles apply, and the same results are obtained. The nature of the integers and of the geometrical relation of Pythagoras' theorem are independent of the notations and methods, the means by which these relationships are expressed.

For the teacher, the theorem of Pythagoras provides a wide range of possibilities at many different levels; simple demonstration, experimental verification, extensions into non-right-angled triangles and non-square areas, trigonometry, three-dimensional geometry, algebra and number theory. All are there for the asking, each giving a different variation to the original problem and linking it with many other areas of mathematics.

But some of the most important things to be gained are not only the specific results, but the questions, conjectures, experiments, generalisations, proofs and methods by which these results are obtained. The nature of mathematics is revealed to us and to children by involvement in the practical, intellectual, social and personal activities which are necessary for a satisfactory solution of a problem.

Symbolisation

The ability to invent and use symbols is a vital and often neglected aspect of mathematics teaching. While we have sorting and classification in primary classrooms, and even hypothesising and proving, by experiment and argument; *transforming* and *symbolising*, the means by which we proceed from the problem to its description, from the reality to its model, are often taken for granted.

Symbols are both cryptic and evocative. Symbols in mathematics are not only the digits and letters we use to represent number and quantity, but the ways in which we represent relations, qualities, functions and situations, and the multiplicity of objects, diagrams, pictures, tabulations and graphs which we use to aid our thinking.

It is important to remember that symbols are conventions, and as such are independent of the situation they represent. Conversely, a given situation may have many descriptions, each similar but each in some sense emphasising a different aspect of that situation.

For example,

$$3 + \square = 5 \qquad (3, 2) \xrightarrow{\;+\;} 5 \qquad \textcircled{3} \xrightarrow{\;+2\;} \textcircled{5}$$

$$\square + 3 = 5 \qquad (2, 3) \xrightarrow{\;+\;} 5 \qquad \textcircled{2} \xrightarrow{\;+3\;} \textcircled{5}$$

can be used for different purposes and emphasise different aspects of the relations between the objects 2, 3 and 5 and of the operations available.

If we have an efficient symbolisation, then this can often carry with it suggestions for alternative versions, for transformations within the symbolism, and for solution of the problem. Our own number notation is a classic example of this efficiency, and in the subtraction of 17 from 43 we have many possible transformations leading to the solution:

$$
\begin{aligned}
43 - 17 &= (40 + 3) - (10 + 7) \\
&= (30 + 10 + 3) - (10 + 7) \\
&= 20 + 3 + 3 \\
&= 26
\end{aligned}
$$

or
$$
\begin{aligned}
43 - 17 &= (43 + 3) - (17 + 3) \\
&= 46 - 20 \\
&= 26 \qquad\qquad \text{etc.}
\end{aligned}
$$

Another example is that of representing a situation by a diagram. A young children's story entitled 'Five jolly brothers' is based on the exciting morning when Tim's five brothers, who are a sea captain, a doctor, an airline pilot, a fireman and a policeman, get up in some haste and go out wearing each other's hats. A picture shows the five men wearing the wrong hats, and it is interesting to try to draw arrows on the picture to show whose hat is on each head. The result of this is shown in Fig. 5.11, which leads to the

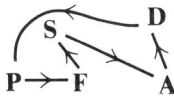

Fig. 5.11

comment that they could all stand in a ring and return the hats by each passing a hat to his left. Does it have to be like that, we may wonder, or are there other ways of being wrongly hatted? A little experiment will make it clear that Fig. 5.12 shows the only other way, if it is insisted

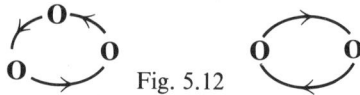

Fig. 5.12

that no one can have his own hat. If this is not a requirement, the men can change hats round a ring of four, or in one or two pairs.

These results give some insight into the situation, and are achieved by representing the situation quite simply by a symbolic diagram. There are clearly many situations in which this or another form of symbolism is useful. This is a characteristic mathematical activity which we think might be worth developing more consciously than it is.

The arbitrary introduction of symbols as shorthand is often confusing, and can produce insurmountable barriers in childrens' comprehension if their real relevance is not understood. On the other hand, helping children to symbolise situations with which they are familiar, not only helps them to describe more easily certain relations they may discover, but also teaches them that the invention of symbols is an important aspect of mathematical activity. The invention of a symbol, exhibits, in a sense, the possession of a concept.

The following account of a lesson shows one way in which the teacher can encourage the invention and use of symbols by looking at the patterns in a multiplication square.

1	1	2	3	4	5	6	7	8	9
1	1	2	3	4	5	6	7	8	9
2	2	4	6	8	10	12	14	16	18
3	3	6	9	12	15	18	21	24	27
4	4	8	12	16	20	24	28	32	36
5	5	10	15	20	25	30	35	40	45
6	6	12	18	24	30	36	42	48	54
7	7	14	21	28	35	42	49	56	63
8	8	16	24	32	40	48	56	64	72
9	9	18	27	36	45	54	63	72	81

Rows and columns give us counting in twos, threes, fours etc. What shall we call the numbers we get when counting in twos? Even numbers – easy! In threes? 'Trebles?'

'Well no, Johnny – actually we call them *multiples* of three.' Oh dear, this jargon! How does one *discover* jargon?

'Please, sir, every number in the "something" row is a multiple of the "something".'

'Very good, Johnny! Let's call that Johnny's pattern. Yes, Rachel?'

'Please sir, every number in the "something" column is a multiple of the "something".'

'That's so. I think we all have Rachel's pattern.'

'Sir! Sir! Sir!!'

'Well, Peter?'

'Please sir, my lines are slopy and they've got a bump in the middle, and they climb up and then slide down again!'

Ten minutes later we have managed, Peter and I, to explain Peter's pattern to some of the class and they are trying, without much success, to extend the sphere of comprehension. Oh, this language problem! Symmetry, commutativity – will the labels mean anything? And the definitions are so long-winded and verbose.

'Please sir, they're all the same pattern!' This from Jennifer, always the awkward one!

'Now hold on – let's try to sort this out! What do you mean, Jenny, when you say they're all the same pattern?'

'Well sir, if Johnny's "something" is Rachel's "something", then Peter's slopy hill is bound to come back down again, isn't it?'

This tour de force leads first to a stunned silence and then to a period of frantic activity and furious argument out of which emerge gradually and sporadically the following ideas:

1. Each of Peter's slopy lines contains products of numbers whose sum is constant.

2. This is like keeping the perimeter of a rectangle constant and varying the area, sticking to whole number sides.

3. The biggest area is a square, or the shortest, fattest rectangle you can get.

4. This is why the lines have a bump in the middle.

5. The number in the 'something' row and the 'something else' column is the same as the number in the 'something else' row and the 'something' column. (Multiplication of whole numbers is commutative.)

This last is a terrible mouthful and many children just cannot grasp the idea because it is so wrapped up in words.

I suggest that we invent our own shorthand to try to make it clearer. No one seems frightened of 'n for any' and 'm for other'.

So $m\boxed{}^{n} = n\boxed{}^{m}$ seems a reasonable way to express discovery 5. No one suggests using the multiplication sign, most people seem to have forgotten where the table came from and to be concentrating entirely on the pattern, or structure, of the table itself.

We like our shorthand way – everyone now understands rule 5.

'Please sir, can we try and shorthand the others?' asks Jenny. We all know what she means and fall to avidly.

Rule 4 presents problems – I have to ask how to write 'any less one' before Alice suggests $n - 1$. 'Other plus one' follows, and rule 4 becomes:

$$m \;\overset{n}{\boxed{}}\; \text{is bigger than}\;\; m+1\;\overset{n-1}{\boxed{}}\; \text{if } m \text{ is bigger than } n.$$

Jimmy remembers that we invented a sign for 'is bigger than' when using Colour Factor rods – we wrote pink 'is bigger than' white as $p \parallel w$, and pink 'is smaller than' light blue as $p \parallel b$.

Rule 4 now reads

and

$$m \;\overset{n}{\boxed{}}\; \Big| \; \Big| \; m+1\;\overset{n-1}{\boxed{}}\; , \; m \;\Big|\;\Big|\; n$$

$$m \;\overset{n}{\boxed{}}\; \Big| \; \Big| \; m+1\;\overset{n-1}{\boxed{}}\; , \; m \;\Big|\;\Big|\; n$$

Everyone is happy with this until Mary notices that it isn't true when m is 3 and n is 4.

$$m \;\overset{n}{\boxed{}}\; \Big| \; \Big| \; m+1\;\overset{n-1}{\boxed{}}\; , \; m \;\Big|\;\Big|\; n$$

$$m \;\overset{n}{\boxed{}}\; \Big| \; \Big| \; m-1\;\overset{n+1}{\boxed{}}\; , \; m \;\Big|\;\Big|\; n$$

follows, though by now no one is very pleased with it since it doesn't account for the squares – when $m = n$, as it were.

Fred proposes $m \;\overset{n}{\boxed{}}\; \Big|\;\Big| \; m+1\;\overset{n-1}{\boxed{}}\; , \; m = n$ and on this note the lesson ends.

Was it an algebra lesson? I wonder? Or does it only become algebra when we bow to convention and write

$$mn = nm (m, n \in N)?$$

Translating 4 gives:

$$mn > (m + 1)(n - 1) \text{ iff } m \geqq n$$
$$mn > (m - 1)(n + 1) \text{ iff } m \leqq n$$

and Fred's proposition becomes:

$$n^2 = (n + 1)(n - 1) + 1$$

or

$$n^2 - 1 = (n + 1)(n - 1).$$

Now that's algebra, isn't it – but has it got so far from the situation that it only pretends to be of value? Shorthand is only useful if it can be rapidly translated into language that anyone can understand.

But for us, *our* shorthand *was* useful – it helped us to say simply what was hard to express in words. It enabled us to generalise from our experience and it somehow enriched our experience.

I can see too that everybody else's algebra suggests an even greater generality: we weren't ready for it today but, who knows whether to-morrow . . . ?

The step taken in representing a situation by a diagram or by symbols is a crucial one. For one thing, it is difficult; for another, it brings with it the possibility of *operating with the symbols* instead of the situation itself, which can give great power. Much of school mathematics is done with well-established symbol systems like numbers, or cartesian graphs, or letters for numbers, and the ability actually to *make* a suitable representation for oneself is almost certainly underdeveloped.

We think it may be useful to collect some situations which could be offered to children to give them opportunities for this. The possibilities are potentially enormous. The mathematical entities which we can encourage children to symbolise may be suggested by the following headings:

Objects, Numbers

We have the digits 1, 2, 3, ... and tally systems ////// // , but the history

of mathematics demonstrates the wide variety of symbols and methods of recording numbers invented by other cultures and should give us as teachers enough confidence to encourage the children to invent their own. Objects can be suggested by initial letters, *n* for any number that we know, a box □, for an unknown, are widely used. The initial letters of the Cuisenaire or Colour Factor rods are often virtually neglected in this context.

Relations

All the words and experiments describing relations of size, position, time, frequency, etc., can be symbolised. The usefulness will obviously depend on the context, but we need not think that '>' and '<' are the only symbols allowed here.

Operations

Perhaps the operations of arithmetic are already too familiar, but even here sqrt. instead of √ may be a more meaningful initial stage. A fruitful field for symbol invention is that of geometry, where movements in space and movements of objects may be described. Left, right; up, down; reflect, rotate, magnify, diminish, and many more are available and the possibility for inverses can also be explored.

Functions

The interdependence of two or more variables can be represented by an algebraic expression, in tabular form, or by some form of graph. Proportionality, both direct and inverse is one of the functional situations children seem to find most difficult to comprehend. Perhaps the teacher's introduction of algebraic symbols before children have developed some form of tabulation method of their own for dealing with proportion inhibits their understanding. Other common relationships, for example, between the sides, area and perimeter of shapes, the edges, vertices and faces of polyhedra, time and speed over a distance, all exhibit various aspects of functionality which can be symbolised by children.

Situations

The idea of deliberately giving children situations to explore which have their purpose as the development of a symbolic representation or a descriptive notation, may not in itself be new, but when we consider that the main objective is to get the *children* to develop *their own* symbols, not to use the situation as a vehicle for introducing *our* symbols we have a much more interesting pedagogical challenge.

The situations listed here may have many aspects. Perhaps one common attribute is the possibility of describing the progress through their stages in terms of some decision diagram or general flow chart; but having invented one set of symbols, we may be encouraged to find others.

Pegboard games: frogs, Lucas' game, etc.
Chessboard games: draughts or checkers, pawn chess (played on a 3 × 3 or 4 × 4 board)
Grid games: noughts and crosses, Go
Logical problems: wolf, goat and cabbage problem; jug problem (given two jugs holding *a* and *b* litres, measure out *c* litres); weighing problem (given *n* similar objects, find the light one in *m* weighings)
Cyclic problems: tower of Hanoi, three penny problems
Logic-block games: shape, size and colour changes, etc.
Geometrical transformations: reflections, rotations, flips on a grid

Most of these games are described in many books of mathematical recreations, but some useful sources are ATM, Domoryad and Tahta.

Principles of Choice

Mathematics is valued as a component of education, partly because it provides quantitative concepts which help in the interpretation of wide areas of experience; but partly also, and perhaps less obviously, because it is built on those mental actions which are fundamental to all cognitive activity. From the interaction of the mind with the stream of data picked up by the senses we 'make sense', that is we fit new factors and ideas into existing generalisations where this is possible, and make new generalisations when the new data make this necessary. We relate bits of knowledge with each other, looking for repeated associations of one thing with another, for reasons, and in general for any kind of pattern in the data. We try to reduce the diversity of the information by 'explaining' it, by finding principles which embrace a whole set of data. Often this involves the learning of new words to describe the classes which we have made.

If mathematics may be regarded as the elaboration and codification of relationships and classification in themselves, distinct from the particular objects or ideas which are being related, it is clearly fundamental to all thinking activity. So fundamental, in fact, that these mental actions are being developed in all mental activity, not just in mathematics. On the other hand, the higher levels of mathematical activity, such as deductive proof and axiomatisation, are relevant only within mathematics. Thus although mathematics may justify itself as a study by both its universality and its uniqueness there remain questions of how to teach it so as to maximise the availability of its ideas and its strategies for transfer to other fields of thought.

At the present time, many fields are discovering the value of having the greater power in dealing with relational aspects of their activity which is given by the use of mathematical ideas and strategies, for example, in the storing, reorganising and retrieving of information. This should give pointers for school mathematics; they depend on fundamental mathematical approaches and the development of new branches of mathematical knowledge rather than the application of existing developed ideas.

Choices about mathematics in the classroom depend partly on the teacher's view about why mathematics is being taught at all, but also on the under- standing of what kind of mathematical work is possible and suitable for the children. The latter is a question which psychology should help to answer.

Two ten-year-old children timed each other on runs in the school play- ground. One took 11 seconds for 25 metres and 23 seconds for the next 50 metres.

What can we do with these data?

One possibility would be to draw a graph and see if it 'bends', bringing up the question of comparing the two parts of the run. But the data give average speeds which are so close to each other that the difference in slope might not be detectable. Indeed, the idea of thinking about the *gradient* of a line because of its connection with speed is not obvious and would pro- bably require the drawing of a variety of lines relating to known speeds. In any case the working out of the speed of the run in miles per hour would be an interesting line to pursue; it could then be compared with the speeds of a car, a bird, a dog (estimated and checked from reference books), and with Olympic records. Once the connection between gradient and speed has been established, many comparisons can be made by plotting lines on the graph, but essential to all these comparisons is the conversion of 11 seconds for 25 metres into miles per hour; or assuming that the 5 miles = 8 km is a known equivalence, to km per hour.

How might this be done?

We might start as follows:

$$11 \text{ s for } \quad 25 \text{ m}$$
$$22 \qquad\qquad 50$$
$$44 \qquad\qquad 100$$
$$440 \qquad\quad 1000 \text{ m} = 1 \text{ km}$$

$440 \text{ s} = ? \text{ min: answer } 440 \div 60 \text{ or } \dfrac{440}{60} \text{ min} \quad (A)$

$\dfrac{440}{60} = \dfrac{44}{6} = \dfrac{22}{3} = 7\frac{1}{3} \text{ min or } 7.3 \text{ min if we use decimals.} \qquad (B)$

Then 7.3 min for 1 km, how many km in an hour?

(In 1 min we do 1/7.3 km.)   (C)

An hour is 60 min, so we shall do 60 ÷ 7.3 or 60/7.3 km, which requires long division.

Not having a method for this we might proceed by trial:

1	7.3	(D)
2	14.6	
4	29.2	
8	58.4	

which is quite near; so the answer is 8 km per hour approximately, which is about 5 miles per hour.

Several points here need comment. First, this conversion contains plenty of difficulties; second, this is an important example in itself, and there are many others like it, also requiring proportion.

The difficulties cannot be avoided by writing off the topic, so let us examine them. At (A) we have the need to divide 440 seconds into parcels of 60 seconds each; unless we are to make a long division of this we need to convert this to the fraction 440/60 with the understanding that this allows cancellation of a factor from numerator and denominator. How may this be learnt? It is equivalent to changing from saying $6 \div 4 = 1$ rem 2 to $6 \div 4 = 6/4 = 3/2$. We may still be asking 'How many fours in six?' but we want the answer wholly in terms of fours and we are prepared to accept fractions.

One line of thought might be to go back to divisible numbers and say

$6 \div 3$ means – how many 3s in 6?   (1)

or – if 6 is divided into 3 parts, how big are the parts?   (2)

or – what must 3 be multiplied by to give 6?   (3)

Do any of these transfer to $5 \div 3$?

If we know or think that the answer is $\frac{5}{3}$, and wish to gain assurance, we could use (3) and see that

$$3 \times \tfrac{5}{3} = \tfrac{15}{3} = 5,$$

assuming that we already know how to multiply fractions.

But this may be asking children to take bigger steps than they can. Even if they understand that

$$35 \div 7 = \square \text{ is asking the same question as } 7 \times \square = 35,$$

to infer that

$$5 \div 3 = \square \text{ must be the same as } 3 \times \square = 5$$

is asking them to be aware of the relation between the left-hand form and the right-hand form *in general,* divorced from the familiar and operable numbers, and to transfer this to a situation where the operation $(5 \div 3)$ cannot be performed and the triad reduced to a single known number. This kind of transfer is identified by Piaget and others who have tried to analyse the source of children's difficulties in mathematics as requiring the formal reasoning abilities which normally develop during the ages 12–14. Observations in the classroom also give support to the conclusion that this kind of step is too difficult for most juniors.

An alternative route to the required conclusion may be:

to divide 5 by 3 it may be helpful first to divide each of the five units into 3 parts, making 15 thirds, which then gives

$$\tfrac{15}{3} \div 3 = \text{divide 15 thirds into 3 equal parts}$$
$$= 5 \text{ thirds}$$
$$= \tfrac{5}{3}.$$

Here we have used interpretation (2) of division.

The full process would then be

$$5 \div 3 = \frac{5 \times 3}{3} \div 3$$
$$= \frac{5}{3}.$$

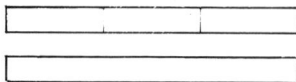

Fig. 5.13

Would it be fair to draw from this analysis the conclusion that it would be helpful if children had plenty of experience of representing situations such as Fig. 5.13, as

$$2 \times 3 = 6, \quad 6 \div 2 = 3, \quad \tfrac{1}{3} \text{ of 6 is 2,}$$
$$3 \times 2 = 6, \quad 6 \div 3 = 2, \quad \tfrac{6}{2} = 3, \quad \tfrac{6}{3} = 2,$$

expressing the relation in all possible ways?

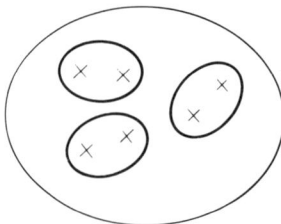

Fig. 5.14

Other representations could be used, such as sets and subsets of crosses (Fig. 5.14). It would seem useful for children to have one or more standard models of counting numbers and of ratio numbers to refer to as a matter of course when questions arise. This is something which children do quite naturally, but their models are often inadequate, and regarded as something not quite allowed in public. We have seen children making and counting heaps of dots surreptitiously, behind a hand; adding 17 and 17 on fingers without realising that ten could be added all at once (and getting 33); trying to compare $\frac{2}{3}$ and $\frac{3}{5}$ for size by dividing freehand pies (Fig. 5.15).

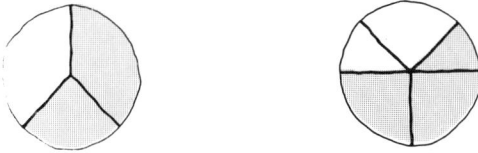

Fig. 5.15

Dots, fingers and pie diagrams are the inadequate models these children refer to. Surely it would be better to develop with them the systematic use of Cuisenaire rods, supplemented by squared paper or something which they can draw or carry round with them as easily as their fingers?

To return to the original calculation, at (*B*) we have the choice between staying in fractions or going into decimals. Although decimals are better for addition, in this case the fraction from $\frac{22}{3}$ is slightly easier for continuing the calculation; and in a case where the choice was between, say, $\frac{3}{80}$ and 0.037, the decimal form would be even less attractive. Generally speaking decimals can usefully replace fractions except when we are dealing with ratios. Fractions as ratio-numbers are indispensable. (They are also useful, though not essential, in establishing the rules for multiplication of decimals:

$$0.3 \times 0.2 = \tfrac{3}{10} \times \tfrac{2}{10} = \tfrac{6}{100} = 0.06;$$

but we could say, once familiar with moving the point (!),

$$= (3 \div 10) \times (2 \div 10) = (3 \times 2) \div (10 \times 10).)$$

At point (*C*) we come to the crucial proportion step, and the choice of unitary or ratio methods.

The ratio argument is:

$$
\begin{array}{ccc}
7.3\,\text{min} & \text{for} & 1\,\text{km} \\
\Big\downarrow \times \dfrac{60}{7.3} & & \Big\downarrow \times \dfrac{60}{7.3} \\
60\,\text{min} \;-\!-\!-\!-\!\rightarrow & & \dfrac{60}{7.3}\,\text{km}
\end{array}
$$

The unitary method says

$$
\begin{array}{lll}
7.3 \text{ min} & \text{for} & 1 \text{ km} \\
\downarrow \div 7.3 & & \downarrow \div 7.3 \\
1 \text{ min} & \longrightarrow & \dfrac{1}{7.3} \text{ km} \\
\downarrow \times 60 & & \downarrow \times 60 \\
60 \text{ min} & \longrightarrow & \dfrac{60}{7.3} \text{ km}
\end{array}
$$

the difference being in the ability to use 60/7.3 as an operator, as a number, that is, without needing to have it reduced to a single recognisable number. This is the same type of difficulty as noted above in the division of 5 by 3 to give $\frac{5}{3}$, and which Piaget assigns to the formal reasoning level. (On this criterion, the problem would not require this level of thinking if the division of 60 by 7.3 to give the decimal number 8.2 was a thoroughly familiar operation – so that it could be seen as 8.2 as easily as $7 - 5$ is seen as 2.)

How do you teach proportion if it is not immediately seen? Does the unitary method help or hinder? Have we·anything to add to Durell here?

At (*D*) we have the question whether or not long division is available. The method shown can give results more accurate than we have obtained, by continuing with

$$
\begin{array}{ll}
\begin{array}{r} 60 \\ 58.4 \\ \hline 1.6 \end{array} & \begin{array}{ll} 0.1 & 0.73 \\ 0.2 & 1.46 \end{array}
\end{array}
$$

so that 8.2 is very near. To go to further decimal places, if needed repeatedly, would lead to something similar to the usual algorithm.

We now give the solutions adopted by two boys to this problem. The first, aged twelve, was asked to find 11 seconds for 25 metres in kilometres per hour. He said, '11s into 60 is $5\frac{5}{11}$ or 5.5 approx., so the distance in 60 s is 25×5.5 or 137.5 m. For 1 hour we need 137.5×60, which is 1375×6 or 8250 m, which is 8.25 km.'

His proportion is therefore

$$
\begin{array}{ll}
11 & 25 \\
\downarrow \times 5.5 & \downarrow \times 5.5; \\
60 & 137.5
\end{array}
$$

he uses decimals and moves the point quite correctly.

The other boy, aged ten, was given 11 seconds for 25 metres, and asked how far in a minute. His first answer was 2 approx. (or $2\frac{1}{8}$ more exactly), and when eventually it was realised that this was the distance in a second and his questioner wanted the distance in a minute, he (1) divided 11 into

60 giving 5 rem 5, and multiplied 25 × 5 and a bit, getting 125 and something, then (2) divided $2\frac{1}{8}$ into 60 (ignoring the $\frac{1}{8}$) getting 30 then, after a lot of talk, decided to multiply the $2\frac{1}{8}$ by 60, getting 120, and (3) finally realised that this 120 and the previous 125 were two different approximate answers for the same results.

What were the sources of difficulty here? Mainly, it would seem, in the proportional relationships; the multiplications and divisions were performed with confidence, by working with approximations which he could handle (5 and 2).

The first boy was also asked if he could do the calculation more accurately which he did by working in fractions ($\frac{60}{11} \times 25 = \frac{1500}{11} = 136\frac{4}{11} = 136.36$ since $\frac{1}{11} = 0.0909 \ldots$ by division).

He was then asked if he could do $60 \div \frac{4}{11}$.

At first he thought 'Divide 60 by 11 ... $\frac{240}{11}$ ... no, that's wrong', then *remembered* that it was $60 \times \frac{11}{4}$. Would he like to 'prove' that that was right, perhaps by trying some simple numbers, like $6 \div \frac{3}{4}$? This produced various answers such as $\frac{3}{4} \times 6$ or $4\frac{1}{2}$, and 18, before he succeeded in thinking $\frac{3}{4}$ × 2, $1\frac{1}{2}$ × 2, 3 × 2, 6 and was sure the answer was 8. This didn't give a rule, so we tried $6 \div \frac{1}{4}$. This also produced a variety of answers and a lot of very valuable thinking about the situation, until 24 was settled on as definitely right. Then almost immediately this was seen as 6 × 4, but still no general rule for inversion. I got him to write down these two results on a clean sheet of paper; then he spotted the inversion rule: 'It's true!' he said. 'You've only proved it in those two cases', said I, 'try some more.' So he wrote $6 \div \frac{127}{369} = 6 \times \frac{369}{127}$. 'That doesn't prove anything', I said. 'Try some easy ones which you can check by thinking them out.' So he wrote $8 \div \frac{1}{2} = 16$, $9 \div \frac{3}{4} = 12$, $13 \div \frac{13}{13} = 13$, but I have no idea whether he actually verified these independently.

What general principles emerge from the discussion of this example? When I started exploring this situation with the children I was originally hoping to say, 'Comparison is a good way of developing an investigation: comparison of one person's running speed with another's, of a person with a car or an animal; other ways of development are by extension or transformation.' In fact other principles have come to the fore: and several questions.

The first concerns the place of applications in mathematical education, and of proportion among these. As well as speed, questions of price and quantity – 3 lb 2 oz of detergent cost 65 pence, 1 lb 4 oz cost 28 pence, which is the better value? – of expansion – a bar 50 cm long expands 0.12 mm on a rise in temperature of 15 degrees, what is its coefficient of expansion? – the lever, density, interest rates – these and many other situations occur in everyday life or in the work of older children and all need the ability to use proportion.

Second, what are the teaching strategies which would help children to progress towards this goal? Is there a place for the organised development of ratios using Cuisenaire material? Equal ratios, similar figures (drawn on grids), the linear function and the straight-line graph – can these be developed?

Third, what kind of explanations or justifications for a generalisation such as $5 \div 3 = \frac{5}{3}$ are acceptable to children? Is it the lack of an explanation, or something else, which leads to the feeling that mathematics is mysterious and to the child's despairing of understanding? Am I right in feeling that a familiar concrete referent would provide the necessary security?

Another piece of children's work may help to give a different viewpoint. Some eight- to nine-year-olds were playing with the logic blocks and some change cards. Some of these were colour-change cards and some shape-changers (see Fig. 5.16).

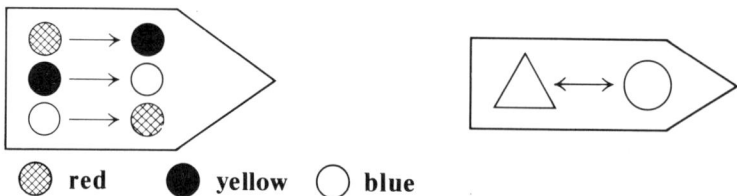

Fig. 5.16

Fig. 5.17

At an earlier stage of the activity a bigger variety of cards was in use but for this particular activity just these two types of card were used, and six blocks – circles and triangles in red, yellow and blue. The children were asked to choose two blocks and then find a sequence of change cards which would change the first into the second (see Fig. 5.17). Then they were asked to find cards to reverse this, going from the second block to the first. They then picked another pair of blocks and did the same again. Soon they were ready to agree that they could get from any block to any other, using not more than one shape-changer and not more than two colour changers.

They were then asked to 'record on a piece of paper what cards were needed to change any block into any other'. Their records were like those in Fig. 5.18: S is a shape-changer, C a colour-changer. This new task reawakened their interest and it was interesting to see how they filled in some arrows straight away, but used the blocks and cards to check certain others. The construction of the diagram appeared to be giving them a new aware-

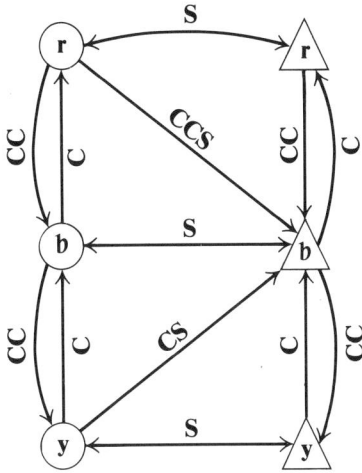

Fig. 5.18

ness of the total situation and of its structure – of the number of changes of each different type which there were.

Another task given to these children was that of making sequences of cards which would change a block into itself. They found that three colour-changers or two shape-changers would do this. They had also noticed earlier that when reversing a sequence of changes, the shape-changer was its own inverse, while the inverse of the colour-changer was two colour-changers.

One aim of this piece of work was to see whether, and how, the children acquired the notions of identity and inverse. We wanted to see whether they could learn the ideas in this situation, and then use them in another one – a number situation, say – but we have not yet had an opportunity to try this. We felt that the possession of these ideas might enable the children to learn more quickly some of the properties of numbers. But we also felt that the under-standing of the nature and inter-relationship of the possible changes in a set of objects such as this was a useful addition to the children's mathematical knowledge – not that they would necessarily meet this particular structure else-where, but that the general notions being used – transformations, combinations of them, identities and inverses – were of quite wide applicability.

Purple Footsteps

... so, as soon as I've finished this list for Mr Jones I'll hear you read. I won't be many minutes.'

The group in the corner are getting along nicely with their mathematics work. That box of beads will give them plenty of practice in using large numbers.

Mark and Michael are all set for a good session at the painting easels – plenty of paper, the light's OK for them. Yes, that should be harmless. 'Mark, put your overall on, please.'

Patrick, John, David and Fraser seem very co-operative today. That wooden model looks promising. At least that will be something for Open Day. Perhaps Mrs D will see some good in these modern methods.

Those new flash cards seem to be working with Susan. She really seems keen and it's much better for her to have some made especially for her. Sunday wasn't wasted after all.

The balances are working properly now. I didn't realise sand was quite so heavy as that parcel seems.

I'm glad I brought that old rug for the Book Corner. It's much better than those hard chairs.

I must do something about Brian's number work next. He's so pleased to get something right at last that he'll carry on *ad infinitum*. I must prod him a bit as soon as I've finished this list for the Head. What comes after that step in addition? Perhaps I should leave him, though?

Mentally checking-off that all is well with my class of six-year-olds; every one gainfully employed and happily integrated, I settle to do the 'small thing that won't take a few minutes' for the Headmaster.

'Miss, Patrick hit my thumb with his hammer. He meant to do it, really he did.'

'Never mind, John, it will feel better in a moment. Patrick, do be more careful please.'

'But he sawed my finger and it's bleeding all over our castle.'

I walk over to investigate just as Jenny arrives, dragging a very wet rug from the Book Corner. Joan stands by with her finger in her mouth and her wet pants in her other hand.

At that moment the group using large numbers start diving through our legs in search of beads. Was it six or seven hundred in that box? It was *supposed* to be unbreakable!

I'd better get Patrick to hospital. That finger is going to need three stitches at least. How did that parcel of sand leak into the clay bin? Who cut that corner off?

Mrs P arrives at the door. Of course, she said she was collecting Mark to take him to the airport to meet her old school friend and must make a good impression. Perhaps I shouldn't have let Mark paint? He's bound to get something on him.

Mark appears from the stock cupboard, purple from head to toe. The large tin of powder paint was just out of his reach. He had to climb up to get it. I told that student not to put it up on the shelf. At least she could have put the lid back firmly.

Oh no! Susan has dropped all the new flash cards and Michael has just knocked over the green paint on top of her and them!

'No, Mr J, I've not quite finished the list. I'll do it straight away.'

'I've come to read to you. You've been lots of minutes so I thought I'd better remind you. I'm up to here. "Look, Janet, look. Come and see the little kitten . . . ."'

What *is* that next step in addition? I must get to Brian. What did that article say?

Mr G, the caretaker, appears.

'Miss C, there are purple footsteps from this room all down my clean corridor . . .'

6

Perhaps, in an ideal world, there would be no need for syllabuses and curricula because teachers would know how to generate a satisfying programme of study out of the interaction of their knowledge, skills and sensitivities with the needs, interests and powers of their students. There would be no need for examinations if teachers on the whole were better judges and if society trusted their judgments.

But beyond these demands on teachers – which are largely the product of other forces, though they are often willingly embraced – are the preparations which teachers must demand of themselves if they are to make the best possible job of teaching they have to do.

What preparations should a teacher make? Draw up a scheme of work? Write sets of assignment and workcards? Furnish the classroom with intriguing games, or with a variety of raw materials to suit many kinds of spontaneous activity? Choose the best set of textbooks she can find? Perhaps all of these, provided that these various means remain the aids they are meant to be and do not turn into permanent substitutes for the on-going active responsive leadership that only a person can provide.

We talk, rather miscellaneously, about some of these things here – not with the hope or intention of offering guidance, but because the consideration of these issues is yet another chance to reflect on aspects of the responsibility of teaching mathematics. The most important preparation a teacher can undertake is to prepare herself.

The Content of School Mathematics for Younger Children

NUMBERS	MEASURES	GEOMETRY
counting numbers	angle	shape of objects
integers	length	symmetry
rationals	area	position
signed rationals	volume	space-filling
number-pairs and lists	mean	
matrices	speed	
	probability	
	frequency	

SETS AND RELATIONS
subset   complement   intersection : symmetric, transitive
equivalence   order

FUNCTIONS/TRANSFORMATIONS

OF NUMBERS	OF SETS OF OBJECTS	OF POSITION and SHAPE
linear (kx)	permutations	enlargement
reciprocal (k/x)	many–one, etc.	translation
square (kx^2)		reflection
exponential (k^x)		rotation

SYMBOLISMS

Venn diagrams   tree diagrams   arrowgraphs   flow diagrams
Cartesian graphs   scale maps   letters and signs

MATHEMATICAL ACTIONS*

classifying   associating   ordering   transforming   combining
undoing   generating

Maps and Charts

A boy of ten asked, 'What is the infinityest number?' I know there are interest-ing things to say about infinity, but I don't know what they are. Where can I find out?

A girl of seven drew and coloured a beautiful and symmetrical pattern using triangles and hexagons. Where could she go from here?

A boy of eight adds up two numbers making a place-value mistake. What kinds of activity could he go back to at this point?

A book suggested modular arithmetic as a junior school topic. I'd never heard of it before. What's the point? Where does it fit in?

What mathematics was going on in our school? What connections could we find between the work in each classroom, and could we get a clearer picture of what we ought to be doing?

Common to all these questions is a feeling of uncertainty, a need to take bearings.

If you want to know where something leads, why not look for it on a map? If no map of the area exists, then why not make one?

A 'map of mathematics' becomes, in practice, words disposed on a page,

* The *other* sections of this 'map' indicate a field to be covered. The actions, on the other hand, indicate ways of exploring a chosen situation.

suggesting space; perhaps arrows between words, suggesting routes through that space.

Maps, diagrams, flow charts, do some things better, some things worse than words strung in sentences. (A sketch map of a walk and a description of it in words: two good travelling companions.)

Like maps, flow charts are easy to scan. (They use space where words take time.) A whole field of mathematics can be laid out on one page.

Complex relationships can be presented with deceptive simplicity. If one word in a box connects with six other words in other boxes, the arrows of a flow chart can show this at a glance. (But what if you have only one other word and twelve connections? . . .)

Arrows are powerful symbols. They are more accessible than words. Because they need to have meaning read into them, anyone can make a start. If you are making your own chart you can use an arrow to indicate a relationship you feel sure exists, even if you'd find it hard to put into words. Because they don't need to explain themselves, arrows can be drawn all over the place in a fit of enthusiasm, to stand for essentially different kinds of connection, or where no good connection exists. In this way important difficulties might be glossed over.

Any map or chart of mathematics has words on it as well as arrows. Because words are reduced to a minimum, each one carries more weight, has more meanings placed on it.

If you didn't write the words on the chart yourself, you may not be able to make sense of them all. Once you can give a sense to the words on the chart, you may wish to push the words around, to add some more of your own. If you make your own chart, then you are forced to choose your words carefully. And the more meanings you place on a word, the harder it is to place it on the page with others. Arrows begin to sprout everywhere and have to be pruned.

When they ask 'Where does it lead to?' people are often implying that in mathematics one thing *ought* to lead to another. Many teachers look to flow charts to help them find a structure in (or for) the mathematics they are involved with in school. But what do people mean by a 'structure'?

Practical considerations may suggest the need for a developing structure for mathematics in school. At present, activities proliferate, teachers come and go. Two distinct kinds of evidence support this call for a structure. Surely mathematics itself is essentially structured? And a child's mental growth is presented to us as an evolving series of conceptual structures.

Reflecting these arguments, two distinct kinds of connection are commonly present in almost all syllabuses and schemes of work. The first connects mathematics with mathematics for mathematical reasons. The second connects mathematics with mathematics for 'psychogenetic' reasons. (If a child has done this, then someone believes he is ready to do that.) Both kinds of connection are usually mixed up together. The 'psycho-genetic' version of mathematical activities is based on a theory of the mental growth of the child. When it comes to the teaching of mathematics, this theory often becomes a preconception, shaping people's approaches, rather than a view itself open to question. So powerful is the hold of the psychogenetic approach that all mathematical topics are likely to be affected. When a topic is to be laid out in a way that will match a child's developing powers, one begins by looking for 'simple' or 'basic' notions, and builds one's 'structure' on these. For example, a complex and essentially non-linear field of activities like space-filling may be squeezed into a linear form. The youngest children are expected to learn the names of common shapes but the problems of symmetry and tessellation are reserved for those of seven years and over.

Whatever their authors' intentions, theories of mental growth often exert an anti-experimental, conservative influence on mathematics teaching. (Teachers can and do argue against new ideas on the grounds that their children are not yet ready for any more mathematics.)

Naturally childrens' minds develop and mathematics has to fit in with this process. What is in question is the influence of the 'high theory' of mental development on mathematics syllabuses, schemes of work and textbooks.

Some syllabus charts represent a distillation of what a large number of teachers already do with a large number of children. The result is a variation of the developmental approach. Flow charts of this kind tend to present the average of what is done by teachers rather than the range of what has been or could be done. They are also likely to be conservative in their influence. (So many teachers can't be wrong.)

We wanted to get a picture of what we were doing in mathematics in the school. We all wrote down what we had done, what we intended to do. It was good to find how much there was and how well it fitted together. And having made the thing ourselves, we understood it and weren't over-impressed by it. In fact, I think we gained more from making it than we did from the finished product.

A mathematics adviser visited us once. He told us that in our mathematics work we needed a structure. We showed him our home grown mathematics syllabuses. 'Yes', he said, 'but what you need is a structure.' He handed us a neatly packaged, printed syllabus-map and left. We never saw him again.

There are several problems that flow charts do not yet seem to have succeeded in solving. One is the problem of 'realising' the arrows. *How do you get from here to there?* The chart doesn't say. Another is how to distinguish the necessary arrow-heads from the arbitrary ones. It may only be possible to traverse certain arrows one way because the logic of the

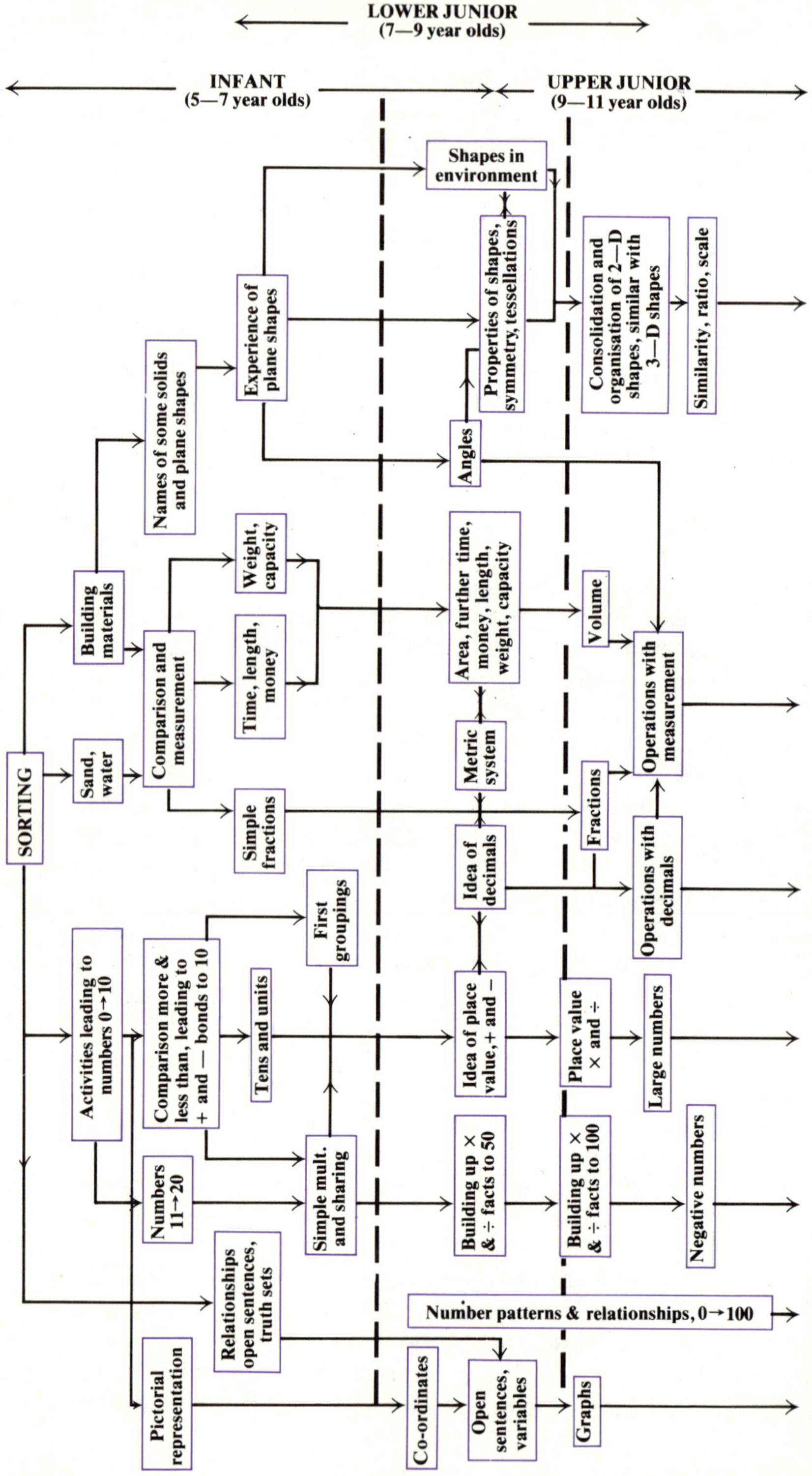

LOWER JUNIOR
(7—9 year olds)

INFANT
(5—7 year olds)

UPPER JUNIOR
(9—11 year olds)

Shapes in environment

Experience of plane shapes

Names of some solids and plane shapes

Properties of shapes, symmetry, tessellations

Consolidation and organisation of 2—D shapes, similar with 3—D shapes

Similarity, ratio, scale

Angles

Building materials

Weight, capacity

Time, length, money

Area, further time, money, length, weight, capacity

Volume

SORTING

Sand, water

Comparison and measurement

Metric system

Operations with measurement

Simple fractions

Idea of decimals

Fractions

Activities leading to numbers 0→10

Comparison more & less than, leading to + and — bonds to 10

First groupings

Tens and units

Idea of place value, + and —

Place value × and ÷

Large numbers

Operations with decimals

Numbers 11→20

Simple mult. and sharing

Building up × & ÷ facts to 50

Building up × & ÷ facts to 100

Negative numbers

Relationships open sentences, truth sets

Number patterns & relationships, 0→100

Pictorial representation

Co-ordinates

Open sentences, variables

Graphs

DEVELOPMENT OF MATHEMATICAL IDEAS WITH YOUNGER CHILDREN

Fig. 6.1

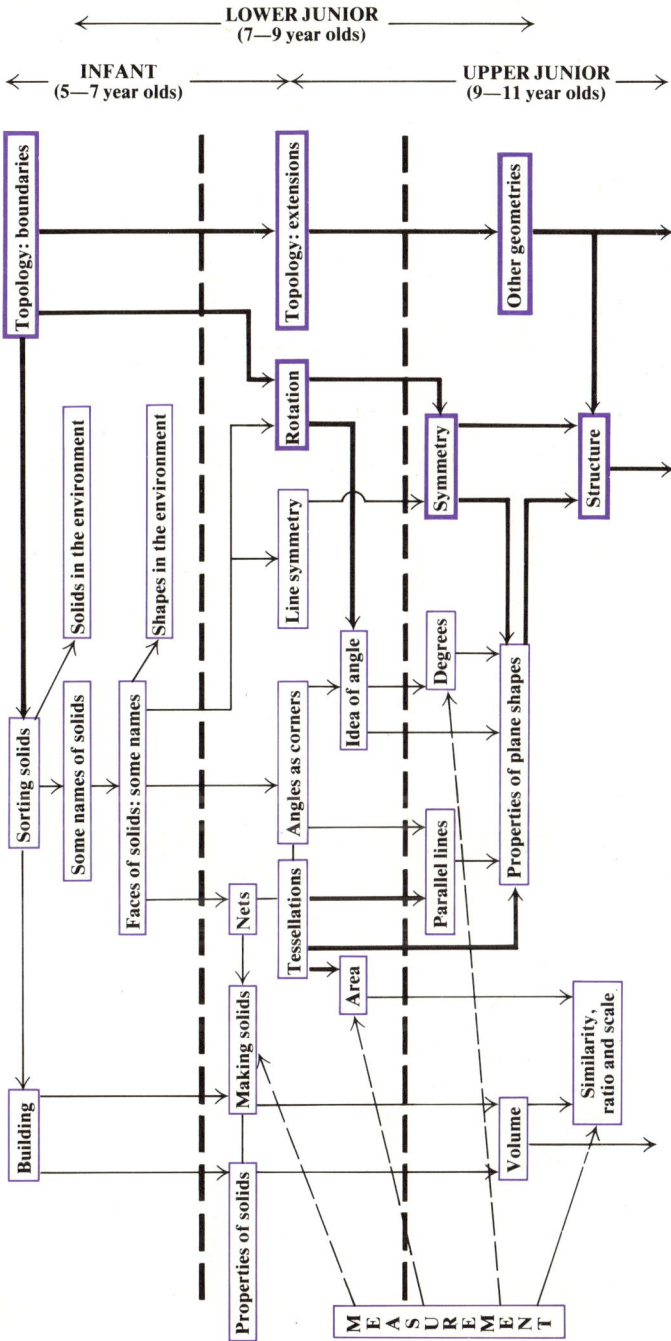

DEVELOPMENT OF GEOMETRY WITH YOUNGER CHILDREN
(THICK LINES indicate newer ideas)

Fig. 6.2

183

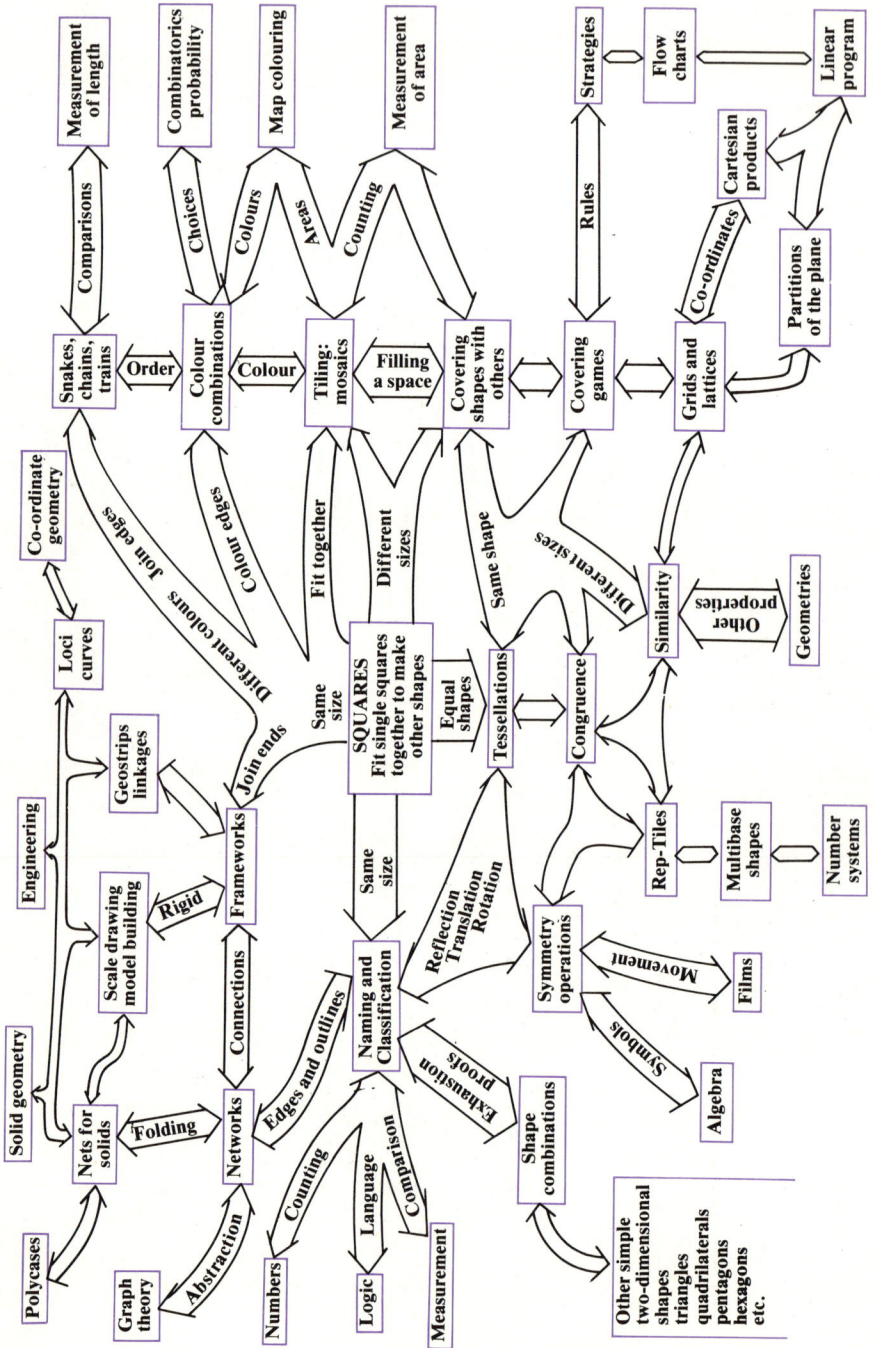

Fig. 6.3

evelopment requires it, but in mathematics it is frequently possible to
everse a sequence of connections. Then there is that characteristic of all
ow charts, that they tend to include all the arrows that *can* be put in, hiding
he fact that the chart may contain several detachable sub-charts which
ould be disconnected and worked on at any time without hurting anything.

A flow chart which reversed the usual conventions would be instructive,
oo – topics written where the arrows are and generating activities put into
he boxes. Unfortunately no one has yet devised a sufficiently economical
anguage of activities to make it possible to label such a diagram in a way
hat would be understood.

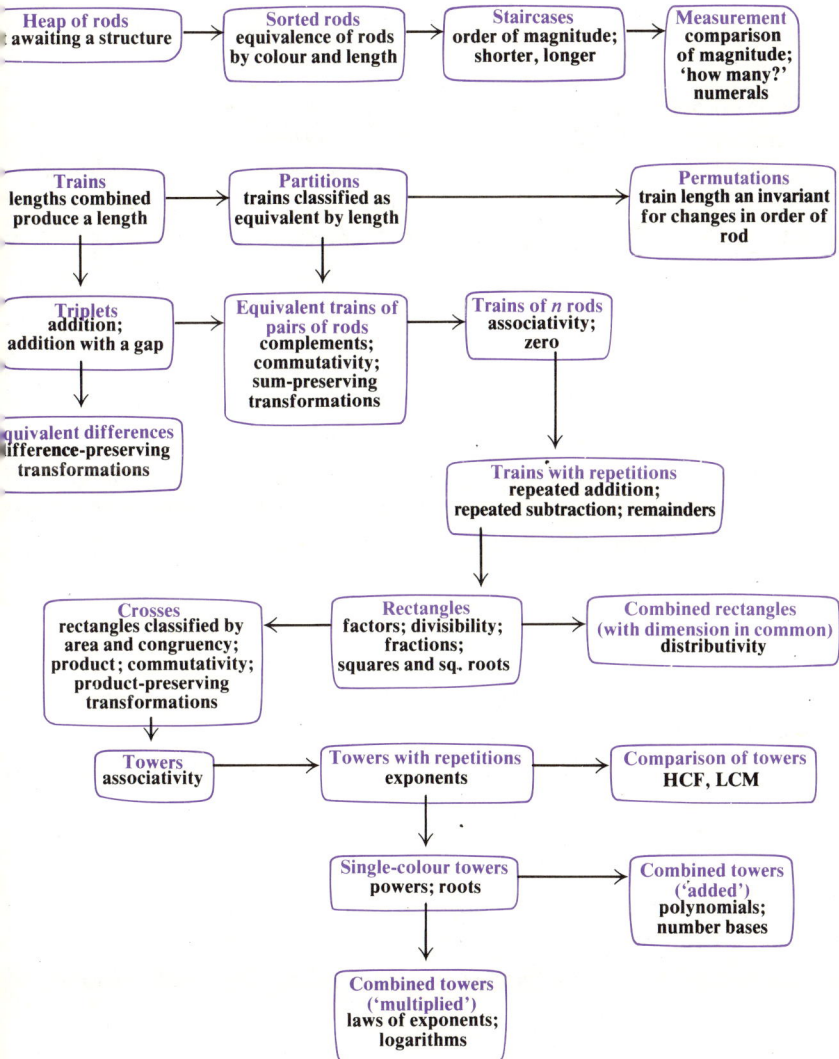

Fig. 6.4

Workcards

1. Workcards have the potential advantage over textbooks that you can more easily add to them, discard some of them, select from them, regroup them. If you don't do any of these, why have workcards?

2. We are still in the Stone Age of workcard design. Too many words. Poor layout. Often scruffy pieces of card. A workcard is a stimulus to do something. Can one not be stimulated to do something by a photograph? A sequence of diagrams? Few words? No words? A sheet of squared paper? Or 'Here are some answers, what might the questions have been?

3. What about *workboards*? (Putting a chessboard on the table is an invitation to start an activity on that board.) Can we not devise workboards for mathematics?

4. (*a*) Workcards enable children to work without the teacher. Too many workcards prevent children from working with the teacher.

(*b*) Cards can be a substitute (and a poor one) for a conversation with the teacher; they may enable the pupil to have some thoughts in a new direction; they will probably need completing by a conversation with the teacher.

5. (*a*) Why *work*cards only? What about *activity*-cards? *play*-cards? *think*-cards? *talk*-cards? *story*-cards? *doodle*-cards? and *practice*-cards: *problem*-cards: *what-if-not* cards: *stand-up* cards: *fold-up* cards.

(*b*) *Work*cards – work, activity-cards – activity. Has anybody seen any cards which lead to pupil involvement in an inquiry?

6. A workcard means that you think you know today what Johnny will find useful or of interest tomorrow. Very often the result is to reveal how wrong your prediction was.

Schemes of Work

1. A scheme of work should be a description of what is going on rather than a pious hope about what somebody would like to go on.

2. If a scheme of work is there basically to impress, anything will do. Stick it up and forget it.

If it is to be useful, then it must be intelligible to everyone who is to use it, and agreeable to everyone who is to use it.

3. A scheme of work can only be intelligible and agreeable to people who have helped to compile it.

4. A scheme of work should be discussed and possibly amended at least once a year.

5. A scheme of work should be a minimum list of suggestions rather than a restrictive list of requirements.

6. A scheme of work should incorporate the collective experience of the people involved. Next year's scheme should have this year's reality as a basis.

7. A scheme of work is a scheme for children to work, not for teachers to work. It should be flexible enough to be stretched to fit any child who comes along and to grow with him.

What is wanted is a 'stretch body-stocking', not a 'straight jacket'.

Keeping Records

1. If you are keeping records for someone else, then you need to consult with that person to find out what he/she wants them for.

2. If you are keeping records for yourself then they need only be intelligible to yourself.

3. Check-list records are too often too involved, too time-consuming; if no one is going to read them, they are useless.

4. (*a*) It is worth recording the unexpected – the sudden spark of interest or achievement or failure or comment which surprised you.

The expected you have within you already.

(*b*) A record of the unexpected is a record of your failure to understand the child's need or potential – not of his failure to meet your requirements or expectations.

5. A piece of work is a better record than a record about that piece of work.

6. The routine record is too often a millstone rather than a help.

7. A record may help you to determine whether you are fulfilling your aims. It is the scheme of work which represents your aims.

So the scheme of work must come before the record.

Numbers and Materials

We can ask questions about numbers or we can ask questions about materials. The two are quite different, even though we may hope for some connections to be made.

The *question* (Fig. 6.5) is about balancing, about a piece of apparatus, *not* about numbers. Whether the child approaches it through numbers $(3 + ? = 8)$, or by trial and error without reference to numbers, is quite irrelevant. If you ask the child to think before it hangs the ring, then you are really asking a question about numbers, and the balance is unnecessary.

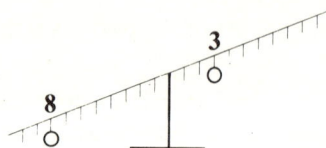

Make this balance by
hanging one more ring

Fig. 6.5

If we introduce material, then we should ask questions about the material.
Structural material for number work is useful because it mirrors certain aspects of numbers. Different pieces of structural material highlight different aspects. Not surprisingly, one piece of apparatus is more effective than another at different stages. You *can* no doubt use bottle tops, or Cuisenaire rods, for everything, just as you *can* add, subtract, multiply and divide, by counting on and back in ones, but it is inefficient.

A reasonable sequence for the use of materials for computation would seem to be:

1. (a) *Any small countable objects* (bottle tops, nuts, counters, plastic animals, etc.)
– for sorting, matching one-to-one, counting up to twenty, putting in piles of three, piles of four, etc.
   (b) *Logic blocks*
– for building up a store of problems, structures, activities, thoughts which will be mirrored in activities with numbers.

2. *Unifix cubes*
– for all the above, with the added advantage that you can make *one* rod of *three* cubes
– for + and − bonds, emphasising counting on and back in ones.
– for the beginning of × and ÷.

3. *Cuisenaire, Colour–Factor or Stern rods*
– for extensive work with + and − bonds, for counting on further in twos, threes, etc.; for the beginning of tens and units; for incorporating a number track to 100
– for moving away from counting in *ones*; for fractions, powers and displaying operations.

3. *Multibase Arithmetic blocks*
– for exploring and extending place value, and computation within it, for powers, base-work.

5. *The abacus*
– for abstracting further within a place value system.

6. *Calculating devices* (Napiers rods, hand calculator, etc.)

In addition to this straight sequence through *computation*, both these and other materials are valuable for exploring *patterns of numbers*. Here, no such obvious sequence is apparent: any of the following can be used at almost any stage:

logic or attribute material
Unifix cubes
Cuisenaire rods
the number balance
pegs and pegboard
hundred squares (+ 81 squares,
64 squares, etc.)
Algebraic Experience Material

square and circular (prefer-
ably 24-pin) geoboards
number tablets marked 1
to 25 at least
square-grid and triangular-
grid paper
dotty paper

Number in the Early Years

Numbers 1–9

Before dealing with any individual number, the children learned number rhymes, number recognition and were used to counting backwards as well as forwards, in ones and twos.

In the initial stages the work was oral; then recorded by the children using ready-made number symbols, drawings and rubber-stamped pictures and, finally, the children's own recording, using both methods 'invented' by them and more formalised methods which were shown to them.

Each number from one to nine was dealt with separately but not necessarily in order. In fact we found that it was often easier to work with the middle range of numbers at the earliest stage as they gave more possibilities than the smallest numbers but were more limited than the larger numbers.

The basic 'four rules' were used with each number but, at the later recording stage, each rule was introduced separately and recorded in a variety of ways.

Having decided on the number to be studied – usually by one member of the group of four or five taking a handful of objects from a box containing nine items – the objects were put in the centre of the working area of the group. We then talked about the collection.

'How many are there?' (The reply was often a random guess.)

'How do you know?' 'Have you counted them?'

When all the group agreed, the number symbol was written on a small blackboard and put into the middle of the working area.

The group was then asked to find as many different ways as possible of partitioning the original objects into two groups. At each stage the children were encouraged to tell the story of their actions to the others. As the children were sitting on four sides of the working area the first problem was almost immediately encountered. For example,

FIONA   I have five buttons. I'm putting four into one pile and one into the other pile. Four and one make five.

ROBERT   No, it doesn't.

F   Yes, it does! Look four there and one there. Five.

R   Yes that's right. One and four make five.

F   No. Four and one make five.

R   You're wrong. I'm right. One and four.

ME   Could you both be right?

R   NO!

ME   Why not?

R   'Cos there's only one answer.

ME   Is there? Why don't you and Fiona change places, for a moment. (*They were, needless to say, sitting directly opposite each other.*)

R   Oh! it's a different way round over here!

For a little he amused himself moving from one side of the table to the other. Fiona just smiled happily.

R   Do you know something? We're both right, aren't we? Does that always work?

ME   Try it with other numbers to find out.

Left to their own for a while they decided that it was *always* so. I shelved that problem for another day! However, Robert marched round the room to the other children and showed them the problem, making them move about to see it from both angles.

Using the same situation of buttons and numbers I wanted the children to think of other ways of expressing the work they were doing so that the rules of subtraction, multiplication and division were part of this work with the single number. Maria was moving the buttons into two piles again and using the words which Fiona had used.

ME   Maria, what are you doing to the buttons?

MARIA   I'm moving them.

ME   Can you use any different words than to explain what you are doing?

M   I've got five buttons. I'm sliding three buttons into one pile and two buttons into another pile.

ME   Good. Now what would you say if you only move the three buttons and leave the two where they started?

Silence. I sat looking at the buttons.

M   I could say I have five buttons. I take three of them and put them over there and I leave two buttons behind.

ME   Yes. Any other ways?

The discussion became general and other ways of verbalising the operation were suggested and accepted as part of the process.

When an even number was being studied there came a stage when the numbers in each section were the same.

JANE   Oh look! There's three there and three in that pile. Three and three make six don't they?

FIONA   Yes. If I've got six and I move three away I've got three left.

ME   How many are there in each pile?

J   Three in each.

ME   How many piles of three are there?

J   Three.

ME   Show me.

J   One pile of three. Two piles of three. No. Two.

ME   Are you sure?

J   I think so. Yes, I told you. There are two lots of three.

ME   How many of three can you make for six?

J   Oh dear. Um. Yes, two lots of three.

During the various discussions which took place the word 'dividing' was used to describe making an even number into two equal parts as was the expression 'half of' a number. Both were accepted into the group's terminology but, at this early stage, no special emphasis was placed on them to expect them to be used in preference to any other. The items were also made into three or more equal piles and so the earliest multiplication factors were introduced.

When a fluency, based on understanding and familiarity, was reached the numbers above nine were studied, by which stage most children were recording their own work in a variety of ways and most of the class had chosen to work individually in preference to a group situation. However, it was interesting to notice that the majority of children returned to a group when presented with new work.

Numbers 10–19

These numbers were discussed by the groups and it was decided to break them down into groups of ten and a number of units.

Again the middle range of numbers was tackled first. This helped when it came to discussing ten.

ROBERT   You can't break ten up like the others.

FIONA   Yes, you can. It is ten and no units.

R   Yes. I know that. But you can't break it up.

F   Look. There are ten in this place and nothing in this place. That's what the number says, one ten and nothing units.

R   But nothing isn't a number.

MARIA Yes, it is. There's a zero there and zero is something so it must b
a number. It's instead of any of the other numbers.

R So if you put zero into anything it's the same. Miss, why do we cal
40 forty when it's really four?

ME Pardon?

R Maria says that you can put zero onto ten and its still ten so if you pu
zero onto four its still four isn't it?

After a long chat in which we went round in ever decreasing circles, trying t
convince Robert that four and forty were very different, light appeared t
dawn.

ME Maria said we use the zero *instead* of another number NOT as well a
the other number! (*Blissful silence*)

ROBERT Why didn't you say that before, Miss?

After that rather trying experience, using the larger numbers seemed to
present very few problems as the method was similar to that used in the
first section.

Numbers 20–29

When these numbers were studied they were broken down into groups of ten
and units.

23 is 20 and 3
   is 10 and 10 and 3
   is 2 lots of 10 and 3
   is 13 and 10.

At this point the group decided to look at the other numbers before
continuing the work with 23.

JANE Is twenty-anything always ten bigger than anything-teen?

MARIA Mn. I should think so because it starts with two instead of one a
the front so that means two tens instead of one ten so it must mean it'
always got an extra ten. Let's try.

*They worked through the 20–29 numbers and went on to the thirties, fortie
and fifties.*

JANE (*to me*) Listen. Did you know that the number of '-ties' always tell
you how many tens there are? Look. All the forty numbers have four ten
and all the fifty numbers have five tens. That's good, isn't it? It makes thing
much easier, doesn't it?

While she was talking she was showing me the pattern-breakdowns which
she and Maria had made, of numbers from twenty to fifty-nine. I felt a glow
of satisfaction. 'That's that done.'

Two days later

JANE   Who invented numbers? (*looking accusingly at me as if I was personally responsible*)

I muttered something about not really knowing but did it matter.

JANE   Well I think they are really horrible. They make it very difficult for me.
ME   Why is that?
J   Well, you know all that very hard work I did about numbers with lots of tens and it tells you how many tens there are? Well, its all right when you write it but they made a mistake when they read it.
ME   How do you mean?
J   Well that number (*writing down* 12) should say onety-two and it doesn't. They said it back to front and called it -teen. Isn't that bad?
ME   (*Floundering badly, to my lasting shame.*) Er, well, perhaps they got teen from ten and said things like 'three and ten', 'four ten' and so on?
J   Then they were stupid. *I* shall call it onety-three. (*Which she did for a good two weeks!*)

That made me look at the numbers again and, in oral addition of two numbers more than ten, we avoided the numbers 13–19 until the pattern of work was established. I think maybe I was wrong, but it worked!

Numbers Beyond 29

Not all the children found the pattern of these numbers in addition and sub-traction so easily or so quickly as Jane and Maria but few seemed to ex-perience much difficulty provided they were not hurried into this stage. With numbers of a hundred and more the children seemed to regard the hundreds as an entity as had been in the case of the ten. In oral work the hundreds were sorted out first and then the tens and units were worked.

Decisions and Options

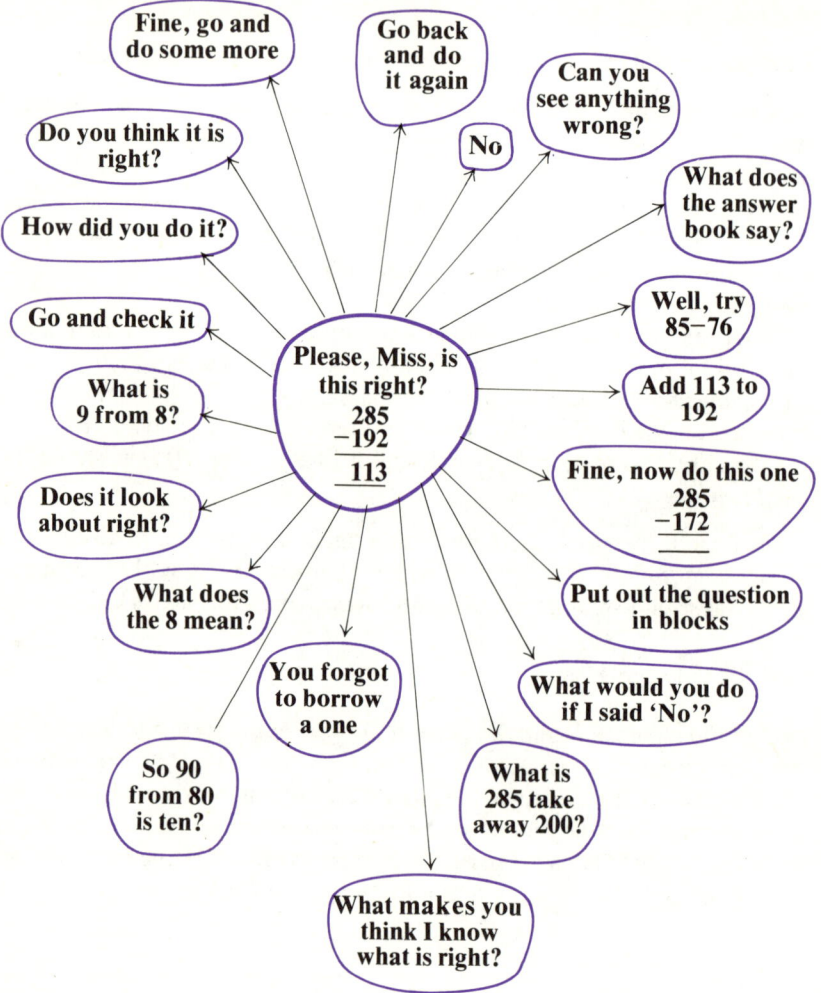

Fine, go and do some more

Go back and do it again

Can you see anything wrong?

Do you think it is right?

No

What does the answer book say?

How did you do it?

Go and check it

Well, try 85−76

What is 9 from 8?

Please, Miss, is this right?
285
−192
‾‾‾‾
113

Add 113 to 192

Does it look about right?

Fine, now do this one
285
−172
‾‾‾‾

What does the 8 mean?

Put out the question in blocks

You forgot to borrow a one

What would you do if I said 'No'?

So 90 from 80 is ten?

What is 285 take away 200?

What makes you think I know what is right?

Fig. 6.6

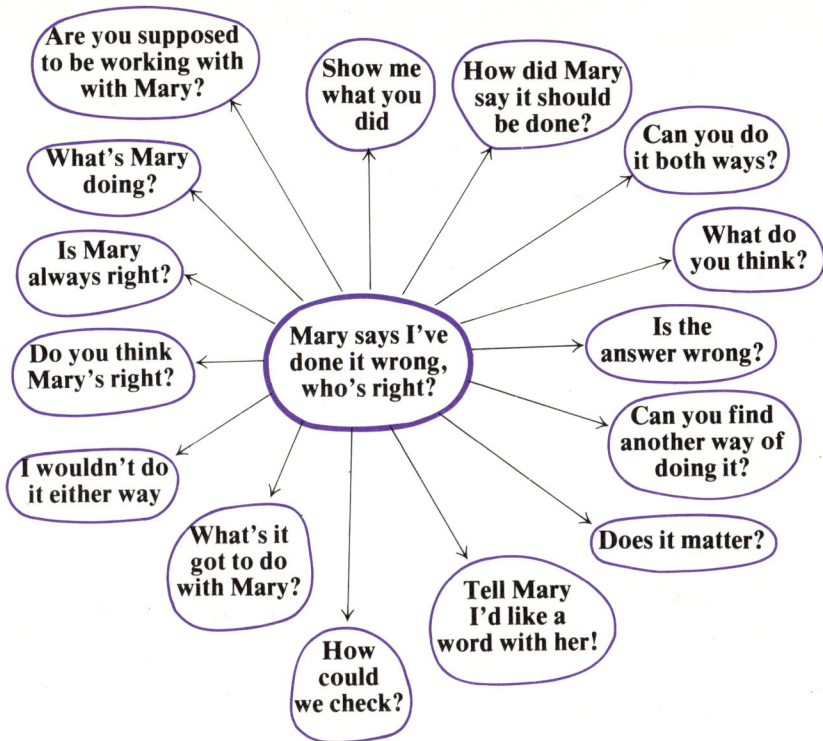

Fig. 6.7

Are you supposed to be working with with Mary?

Show me what you did

How did Mary say it should be done?

Can you do it both ways?

What's Mary doing?

What do you think?

Is Mary always right?

Is the answer wrong?

Do you think Mary's right?

Can you find another way of doing it?

I wouldn't do it either way

Does it matter?

What's it got to do with Mary?

Tell Mary I'd like a word with her!

How could we check?

(centre) Mary says I've done it wrong, who's right?

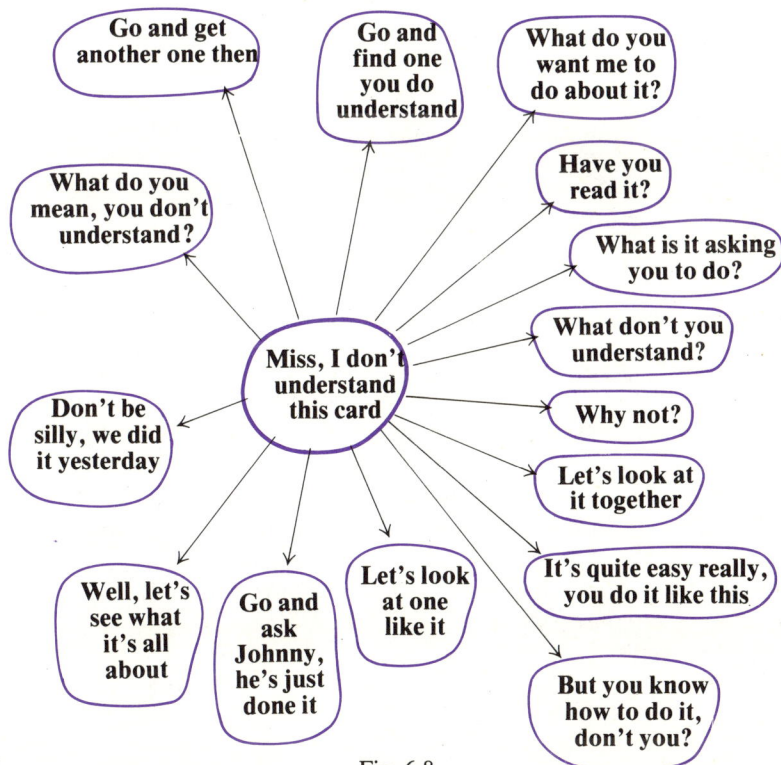

Fig. 6.8

Go and get another one then

Go and find one you do understand

What do you want me to do about it?

What do you mean, you don't understand?

Have you read it?

What is it asking you to do?

What don't you understand?

Don't be silly, we did it yesterday

Why not?

Let's look at it together

Well, let's see what it's all about

Go and ask Johnny, he's just done it

Let's look at one like it

It's quite easy really, you do it like this

But you know how to do it, don't you?

(centre) Miss, I don't understand this card

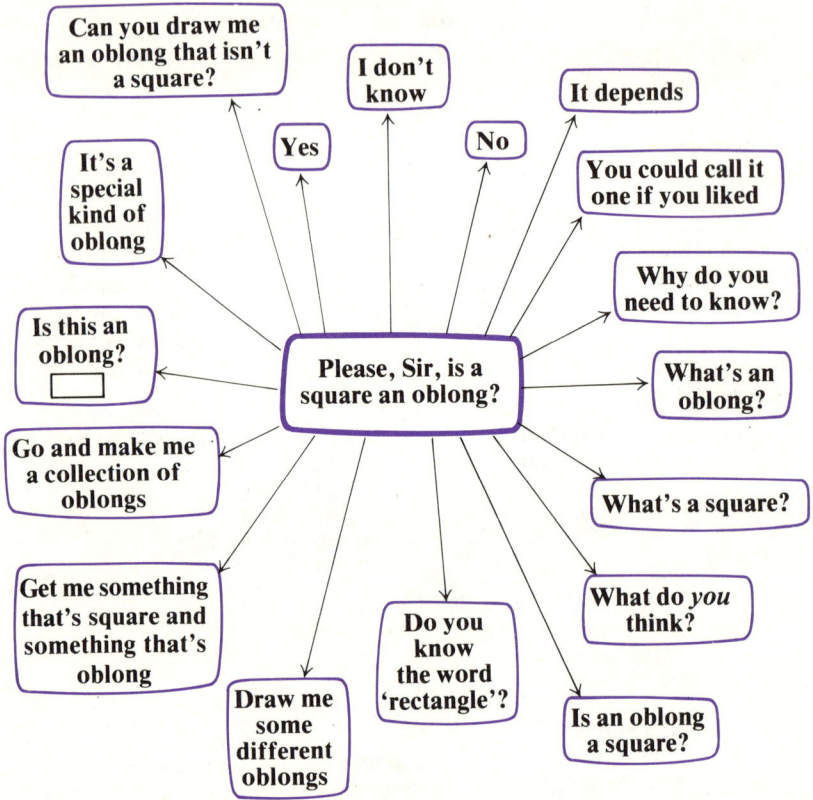

Can you draw me an oblong that isn't a square?

I don't know

It depends

It's a special kind of oblong

Yes

No

You could call it one if you liked

Why do you need to know?

Is this an oblong?

Please, Sir, is a square an oblong?

What's an oblong?

Go and make me a collection of oblongs

What's a square?

Get me something that's square and something that's oblong

Do you know the word 'rectangle'?

What do *you* think?

Draw me some different oblongs

Is an oblong a square?

Fig. 6.9

Inside Classrooms

An extract from a tape-recorded conversation with teachers of younger children.

Q   I wonder whether there is anything which is the same about your class-rooms, whether you would recognise each other's rooms if you went into them, or whether each room is so different from every other anyway?

T_1 I don't know that you would recognise them as an individual's room but you would possibly recognise them as, oh yes, this is a certain type of room. This person has a certain type of attitude towards something or the other.

Q   What would you think would stand out in your room?

T_1 Mess – organised chaos.

Q   Deliberately?

T₁ Yes, because I think it is an attitude of mind as far as I am concerned that the room belongs to the children as much as it belongs to me, and there the responsibility is a communal one, and I think that the first thing that would appear to anyone is a feeling of dis-organisation. It would only be later when they really knew the room that the structure would begin to emerge.

Q It's not chaos to you?

T₁ It's not to us. I won't say me personally; it's not to *us* because if I want something or a child wants something you merely raise a voice and say 'who knows where so and so is?' if you don't know, and somebody will produce it.

Q That would seem different from yours. The first picture of your room is not one of chaos, not so far as furniture or materials are concerned; possibly activities.

T₂ It is rather different when there are three adults, because if you have to consider other adults as well you can't work if you are a messy person as I am, you have to know that this is perhaps not acceptable to the other two and you have to watch it a bit; but I think when I was working in a room by myself one of its prime characteristics would have been a mess like B's with the same feeling that it didn't matter because there was an order and it was a workshop in which there was a lot of messy work going on, but that the essential feature of an order was there –which was that the important things had resting places where they ended up at the end of the day, or the end of the week.

T₁ Yes, our criterion is: provided the cleaner can sweep certain parts of the floor most of the time, provided bits of apparatus aren't left around, for instance, Unifix scattered to the four corners of the earth, then it's O.K. But things aren't in a tidy pile. I mean, loosely speaking the sort of art stuff would be in a section of the room, but you won't have a beautifully tidy pile of newspapers and a beautifully tidy pile of clean paper to be used.

Q Are they comfortable rooms for children, I mean mentally comfortable?

T₁ Well, the room is their design, in that when a class comes to me in September I always leave it deliberately bare and stark, with nothing out and nothing up. Partly because I want to see what the children want to make of it. Partly because it is a shock tactic that makes them observe things and if things are introduced gradually, I think they take far more notice than if they go into a nice tidy orderly room and see where things are. And then as we want to use things my attitude is, well, where do you think the best place would be – where shall we keep this?

Q I can see that in this context the walls might get covered with lots of collages and lovely paintings and things but I can't see that maths would necessarily enter into your room at all.

T₁ Maybe not, so does it matter?

T₂   It does to you, over the course of a year.

T₁   Yes, over the course of the year because if it doesn't enter in somewhere then things are going to be rather lopsided, and there is an area of things in which the children are being deprived.

T₂   Do the kids bring maths in?

T₁   Yes. Well, last year the first thing maths-wise that arrived was a wasps' nest. Shapes, say we talked about shapes; so we then had one wall covered with boxes of different shapes, and they put some hoops up because I couldn't find anything else and collected all the shapes with corners in one bit and all the round shapes in another one. So maths came into it that way and the first thing we did was shapes.

Q   Would you think this was true of your situation, that you wait for the children to bring the maths in? I would have thought you would have set out deliberately to involve them in something.

T₂   Well, there are times when there is a piece of apparatus around of some kind which interests me either for itself or in connection with young children and I want to see what happens if I bring it into the room and leave it lying around.

T₁   Like what?

T₂   Well, it could be snakes and ladders or logic blocks or some Cuisenaire rods or some sand and water or some plasticine, and sometimes also a hundred square and some windows to put over the numbers or plastic numbers. And sometimes they can lie around for quite a time and children won't take any notice of them much, and then perhaps someone will pick up something like the hundred square and start playing with it and if their playing goes on for long enough, and I'm not doing anything else, I can manage to to get across and sit down and see what is going on. Sometimes, of course, things don't take, but that doesn't matter either. It is nice to have these starting points in the room because I am not sure how far it is easy to bring recognisably mathematical things into the room from the outside world. I mean in the case of the wasps' nest for example, B's wasps' nest, I think – would it be fair to say? – that B had to bring her interest in shapes in and to add this to the wasps' nest itself and that these two *together* are both essential elements which end up generating for the children an interest in both understanding that shape, the shapes of the wasps' nest, and other shapes; so there are two things. Whereas if you want something which is a thing by itself which, without you, will begin, or may begin, mathematical-type things for the children, even when your back is turned, you may look for something more specially manufactured for the purpose, something with numbers in it for example.

T₁   Oh yes, I agree with that, but this I did say was only in the beginning, the *very* beginning, because I want to see what the children are and where I've got to compensate, I suppose, by adding interests to theirs.

Q   Have you got some goals in the back of your mind, things that you are going to be bringing in almost certainly after that?

T₁   Yes, very loose, very wide possibilities of things that I will bring in, but this is only in the first two or three weeks when I am getting to know the children. Very much in those first two or three weeks I tend to sit back and let the children take over with their interest in things, but I will have things, as John said, hundred squares, Unifix cubes, Cuisenaire, number lines, shapes, circles, that type of thing.

Q   I'm wondering whether from one year to the next you are now fairly confident of the range of things that are likely to come out each year?

T₁   I wouldn't say confident of the range of things that are likely, but the range of things which I think might come out and which perhaps I might like to tackle – but that changes from year to year in the peripheral area because it would depend a lot on what is my interest as well as what are the children's interests.

Q   So in fact the maths runs itself, you are not very bothered about it?

T₁   Not particularly.

T₂   I find it important, and it sounds as though you may as well, to try and change, as far as you can, a lot of the details of the things that are going to happen in maths or in any other area because it seems to me you can get very bored if you think that you are going to face the same kind of situation again, although it's with new children. It's nice to tackle a new topic in maths, say, that you have never done before in that way or with that age children, and to keep experimenting around a bit.

T₁   Yes. This is what I was meaning by saying that it to an extent depends on my interests that year. There are certain things which I feel, perhaps, that my six-year-olds need to cover in a very general sort of way, but to stop me being bored, and therefore being interesting and creating an interest, then I rely on what I am particularly interested in that year as well.

T₂   This could be seen as just selfishness on our part, if you like, but perhaps, I like to say, there is more to it than that, it's a question of whether you are play-acting when you are working with children or not, and if the investigation is genuinely new and surprising for you in some respects, then you are not pretending to be surprised when you really know exactly what you expect to happen; it helps to keep you in an honest human situation as far as you and the children are concerned.

T₁   I think children are very, very clever at finding out what is really true and when you are putting on a big con act.

T₂   And when in fact you are a bit bored yourself they can catch boredom off you.

T₁   Yes, and I mean if you are interested in a particular thing then your attitude, the way you talk about it, is going to be lively and you are looking at it in a totally different way and therefore you are going to create interest in other people. If you listen to someone talking on their hobby-horse they *can* be boring but, usually, to start off with, they are very interesting and they can grip you. Well this is what I do with the children, I hope.

T₂ This of course means that we are both of us hoping to find areas where we don't know things in maths and work at those.

T₁ Well, heaven knows that is not very difficult, is it?

T₂ No, what it means is that when we avoid sticking to the little we know and adding to it and only approaching children when we are sure of the ground, we are perhaps looking for uncertain ground, shaky ground, ground that is at least partly new for us.

T₁ Yes. I think that one of the things that really struck me when I started teaching very young children was that for the first time I was having to understand what I was teaching and it wasn't until I started trying to teach it that I began to understand the maths I had been doing. And, therefore, the more maths that I touch upon in a new sort of light the greater my understanding is becoming because I am working through it with the children, but having had vastly more experience than they have and knowing other fields, I create not ignorance but the opposite, a knowledge, and an understanding for myself, and therefore make myself a better teacher, I hope.

Q You are both describing a situation in which you really know the sorts of things you are trying to do; and you are trying to create, in a sense, problems for yourself because that makes life more interesting; and yet a lot of would-be helpers from outside like advisers, college lecturers, textbook writers and so on, I think you would say, seem to miss the point of a lot of what is going on. They seem not to understand quite what it is like in a classroom. What is it that they seem to miss?

T₁ Well, the reality, basically, I think, because when a visitor comes in, the majority of people put themselves out to make things go right and look good and most of the time things don't go right and it doesn't always look good. I mean when a supervisor comes in to see a student taking a lesson, that lesson has been beautifully prepared, more so than any teacher can expect to prepare every lesson or every moment of the day, and therefore they try to cover every eventuality and make a success, if you want to use that word, of that lesson. Now when you are in this classroom all day, every day you can't do that with every lesson and there are going to be so many unexpected interruptions and things that are avoided in that particular situation. It's a different standard. When you are being watched your standard is not quite the same as it is when you are relaxed and at ease and by yourself; and always a visitor brings into the situation another influence and therefore, because that person is just there, whatever they are doing or not doing, they can't help but influence the scene as it is.

Q What about the second-hand visitor, by which I mean the written material, the textbook, the workcard which is written by somebody or a group of people with an intention that it should come into a classroom and help? I don't see many of those being used, in your area, J, at all.

T₂ No, I've got to the arrogant stage of not finding other people's textbooks or workcards, or even my own of last year or for another school or for another group of children, much use. Do you feel the same, B, at all, or do you still find books useful in the classroom?

T₁ I find them useful because it takes some of the kids off my hands while I'm dealing with a group of children. To an extent my workcards are not for the mathematical activity that comes from it but as another aid to reading, a practice for reading skills. I use books and workcards to set a group of children off while I'm dealing with a particular group I want to deal with.

T₂ You think we're presenting a picture of us coping very nicely with a group of children and a room and some materials and it sounds very relaxed and reasonable.

Q Yes, and it doesn't sound as though you are asking for any outside influences on the thing, that you have any worries about the situation that you can't live with.

T₁ I wouldn't say that at all. As far as I am concerned what appears in my classroom is another big con trick. It's like having children in a thunderstorm, isn't it? You might be terrified out of your wits, but if you let the children see that, then they are going to be equally terrified and chaos ensues. So in the classroom you've got to make it appear calm and serene or at least you've got to make it appear to work. What you think inside and what you think out of the classroom are completely different things.

Q What do you think out of the classroom then?

T₁ I think what a miserable failure I am.

Q Why?

T₁ Because I could do so much better in other circumstances if I had more knowledge, if I had more know-how, if I had more time, if there was more of me, if there were less kids, if I had more apparatus and knew how to use them, all those kind of things.

T₂ Yes, I think that teaching from the time that you are a student teacher onwards is set up by people who are not teachers, who write books and who work in institutions other than the sort of schools we teach in, in such a way that you're bound to fail to do the job as they set it out. You cannot possibly teach successfully in the way that it's laid down that you should do – that is, unless you totally ignore the amount that the children are learning and just concentrate on your speech delivery and the kind of things you do as a teacher. And I think you can see something happening to teachers after a year or two, they suddenly notice that they are dashing round frantically from child to child in a desperate attempt – I did this myself – you catch yourself out dashing around trying to do the impossible, trying to split into thirty different people, to cope with thirty or forty different children, and once you've done this you have to face the fact that you're failing that way, and that perhaps any other way you can think of acting you will continue to fail to meet the needs that you can see you could meet if there were thirty of you. You can always see many more times the amount of work you could do than you can actually get done in a day. But you have to learn to relax and B and I have both been doing the job long enough to have passed through this stage of frenzy.

Q But you say you catch yourself doing the impossible, or trying to rush round to meet the needs of thirty children. One solution to that would appear to be to teach all thirty as a unit.

T₁ Yes, that is one solution, but that's an even bigger failure.

Q Why?

T₁ Because there are thirty different people not one person. There are thirty different mentalities, intellects, abilities, range of interests, ways in which they learn and stages and speeds at which they learn.

Q But J says it's impossible trying to cope with thirty as individuals and you're saying it's impossible to cope with the thirty as a unit. Why is the one preferable to the other? You both seem to have chosen the thirty as individuals.

T₂ I look at it now this way: whatever I do I'm going to fail most of the children most of the time. I'm going to fail to be with them, I'm going to fail to be part of their learning experience in school. So I can do various things about this; I can choose the way of failing which I as an individual find least unsatisfactory or most satisfying. One of the ways I like best is to try and work with a group of children until they are happy with their place, their room in school, and happy with one another enough to come in and get on with a variety of activities there which don't require my presence as a policeman or referee of helper of any kind. Then I can turn my back on them and sit in a corner with one, two, three or four or however many I choose of the class, and I can be confident that for half an hour, or an hour or a whole morning if necessary, or even a whole day, I can basically ignore ninety per cent of the children who are in my class and who are my responsibility. This is just one way of coping with failure. It seems to me that all the people who don't teach in this situation, starting with non-teaching Heads, do go in for the most incredible fantasies about what is actually happening in classrooms and what would help in classrooms. I think that this makes a lot of the advice that is given by non-teaching Heads, by advisers and teacher-trainers, and a lot of the advice written in books, come from a different world and that's why it often seems, to people who are actually teaching, very unhelpful. I am not prepared to say that reality is all on our side and fantasies all on their side, but their visions of what's going on, and what is possible, are just different visions, and there is possibly less communication between these two kinds of vision of what is going on in the school and the classroom than is normally admitted.

Some Dilemmas

1. A teacher must cope with about 30 children.
   – The majority of useful exchanges occur between a teacher and no more than four children.

2. In order to operate we need a degree of uniformity.
   – We want to encourage diversity of activity/response/experience.

3. We recognise that concrete materials benefit most young children.
   – We want to encourage children to think about abstractions.

4. We want children to discover things for themselves.
   – We want them to come to *some* common conclusions.

5. We want to know what we are trying to do.
   – We want to encourage exploration of new situations.

6. We learn from our experience.
   – This can lead to stereotyped actions.

7. We want to give children the security which comes from repetition.
   – We want children to be able to deal with insecurity.

8. We need to make some plans for children in advance.
   – We don't know our children until we have met them.

9. No textbook is satisfactory.
   – We cannot make up everything from our own resources.

10. We cannot tell in advance the effect of anything we ask children to do.
    – We have to act on the assumption that we can.

11. No teacher wants a syllabus.
    – Every teacher wants a syllabus.

12. Mathematics gains its present place in school through its usefulness to society.
    – Mathematics earns its place in children's experience through its enrichment of that experience.

13. We want children to understand what they are doing.
    – We do many things fluently precisely by *not* thinking about how they work.

14. The range of mathematical activities in which children can now engage is infinite.
    – Children have only a finite amount of time in school.

15. We want to know the best way of doing things.
    – Often there is no best way.

16. We aim to build up confidence in children.
    – We are lacking confidence in ourselves.

17. Children should be treated as individuals.
    Children need the stimulus of other people for their intellectual growth.

Pictures

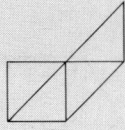
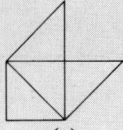

(a)　　(b)　　(c)

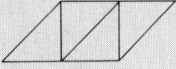

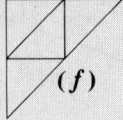

(d)　　(e)　　(f)

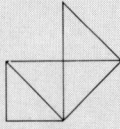
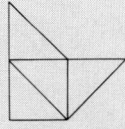

(g)　　(h)

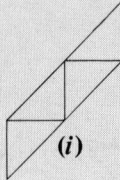
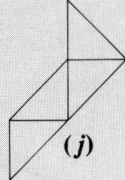

(i)　　(j)

(k)　　(l)

(m)　　(n)

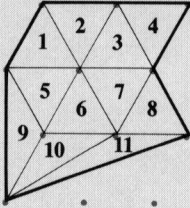
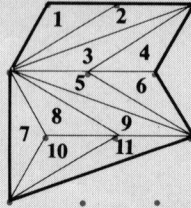
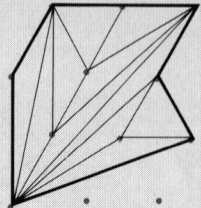

How many?

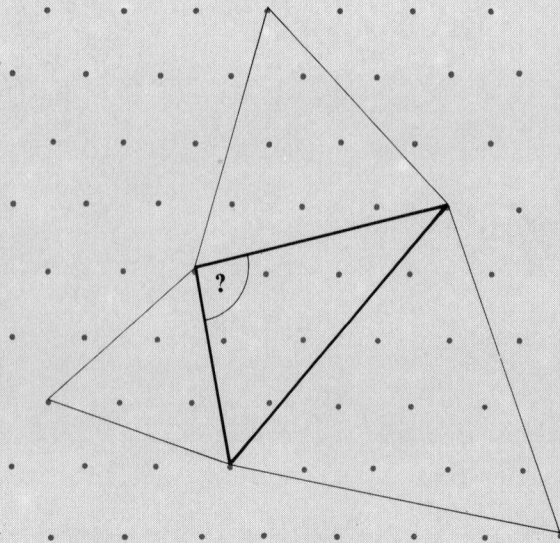

What angle?

1	2	4	7	11	16	22	29
3	5	8	12	17	23	30	
6	9	13	18	24	31		
10	14	19	25	32			
15	20	26	33				
21	27	34					
28	35						
36							

				34	23	21	36
			33	24	20	11	35 22
		32	25	19	12	10	
	31	26	18	13	9	4	
30	27	17	14	8	5	3	
29	28	16	15	7	6	2	1

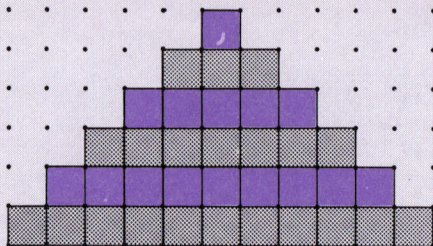

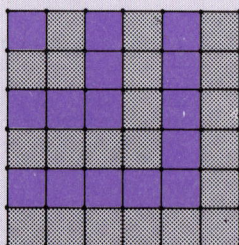

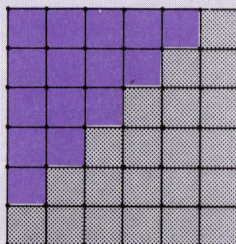

Triangles and squares

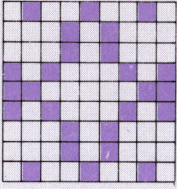
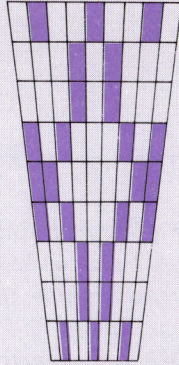
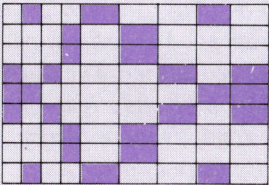
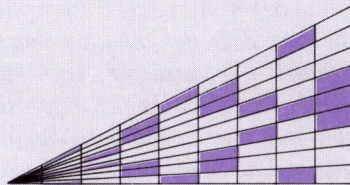
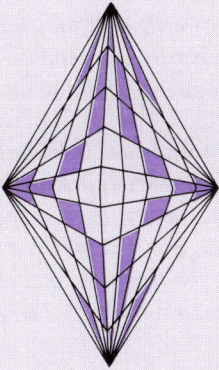
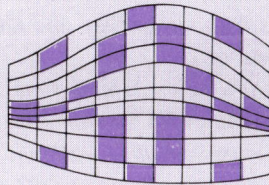

7

It is a pity that it has become a cliché to say that the more a person knows, the more he knows how much there is still to be known. As with most clichés, it is uttered more often than not with only a modest amount of conviction. Situated as we are in this half century in the track of an 'information explosion', it is probably easier for us to be convinced that the world shows itself vastly too complex for any individual to stand a chance of getting on terms with very much of it. Both beliefs make acknowledgment of the inevitability of human ignorance, but the first does not question that we can advance – and, indeed, makes it clear that it is because we reach farther that we see farther. The distinction between the two lies in the difference between knowing one's ignorance and knowing that one is ignorant. The former is substantially more precise, more specific; and more useful and more hopeful because more aware.

Knowing parts of one's ignorance is as hard to achieve, requires as much effort, and is as subject to the same limitations of relativity and non-finality, as knowing anything else. In fact, knowing what one does not know and knowing what one knows, go together, equally legitimate and successful outcomes of the human urge to know. It is only putting them into words that may make them seem paradoxical or contradictory; in our experience we can readily hold both knowings without anxiety and know that we are better off for any small increment in either.

The following are five personal statements, more concerned with the teacher's ignorance than with the children's. We print them because they acknowledge that teachers must somehow work with the fact that what their role presupposes they can do, they are often at a loss to know how to do. But we aim to be realistic, not fatalistic, because we know that it is possible for teachers to take steps to get closer to dealing with those problems in the classroom that otherwise seem either unmanageable or inscrutable.

Anatomy of a Failure

6 December

Ian has drawn Fig. 7.1.

We have been counting the white rod as 'one'. So Ian has put a green rod where he needs a yellow one. He has represented $2 + 3 = 3$, not $2 + 3 = 5$.

210

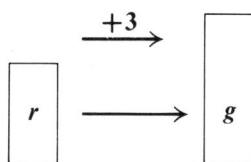

Fig. 7.1

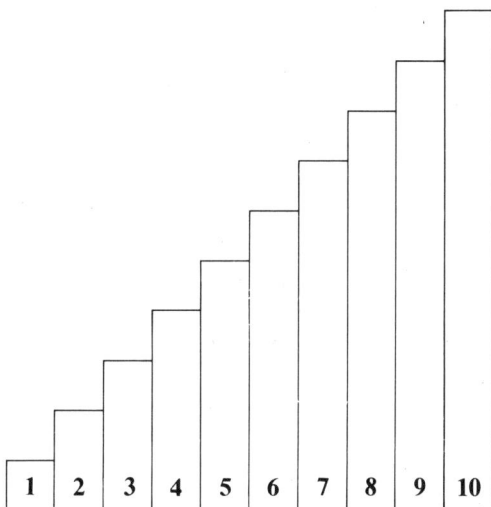

Fig. 7.2

I think Ian is at that stage of terror where the only thing he is sure of is that we have used the rods to exemplify the numbers from 1 to 10 in a staircase (Fig. 7.2).

Bearing this much about Ian in mind, I ask him:

'How do you add a green rod to a red one?'

Ian suggests we could take away a white rod from the green one. That is, make the green rod as long as the red.

ME   You mean, by adding, put the red beside this green? (Fig. 7.3)

Ian says, 'Yes', and adds the white rod to these two, making a piece of that staircase (Fig. 7.4).

Fig. 7.3

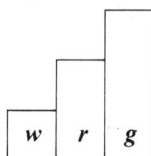

Fig. 7.4

So I remind him of the different action which I want to call 'adding two rods' (Fig. 7.5).

In fact, Ian has been using the rods for months in this way. And my action releases a little more of what I'm sure he knows.

IAN   Oh, I know, you add a red onto a green and put a yellow beside them. (Fig. 7.6).

| g | r |

Fig. 7.6

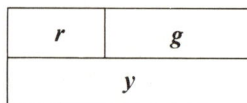

| r | g |
| y | |

Fig. 7.5

He needs encouragement, but these words and actions sound too automatic.

ME   That's very nice. Now, why is that called adding?
IAN   I don't know.

So I show him the same operation using white rods (Fig. 7.7).

Fig. 7.7

As I do this, I tell him once again that we are working a model of adding 2 and 3, using bits of wood to help us. I'm none too confident that Ian gains much from my words. I want to explore the extent of his insecurity. So I scatter the five white rods about on the table. Then I ask him:
'Are there still five?'
Ian says 'Yes', but counts them to make certain.

ME   Why?
IAN   I don't know.

He takes another white rod and plays at re-arranging and counting this collection.

I don't think that either Ian or I is that daft. But we have edged towards a fairly complete state of incomprehension. Perhaps my last question is a silly one to ask and I've put Ian off. I am beginning to wonder whether I am uncovering or creating Ian's problems at the moment. So I simply say

that 'five' is the name for any set with that number of things in it, and move
back to the action:

'Could you try getting two white rods; and then three white rods joined
together in a green rod?'

Ian gets them, and checks that the green rod is the same as three whites.
I 'add the whites to the green'. (Fig. 7.8).

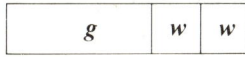

Fig. 7.8

ME   Well, now what comes at the end of your arrow. Two add three is . . . ?
IAN   Five.

I agree. Ian writes in '5', then leaves for his bottle of milk. So the incident
has been tidied up. But I'm very uneasy about the conversation.

I have more general grounds for concern about Ian. His parents are warm-
hearted and concerned. But they have ambitions for him. He has an over-
anxious attitude to the world, compounded by a tendency to asthma. And
he has a three-year-old brother who can't wait to get to school.

I decided to keep a special look-out for Ian in the next few weeks.

8 December

Ian and I are working with the rods. We have made the staircase which uses
all ten of the rods. Now I begin a staircase which uses every other rod. This
is like moving from counting 1, 2, 3, . . . , 10, to counting 1, 3, 5, 7, 9. I put
down a white, green and yellow rod, and ask Ian to carry on with my staircase Fig. 7.9).

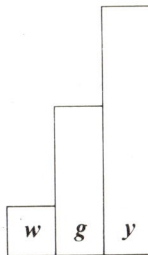

Fig. 7.9

This action with these words usually communicates what game I'm playing to children. Ian puts down the dark green rod next. Then he opens up
my staircase and puts in the 'missing' rods. He ends up with all ten rods.
He is doing the equivalent of counting in ones again.

Not to be defeated, I take away every other rod from this staircase and push the remaining five rods together to make the pattern I was after in the first place. I ask Ian what is different about my staircase. He replies that there should be a red between the white and the green rods, a pink there, and so on ... In other words, he can only describe my staircase as a failed version of his. He has a really powerful mental picture of the complete staircase, which prevents him from using the rods as I meant them to be used.

On both these occasions, Ian was reduced to a form of counting in ones. This is a common and disastrous failing. Counting aloud, on the fingers, with buttons or counters; counting every Unifix cube: the activity takes many forms. These actions can hardly be bad in themselves. But they are only a beginning. Many children spend most of their first years at school relying on counting alone. In other words, they only trust the number rhyme 'one, two, three, four, ...' and some corresponding set of things to be tallied. It is possible to find older children who, under pressure, will secretly set out acres of little dots to get an answer they know to be right.

Clearly, anyone who has to work in this way is at the cave-man stage in his calculations. Yet I'm not suggesting that these children are 'too stupid' to work in any other way. Rather, at some point they have come to distrust their own mathematical powers. They have been made afraid of arithmetical statements like:

$$\text{if} \quad 2 + 3 = 5 \quad \text{then} \quad 20 + 30 = 50,$$
$$15 + 7 = 10 + 5 + 7,$$

and so on.

Many people have tried to make arithmetic less baffling for young children. I have seen all kinds of structural apparatus help a great many children to attack arithmetic, with increased enjoyment and success. At the age of six, Ian was already exhibiting deep worries about the apparatus that I had hoped would help to cure his worries. Ironically, Cuisenaire rods are ideal for helping children out of the specific habit of counting in ones. Yet Ian was able to 'bend' this situation and the rods till they modelled his need to do this very thing.

Surely, for some children, structural apparatus may only serve to confuse the issue. A doctrinaire insistence on any one approach to arithmetic seems a bad idea.

Why did I allow Ian to spend so long getting nowhere with the rods? The answer isn't simple. Basically, it was his decision, not mine. I didn't feel clear enough about what Ian's problems were to intervene decisively at the time. I failed to think out my own part in his failure.

So why did Ian keep working with the rods when it appeared to give him pain?

14 December

Ian isn't sure of the reason for the arrow here:

$$4 \xrightarrow{\;+2\;} ?$$

We are working with the rods again. He takes the notation as an instruction to move the pink rod across. So the addition ($+2$) seems to be a second unconnected action to him. I make a picture and help Ian to put in colours to symbolise rods (Fig. 7.10).

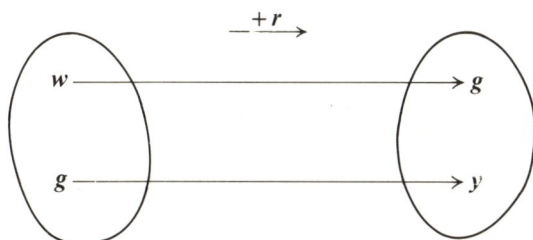

Fig. 7.10

He is still confused, so I decide to go right back to the beginning, which in this case is the most concrete situation. We fetch two hoops and put rods in one. A length of wool joins each rod in one hoop to a corresponding rod in the other hoop. Ian still looks worried after we've played with this, so I give up.

4 March

Ian, set to represent 40 with rods, records 'oooo' – that is, four orange rods, or four 'tens'. But I have many doubts about what he understands. So I ask him:

'How did you know that stood for forty?'

IAN   I don't know. I just found out.

As the crudest of tests, I set out three orange rods, and asked him if that made forty. He said, 'No'; and added one more. I altered the form of my question:

'How do you know that's forty?' (*pointing at the rods*).

IAN   I don't know.
ME   It's forty what?
IAN   Forty orange rods.
ME   How many orange rods there?
IAN   Four.

ME   So it can't be forty orange rods, can it. Why do we say that is forty?

IAN   So you don't have to count on your fingers?

This is one of the reasons for calculating with rods that I have mentioned to the children in the past. It hardly seems in place here. However, Ian's words suggest my next question:

'So can you count these rods?'

IAN   One, two, three, four.

ME   Why is four the same as forty here?

If Alice in Wonderland had been with us, she might have put me in my place:

'Four is forty here? Curiouser and curiouser!'

Ian's reply lacks Alice's self-assurance:

'Because there are two fours?

ME   Why can these four orange bits of wood stand for forty?

IAN   I don't know.

I decide to talk less and move on.

ME   So what about the next one on this card? It asks you to make forty-two.

Ian pushes the four orange rods around but gets nowhere. So I get dragged back into the general question of what these coloured rods are modelling. This seems to be Ian's fundamental problem. He doesn't like the model at all really. He accepts it because – well, because he is who he is.

ME   Why call this orange rod ten?

IAN   Because it's orange.

ME   Why not call the blue rod ten?

IAN   Because it's not orange.

ME   Why is the orange one the ten, though?

IAN   Because it's the highest number.

ME   What do you mean, it's the highest number?

IAN   I don't know what I mean.

ME   What do you call that rod?

IAN   A green.

ME   Yes; and what number do you call it?

IAN   Three.

ME   Why?

IAN   Because it's green.

ME   O.K. What do you call that one?

IAN   Two.

ME   Why?

IAN   Because it's red.

ME   And this one?

IAN   One.

ME   Why?

IAN   Because it's white.

ME   Why not call this orange rod one?

IAN   Because it's too big?

ME   Who decided that this white rod should be called one?

IAN   You did.

ME   Can I change my mind?

IAN   Yes.

ME   Can't you decide what number this orange rod will stand for?

IAN   No.

ME   Why not?

IAN   I just can't.

A learning process which works is often mysterious. When it goes wrong, one may be able to see into it more clearly. There follows my analysis of this particular failure, and my attempt to learn from it.

I am more concerned with my failure to teach than with Ian's failure to learn. In any case, it isn't clear how far Ian was failing to learn, unless you narrow down 'learning' to that period in his life and to those uses of the rods.

There were three ways in which Ian and I were more or less failing to communicate: with Cuisenaire rods, with marks on paper, with words.

First, the rods. Ian's apparent obsession with Cuisenaire rods is bound to reflect on me. I was largely responsible for the mathematical environment in which he worked. So, why my obsession with the rods? Why didn't I provide Unifix cubes or buttons to count?

Well, I did. But that year I was deep in an experiment. I introduced calculation by means of the rods almost exclusively. My workcards all instructed children to use rods. In my explanations, I always had them to hand. I hoped in this way to help children quickly over counting in ones and on to more efficient ways of calculating. At the back of my mind were accounts of the amazing results Gattegno had achieved with five- and six-year-olds, using the rods. I think I had some success with many of the children in the class. On the whole, they used the rods as an aid to understanding arithmetic, not as a substitute for it. The rods served to provoke and communicate thoughts through actions and patterns. They helped children to gain power over numbers. They made children less dependent on me for their insights. All of this was true of most of the children at some time, but not all of the children all the time. And in Ian's case, none of these desirable things were true. He invested me and the rods with magic powers. He appeared to have no control over the rods; for him the white rod 'was' one. Yet he wouldn't stop using them.

Thus my successes were bought at a price. By my intensive use of them, I must have given the rods great prestige. Mathematical success for those children must have seemed to entail success with the rods.

While thinking about Ian's view of the rods I have become clearer about my own. The rods seem to me to be a kind of model. They are supposed to help children gain insight into the nature of numbers, operations on numbers and ways of recording situations which involve numbers. A model either helps you to grasp a situation, or it doesn't. If the model in itself is a worry, so that you have two sources of confusion where you might have had only one, then throw it away. On the other hand, Cuisenaire rods only begin to work for a child if you press on with them until they become mental entities that the child turns to habitually and with complete confidence. (I have since read the work of Madeleine Goutard, which has made this really clear to me for the first time.) At that time I was too busy and too unclear about the value of pressing on, to challenge Ian's primitive view of the rods. I now think I should have followed through one or other course of action.

Secondly, we communicated by means of marks on paper. The notation we used was partly pictorial. I'm not sure whether this helped of hindered Ian. (See his confusions on 14 December.) As with the rods, I didn't risk varying the situation when I might have done. Nor did I find time to discuss what notation is for, or suggest to Ian that he could change what he didn't like.

Neither the rods nor the notation seemed to help Ian very much, but what strikes me most now is the inadequacy of my words.

Words can only convey so much, however hard one tries to elaborate and refine what one says. Without a tacit agreement about what is being discussed, conversation cannot take place. I find the rods particularly useful because they make up for some of the deficiencies of words. I find that a child and I can often work effectively with rods, though our words by themselves appear halting and vague.

At first sight, the rods may seem unambiguous. There they are to be looked at, pushed around, named. But they aren't that straightforward. Ian's view of them and mine were so different that words failed us and the whole teaching and learning game ground to a halt.

Listening to my words, I think Ian may have doubted his ability to understand mathematics, whereas in fact my explanations relied on his ability to make sense of the rods. I think I should have made it clear to Ian that my words were at fault rather than his understanding.

Whenever one fails at a specific teaching or learning task, one is likely to step back for a more comprehensive view of the situation. It would be senseless in any case to divorce a piece of mathematical teaching and learning from the people involved or from their more general views about school and of one another.

In this context, I am not prepared to see our exchanges as a complete failure. As Ian continues to grow, he will draw on the past and in doing so he will alter it. The incident is not closed. And Ian's view of himself in school wasn't dominated by his work in mathematics. His picture of himself, of his friends and of me was mediated through countless activities. I think Ian would have described mathematics as his least favourite activity.

I shall have to step back still further from the mathematics of it in order to complete this anatomy of a failure.

I am not trained in psychiatry or psychology, yet every day I make judgement or have hunches about why certain children act as they do. These judgements and feelings have a great effect on my behaviour towards the children. To an extent I am caught up in both 'diagnosis' and 'therapy' whether I like it or not. The childrens' problems won't go away just because there are no experts around to help them. To ignore the whole person seems impossible when the whole person is there, asking for help. When one is confronted with a child's personal problems it seems to me that one has to act with humility and honesty.

After working with thirty-five children for two years, I got to know them pretty well. I had time to think about each individual. I had a pretty clear picture of Ian, but it didn't help me to sort out his mathematical problems. I know that if Ian were my son I wouldn't have cared how much mathematics he ever learned. But as his teacher I was caught up in his paradoxes and my own.

It seemed to me that Ian had identified his own success in life too closely with his success in school work. In doing so, he was, I think, acting quite rationally. I came to feel that his own nature, the character of his younger brother and the attitude of his parents, presented him with problems of which his mathematical troubles were only aggravating symptoms. He felt keenly that his parents wanted him to do more at school. (How much more is more?) His three-year-old brother was lapping up experience with great relish. Ian spent so much time worrying that he found it hard to think. He could tell that his closest friends in the class were somehow better able to cope with mathematics than he was.

Sometimes I felt that Ian's attitude to mathematics distorted its whole purpose. And that he had involved me in his distortion. I hadn't been able to bring about a cure, which made me his accomplice, not his physician. At other times, feeling less guilty, I admired Ian. I was impressed by his enormous determination to get somewhere with this damned subject. At such times, I felt I had to help him.

I had a more positive reason for trying to help Ian with his mathematics. He set great store by success in school work. He had chosen to put his personal problems to himself in that way. To persuade or order him to give up mathematics for a time seemed much the best course of action, until I realised that this would have challenged the way he put himself to himself. And on the other hand, if I could help him to succeed in mathematics, I felt sure he would be helped with his more general problems. So I felt obliged to meet his request to be taught mathematics along with his friends. If Cuisenaire rods or even mathematics got contaminated in the process, so that Ian came to reject them, then would that matter so very much?

I went to see his parents on two occasions. I tried to explain to them how I felt about Ian. But it's very hard to say to parents that you think you know their son better than they do, and that you question the form their love for him is taking. It sounds so arrogant and so unjustified.

In the last analysis, I noticed very little difference in Ian's behaviour during those two years. He became generally more self-confident, but that might have happened anyway. What I did do was try to notice who he was and to speak to that person rather than to some half-perceived figure. And to help Ian to take hold of his own learning process as he saw it, not as anyone else wished it to be. The most fundamental actions one takes in school are based on feelings and carried out in faith.

Observations

1. A boy in the 7–9 area was counting buttons. He was counting them in twos, then arranging five pairs of buttons to make piles of ten. Obviously helpful, I thought, until I found that he couldn't count in tens. So having got one pile of ten, he put the next pile of ten by it and counted . . . , 11, 12, 13, 14, . . . , 20. I put a third pile of ten near. 'How many altogether now?' 'Fifty?' he suggested.

2. A girl was doing a page from a textbook. 'I've done all these pages', she said, 'and now I'm on this.' (Fig. 7.11)

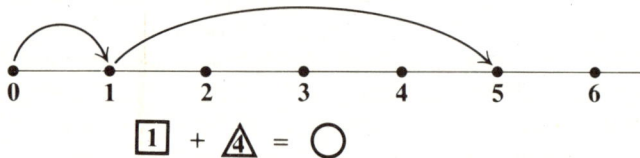

Fig. 7.11

We discussed what it meant. She was confused because, going from 0 to 5 there were *six* spots, although she was clearly perfectly confident that 1 + 4 = 5. About ten similar problems followed.

'Just write down $\boxed{1} + \triangle\!\!\!\!4 = ⑤$ ', I said. But she was unhappy, because the instructions on the page told her to copy out all the number lines with their arrows as well.

I'm not confident that she was gaining anything from doing this, in view of her obvious ability with the number bonds.

Near her another girl was using the same book. She pointed with pride at four pages of work. 'I've done all this', she said, and waited for anticipated approval. 'Are they easy?' I asked. 'Oh yes', she said.

It seemed to me that in both these cases, the girls only *learned* anything when they *asked* about something they did not understand. Perhaps it is rather rare to *learn* anything new from textbooks: perhaps they only serve to *show* you that you have learned something, and to practise it.

3. In the dinner-break a girl was writing on the board:

$$18 \div 7 = 5$$
$$15 \div 10 = 6$$
$$10 \div 10 = 10 \text{ ('No', she said, and wrote } 10 \div 10 = 1.)$$
$$2 \div 2 = 1$$

'How do you do those?' I asked.
'I *can't* do them', she said.

4. Eight children sat at a table taking turns to spin a spinner die to produce two numbers for a subtraction sum. The first rolled 3 and 7, and wrote down $7 - 3 = 4$. Why did they not write down any two numbers? This would be quicker and give them more practice, but the spinning did seem to hold the thing together.

5. Four boys were playing number bingo, calling out numbers written on small squares of card, and covering up the numbers with bottle tops if they were on their card. Several numbers were missing from the set of cards so that the same card 'won' each time. They showed great pleasure and pride in 'winning', although 'winning' required no skill. *Is* this a game?

6. A girl had coloured pegs and a plastic ten-by-ten pegboard. She had filled the pegboard with one hundred pegs. 'How many pegs in this row?' I indicated the top row and covered up the others with a book. She counted. 'Ten.' I pointed to the second row. 'How many here?' She counted again. 'Ten.' I pointed to the third row. She counted again. 'Ten.' 'How many in these two rows together?' She counted from one again. 'Twenty?' Throughout this she looked bemused and blank.

7. This was by all accounts 'one of those mornings' and I found relationships between children absorbing more of my time than mathematics. Restlessness was much more apparent than on previous visits.

Some girls were sorting a large pile of counters on the floor. They put all the orange counters into a tin. Then some black ones. 'Isn't that lovely?' 'Yes, it is.' Suddenly one of the girls plunged her hands into the pile of counters, lifted a handful to her face, and cried out, 'Look, I'm washing.' Counters went everywhere.

A boy in a purple shirt was working at a page of addition. Suddenly he became awkward, slightly aggressive, disruptive, uncontrolled. Moments later he was quietly asking for his sums to be corrected. Why was it? Boredom? Repression gradually building up? Jealousy because I wasn't paying attention to him? A single incident, but representative of many which make it obvious how much more important is the building up of personal relations than starting with academic considerations. And how important at the time that Andrew could pick up his book and materials and settle naturally at another table because he didn't want to be disturbed.

Pressures on a Teacher

As a teacher it seems that there are so many ways in which pressure is put upon me to prove any statement which I make that it is not surprising that I lack confidence in my own ability to govern the method and content of my work.

In almost every field connected with education I feel subjected to a constant battering whenever I venture an opinion. 'Why did you say that? What are your reasons? What research has been done in this field?' The questions pour out and the feeling I receive is not one of a genuine seeking for information but of an aggressive response, 'Who does she think she is, to hold such views?' Humbly, I suggest that I am one of the people doing the real work of teaching, class management and generally making the educational machine work – often despite the administrators and educational experts.

I feel that these pressures build up particularly when the word mathematics is present.

At school mathematics was all bound up with 'being right' and with proof. Whatever was produced in this field was either right (if I could show sound indisputable facts to support my answer) or wrong; proved or totally mistaken. I learned to accept the fact that what I thought or felt to be so was based on my stupid lack of understanding and so was dismissed as nonsense. It was at this stage that I was brain-washed into feeling that, as long as I could support my statement by quoting what someone else had said, then everything was well. However, once I could only say '*I* think so. *I* feel this is true', then the response was a paternalistic smile which was totally lacking in kindness and tinged with pity.

The general atmosphere surrounding the subject of mathematics is still the same now that I am a teacher. The impression I receive is that many people consider that I know enough about the subject – which becomes translated into any subject – to teach young children but not enough to teach older children. At that level more specialised knowledge is required, so a teacher of older children becomes 'a specialist' or some kind of an expert in the subject. With my kind of teaching, I am a non-specialist, a second-rate teacher (and person), a failure at understanding and obtaining knowledge. Therefore my views, opinions and ideas are considered to be second-rate, listened to in the way one might listen to a baby's first attempts at talking and disregarded in the same manner. It is considered that I do not have the specialised knowledge of mathematics to decide either the content of what I teach or the method by which I teach it.

This is an attitude which I feel that I encounter time and again. At one stage I accepted it as a true evaluation of my capabilities and responsibilities. However, I am not quite so certain now. I have listened to so much good advice, so many experts, so many irrelevant impractical words.

In the classroom situation I have often watched young children exploring ideas and apparatus. To come to terms with the way they work the child seems to have a feeling, an instinct, which he then sets out to prove to his own satisfaction. At a later stage this 'proof' might be rejected in favour of more sophisticated reasoning but it remains a step in the process of discovery, a stage through which one must grow. There is no true 'short cut'.

While not using this observation as a justification for irresponsible experiments involving the children I teach, I do feel that it is something which must be borne in mind if it is accepted that every human being changes and develops intellectually and in experience throughout the whole of his life-span.

So, perhaps I might be allowed to decide on the contents of what I teach and the way in which I teach it? By all means help to increase my knowledge of mathematics, to give me a wider vocabulary of topics, ideas and approaches from which to make a selection. But I have lived a life too, just like the mathematician and the expert. I know what mathematics is necessary to my everyday life. I know what mathematics I have found fun to do, absorbing to discover, interesting to pursue. I know the feeling of mathematical failure; I have experienced the specialist's inability to communicate and impart knowledge. I was involved in the teacher's incomprehension of the problems of the subject. Above all, apart from being an expert in the failure of mathematics teaching, I do specialise in children, their relationships and their work. I am involved in the process of child development every working day of my life.

Every proof that ever was or that ever will be started as an instinctive feeling that someone had about something and this was later proved to be 'true'. Please leave me my instincts – and, perhaps, my ignorance.

Creative Ignorance

1 Discovery: Communication

A man sees, grasps or understands something that no one else has seen. (It may be a pattern of events, a relationship between things or ideas . . .) If he wishes to share his discovery with other people, two things must happen. (i) Some other people must see, grasp, or understand what he has. (ii) Some other people must accept that there is indeed something there to be seen (that he has truly discovered a pattern, a relationship), whether or not they can see it themselves.

1.1 PROOF, ACCEPTANCE. HENCE, THE LANGUAGE OF PROOF

A proof is constructed to get other people to accept the thing proved. This makes proof a special kind of communication.

Proofs are not intended to be descriptions or explanations of anything. So they rarely contain the whole story about the thing proved.

A proof is a specialised communication, aimed at specialists. The language of proof is limited, in order to make its terms precise and forceful. This jargon is baffling if you aren't familiar with it. Once the specialists have accepted a proof, other folk take their word for it. A proof may be widely accepted as valid when only a few people can actually follow it.

1.2 DISCOVERY, BEFORE AND AFTER PROOF

The original discovery is the important thing.

When a proof is accepted, everyone adjusts to the thing proved, not to the proof. If the thing proved is of great general interest, many people may try to understand something of it. They probably won't bother with the proof (e.g. relativity).

1.3 DISCOVERY, EXPLANATION. HENCE, THE LANGUAGE OF EXPLANATION

In order to understand something of another man's discovery, what is needed is a description or an explanation, not a proof.

Understanding is a private, personal matter. Each person's route to understanding may well be unique.

So explanations need to 'translate' their subject into another form, other words. They should be imaginative, discursive; they should re-present their subject in several ways.

1.4 PROOF VERSUS UNDERSTANDING

Proofs aren't translations; they are themselves. They are designed to stand up in public to expert cross-examination.

One may understand an idea, but be confused by the proof. (One may follow it, but fail to see the connection, or one may fail to follow it, and doubt one's original understanding.)

1.5 CONCLUSION

A proof gains acceptance for the thing proved; this affects the language of proof. Understanding is a complex and private process; this affects the language of explanation.

2 The Language of Teaching

Proofs are often given to children who have asked for explanations. Is it any wonder that children find mathematics bewildering? It is the subject in which you reason for no reason.

2.1

I have been working on this *dichotome:*
discovery – understanding – explanation
proof – following and accepting – proof – thing proved
Thinking of mathematics, this dichotome may seem too strong (many proofs do help to explain the thing proved, for example). But it is a vital distinction when it comes to teaching.

2.2

For example, I remember how, when I was at school, I would follow a proof admitting each step, yet finish by not really understanding the proof as a whole. Even more frequently I remember following a proof, yet having no clue about why the proof was ever devised, let alone why it was given me to learn.

Official or standard explanations of mathematical ideas for children have largely failed: most children give up the attempt to understand mathematics.

Perhaps official explanations, when they are not proofs, remain too proof-like, too cryptic, too rigorous.

From the start children are prepared for proofs. The right answer is a relation of proof. To have the right answer proves that one has done some mathematics correctly. Already the ritual has begun, the emphasis is on a closed and narrow rightness. From the start, mathematics is presented as a series of rules and recipes which, correctly used, give right answers.

2.3 A LANGUAGE OF LEARNING?

If people are now trying to get children to understand mathematics, then that means a revolution in teaching. No one knows how to bring about understanding. But in teaching, the language of explanation is nothing like the language of proof.

Understanding between teachers and children involves feedback; it has to be a dialogue.

So all standard explanations, however, expressed, are bound to fail with children. They need individual, idiosyncratic explanations. No printed page (no programmed text) can hold a dialogue with a child.

2.4 CONCLUSION

Teaching – the discovery (the idea or relationship) – understanding – explanation – dialogue.

Teaching – the proof (of the idea, the relationship) – following and accepting – monologue.

3 Teaching

It is very hard to teach mathematics well. The subject itself seems to suggest a narrow proof-like approach: when it is taught in this way, it hardly matters how much or how little mathematics a teacher knows (the less one knows, the more hopeful the situation). Yet it seems clear that one cause of poor mathematics teaching must be lack of mathematical knowledge. However, increased knowledge of mathematics won't by itself help people to teach better.

More hopeful would be a fresh approach to the teaching of mathematics using each teacher's existing knowledge and ignorance as a starting point.

The direction of gaze would be not towards mathematics texts. If we hope to bring about change in the classroom, why not enlist the active support of the children? To point to the mathematical actions that already exist in every classroom: is this possible? A book of childrens' (and teachers') reactions. Mistakes and confusions assume a central importance: one doesn't feel need of help with successes.

The problem is how to teach mathematics effectively when you know very little yourself. The ingredients are: a teacher who knows little about mathematics but quite a lot about how to teach, indifferent to mathematics but not to children; someone's mathematical starting point (textbook, workcard, piece of apparatus); children acting on this starting point, and involving the teacher. The outcome hoped for: a new insight into mathematics and how to teach it. The agent of change: feedback.

3.1

I can only say what happened to me. First: my own ignorance and indifference. At school we learned the recipes for doing sums and so on, but they didn't explain the reasons for the recipes. I never had the feeling that I had been 'inside' the subject. Or perhaps it had no 'inside'. Naturally I didn't do well at mathematics and learned to dislike it.

When I became a teacher, 'the system' was prepared for my ignorance and dislike of mathematics. Inside battered desks and cupboards were battered textbooks. I had been given sums to do with the children. This method of coping with my attitude to mathematics left it unchanged. There were three ways in which I might have been persuaded to change my attitude to mathematics: by the teachers, by the textbooks, by the children. The teachers talked about knitting patterns, food, holidays, not education. The textbooks were full of perfectly judged problems: I found them easy, the children didn't. The children and I had been given our text; my job was to interpret it to them. (The crucial thing with any ritual is to perform it, not to convey its meaning to the congregation.) The children were a worry. So many of them were clearly bored and confused over their mathematics (and not only over their mathematics). The effect of the children.

For the first two or three years I didn't enjoy teaching very much. I was worried about the children, but not worried enough to take action. Naturally I blamed the system and the children rather than myself for the bad effects of my (mathematics) teaching. But at least I had noticed that things were badly wrong, and was feeling guilty.

Also, I began to notice a pattern in the mistakes the children made in their sums. They would write one hundred and seventeen as 10017, for example. All the recipes for carrying, borrowing and so on led to this kind of mistake:

$$
\begin{array}{r}
36 \\
+\ 28 \\
\hline
514
\end{array}
$$

Although I didn't know it, the children were leading me towards a mathematical insight.

I went to work in a school where the children were taken more seriously. I became far more committed to the children. I began to do all sorts of enjoyable work with the children. But there was still mathematics. We had a set of textbooks, and the children were still doing sums. They were making the same kinds of mistakes,, and they didn't enjoy the subject. In this school, then, the children's attitude to mathematics was in marked contrast to their general feelings about school work. I felt that something had to be done. I felt more confident that something could be done. I tried to find out why mathematics was so hard to teach.

The key to my problem lay in the children's mistakes. There were some Nuffield guides around, though I didn't think they were used. Reading one, I came across the notion of place value. Once I had met it, the idea seemed obvious. I 'knew' it all along, but the children didn't. Their mistakes were systematic because they didn't understand the system. I also read about working in different bases. As long as you stuck to base ten, the places were hard to distinguish from the numbers you wrote down. But now 5, in base ten, could be written as 10, 11, 12, 101. The numerals shifted as you moved from one base to another, but the places themselves remained a constant underlying structure. I could see why one spoke of a number system.

After that there were no end of fresh questions, and all the problems of how to work with children. (For example, in any base but ten should we call 10 'onety'? What name for 100?) I was 'inside' a piece of mathematics, perhaps for the first time. I soon grew interested in finding out more about mathematics for my sake as well as for the children's. Their mathematical education and mine have gone hand in hand ever since.

3.2

How can this story help another teacher? People teach in such opposed ways. I have in mind anyone who finds he can't resolve a child's mathematical difficulty.

3.3

Teaching ... mathematics. Two words, each a focus for the teacher's thoughts. I want to suggest that the key to teaching mathematics lies in the teaching rather than in the mathematics.

(i) *Listening to children.* However divergent their methods may be, I suspect that all teachers use some feedback from the children.

My own attitude to mathematics began to change when I really listened to what the children were telling me. They didn't understand or enjoy the subject. My explanations didn't seem to help. I was feeling guilty about the situation for some time before I found any way to improve it.

(ii) *Thinking.* Next, I had to see that I knew just enough mathematics to prevent me from thinking about it. What I did know was even more harmful than what I didn't. It is very difficult to teach for long without thinking about the children's mistakes. Many teachers who are on bad terms with mathematics are skilled at dealing with a great number of learning problems. However little mathematics a teacher may know, he can bring his problem-solving ability to bear on the children's mathematics difficulties.

4 Thinking Mathematically

So this gives everyone a way to work on and within their own little knowledge of mathematics. The answer is not to learn more mathematics, but to think mathematically. This is the child's problem as well as the teacher's.

4.1

Whenever you are thinking about a child's mistakes in mathematics you are probably thinking mathematically. Once you recognise that you can, that you do, think mathematically, then you are on the 'inside' of the subject.
    The result of this realisation for me was a feeling of power and of pleasure.

4.2

I saw that I could turn my lack of knowledge into an advantage when I was teaching. Once I had focussed on my own mathematical problem, I was able to focus more clearly on the child's. After all, he and I were in a rather similar state. His problem, like mine, was much bigger than the particular sum or whatever that was holding us up. What we needed was the ability to work on mathematical problems.

    (i) *Creative ignorance*? What does it feel like when 'I don't know the answer'? When I'm trying to understand a problem I weigh up any offered explanations. I have to be convinced, to see for myself. I have to resist being bullied by impressive presentations. Jargon words are danger signals. To make an explanation my own I must get it to fit with the rest of my understanding of the subject. I usually have to play with a new idea before I can get hold of it. The more unfamiliar an idea, the more need there is to re-frame it in my own terms, in order to grasp its form at all.
    (ii) A teacher who does not know the answer to a child's mathematical problem is in many ways better placed than someone who does. Every child's abiding problem is how to cope with mathematics, not how to solve this or that problem, how to apply a proof or get a right answer. Anyone who is conscious of what it feels like to grope for understanding is well placed to help children to achieve their own understanding. If I have just understood a problem for the first time, then it will also be a first-time experience to work on it with the children. We shall probably find all kinds of difficulties I hadn't thought of. We are on shaky ground, and used to the sensation. As well as, because of, the false starts, gropings, confusions, there are, eventually, clarities. When we do get somewhere with a problem, there is a good chance that the children know what they are doing and why.
    (iii) *Conclusion* When I'm working on some mathematics in the classroom, my knowledge or understanding is liable to run out. Very often it's possible to work on the problem there and then, with the children. This seems to me to be the most fruitful use of ignorance.

4.3

There is another virtue in treating mathematics as a joint exploration. Mathematics is a rich field of interconnecting structures. In order to understand a mathematical notion (say, place value) it is unlikely that a single explanation will do. Conversely, any particular sum, problem, piece of apparatus is certain to bring into play many mathematical notions. If a child is trying to understand what is happening, then any given sum, problem, piece of apparatus, can only be a starting point. He will move away from that starting point in one of many directions. In this light any piece of mathematics is potentially open-ended. The answer to a problem may be the least important thing about it.

5

Mathematical knowledge, on the other hand, can be a barrier to effective teaching. I can imagine a teacher who understood long ago all the mathematics that the children in his class attempt to learn. Given a child with a difficulty, such a teacher might present the mathematical answer to the difficulty and feel that he had done his bit as a teacher, whereas I'd say that he hadn't even begun. The more mathematics a teacher knows, the harder he may have to work to communicate with children about it. He may have to recall that ignorance is not dishonourable and his own knowledge not necessarily a virtue. He may have to be on his guard against 'being patient' with the children until they are subdued by his repetitions; a nasty habit, guaranteed to make the questioner feel a fool. To teach effectively he will have to get back 'inside' what he knows.

6

In other words, when it comes to teaching the subject, it may be of little importance how much mathematics one knows. What matters is a teacher's attitude to his own knowledge and to his and the children's lack of knowledge.

7

Yes, the danger of ignorance.

I can feel the need of help with some mathematics, and not know what could help. If I don't know what mathematics there is, how can I look for it (a classification problem)? Some teachers give up and rely on textbooks, workcards.

8

Revised curricula, maps of mathematics, etc.

Where does it all lead? What about a structure? What are the foundations? I would love to go on a crash course, to extend my understanding of mathematics. Maps, syllabuses and so on, provide the ignorant with some reassurance, but can only really be useful to people who have begun to work on their ignorance. I think these anxieties lessen as one gets to work on the problems to hand.

What Was Shirley Doing?

Shirley had some plastic shapes – lots of them. The different shapes are shown in Fig. 7.12

Fig. 7.12

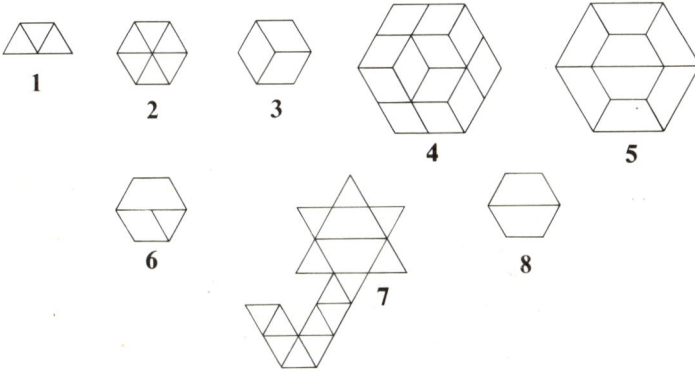

Fig. 7.13

She had not been told what to do with them. She had been making different shapes with them for about twenty minutes. Fig. 7.13 shows some of the things she had made.

They weren't all laid out like this together, of course. She doodled with the shapes, made, or half-made something, then started something else, sometimes using pieces from previous makings: and towards the end she was making a large mosaic which grew and grew.

I sensed, as this large mosaic developed, that she might welcome an intervention by me. I'm not quite sure how I sensed this – the increasingly spasmodic growth of the mosaic, a look, the slant of her shoulders, a lack of vigour as compared with the first fifteen minutes – or was it my own feelings I was transferring to her?

I had at least a few moments to reflect. What could I do or say?

I could ask her how many triangles made a diamond, or a hexagon. It would bring out into the open what she had done in (2), but it might kill the activity.

I could ask her to make a hexagon in a lot of different ways. That would allow her to continue to act, but it might be too structured.

What about the angles? Could I point out how they fitted together, or ask her something about them? That might focus her attention on an aspect which she had not noticed, and could be stimulating.

Or could I pursue the patterns of numbers? Three triangles make a trapezium, two trapezia make a hexagon, and six triangles make a hexagon. And $3 \times 2 = 6$. She might like that idea: would it enable *her* to do something?

Or the area aspect. Three diamonds to make a small hexagon (3). Twelve to make a larger one (4). Also two trapezia to make a small hexagon (8), and eight to make a larger hexagon (5).

$3 \to 12$. $2 \to 8$. Four times as many. I could ask her to make squares, or to make larger hexagons and guess how many triangles, or diamonds, or trapezia she would need. That would certainly be interesting, but I might have to direct things too much, and I don't want to take over the activity.

What about the flower (7)? I'm not so keen on those 'make a man out of shapes' activities, but it might give a welcome twist to the proceedings: she may have got into a rut just because she is fitting the shapes together so compactly and abstractly. It might be just the relaxation she needs.

Perhaps I could give her a little problem like 'make this shape

in as many different ways as possible using two diamonds and two trapezia. I know there are seven ways, and she would be involved in discarding rotations and reflections, in trying perhaps to prove to herself that she had found *all* the ways – and all in the confines of a simple puzzle. But perhaps that is too circumscribed for the moment.

I wonder whether she has really noticed that all the sides are the same length – except the long side of the trapezium? Or that the dimensions of her large hexagons are twice those of the small hexagon?

Or is the large mosaic more important than I think? Perhaps the smaller patterns have given her some sense of power over the pieces, some skill in fitting them together, and now she is allowing that skill and that power to burst out and take her where it will.

Perhaps I should just ask her what she is doing, or what she is going to do now. But she may not want to tell me, or may not be able to, and she'll feel obliged to say something.

I see she hasn't used the squares or the thin diamonds. I think I'll sit by her and start a mosaic of my own using these pieces as well, and see what happens. I'd like to have tried some of my other ideas and perhaps I will, but this will ease me into the situation.

I can't learn what to do unless I make some mistakes.

Select Bibliography

Association of Teachers of Mathematics. *Notes on mathematics in primary schools.* Cambridge: The University Press, 1967.

Banwell, C. S., Saunders, K. D. and Tahta, D. G. *Starting points.* London: Oxford University Press, 1972.

Biggs, E. E. and MacLean, J. R. *Freedom to learn – an active learning approach to mathematics.* Don Mills, Ontario: Addison-Wesley (Canada), 1969.

Boyer, C. B. *A history of mathematics.* New York: Wiley, 1968.

Davis, R. B. *Mathematics teaching – with special reference to epistemological problems.* Journal of Research and Development in Education Monograph No. 1: Athens, Georgia, 1967.

Domoryad, A. P. *Mathematical games and pastimes.* Oxford: Pergamon Press, 1964.

Gattegno, C. *For the teaching of mathematics.* 4 vols. Reading: Educational Explorers, 1963 – (in progress).

What we owe children. New York: Outerbridge and Dienstfrey, 1971. London: Routlege and Kegan Paul, 1971.

The common sense of teaching mathematics. New York: Educational Solutions, 1974.

Goutard, M. *Mathematics and children.* Reading: Educational Explorers, 1964.

Mathématiques sur mesure. Paris: Classiques Hachette, 1970.

Hawkins, D. *The informed vision – essays on learning and human nature.* New York: Agathon Press, 1974.

Kline, M. *Mathematics in Western culture.* London: Allen and Unwin, 1954. Harmondsworth: Penguin Books, 1972.

Mold, J. *Topics from mathematics – Workshop Manual 1.* Cambridge: The University Press, 1974.

Niven, I. *Mathematics of choice*: New Mathematical Library No. 15. New York: Random House, 1965.

Tahta, D. G. *Pegboard games.* Nelson, Lancs: Association of Teachers of Mathematics, 1967.

A boolean anthology. Nelson, Lancs: Association of Teachers of Mathematics, 1972.

Wilder, R. L. *Evolution of mathematical concepts.* New York: Wiley, 1968.

Readers may like to refer to the longer bibliography included in *Notes on mathematics in primary schools*, particulars of which are given above.